ATLAS OF RUSSIAN HISTORY

OTHER BOOKS BY MARTIN GILBERT

The Churchill biography
Volume III, 'The Challenge of War', 1914–1916
Volume III, Documents, Parts I and II
Volume IV, 'The Stricken World', 1917–1922
Volume IV, Documents, Parts I, II and III
Volume V, 'The Prophet of Truth', 1922–1939
The Exchequer Years, Documents, 1922–1929
The Wilderness Years, Documents, 1929–1935
The Coming of War, Documents, 1936–1939
Volume VI, 'Finest Hour', 1939–1941
At the Admiralty, Documents, 1939–1940
Volume VII, 'Road to Victory', 1941–1945
Volume VIII, 'Never Despair', 1945–1965

Historical works
The Appeasers (with Richard Gott)
The European Powers, 1900–1945
The Roots of Appeasement
Britain and Germany Between the Wars (documents)
Plough My Own Furrow: the Life of Lord Allen of Hurtwood (documents)
Servant of India: Diaries of the Viceroy's Private Secretary (documents)
Sir Horace Rumbold: Portrait of a Diplomat
Churchill: a Photographic Portrait
Churchill's Political Philosophy
Auschwitz and the Allies
Exile and Return: the Struggle for Jewish Statehood
The Jews of Hope: the Plight of Soviet Jewry Today
Shcharansky: Hero of our Time
Jerusalem: Rebirth of a City, 1838–1898
Final Journey: the Fate of the Jews in Nazi Europe
The Holocaust: the Jewish Tragedy
The Second World War
Churchill, A Life

Atlases
Dent Atlas of American History
Dent Atlas of the Arab–Israeli Conflict
Dent Atlas of the First World War
Dent Atlas of the Holocaust
Dent Atlas of Jewish History
Dent Atlas of Recent History (*in preparation*)
Dent Atlas of Russian History
The Jews of Arab Lands: Their History in Maps
The Jews of Russia: Their History in Maps
Jerusalem: Illustrated History Atlas
Children's Illustrated Bible Atlas

ATLAS OF
RUSSIAN HISTORY

Second edition

Martin Gilbert

Fellow of Merton College, Oxford

New York

OXFORD UNIVERSITY PRESS

1993

© 1972 and 1993 Martin Gilbert

First published in Great Britain by
The Orion Publishing Group Limited
5 Upper St. Martin's Lane, London WC2H 9EA

Published in the United States of America by
Oxford University Press, Inc.
200 Madison Avenue
New York, N.Y. 10016, U.S.A.

Oxford is a registered trademark of
Oxford University Press

Library of Congress
Cataloging-in-Publication Data
Gilbert, Martin, 1936–
    Atlas of Russian history / Martin Gilbert
      p.   cm.
  Rev. ed. of: Russian history atlas / Martin Gilbert. 1972
  Includes bibliographical references and index.
  ISBN 0–19–521041–7 (hardback)
  ISBN 0–19–521061–1 (paperback)
  1. Russia—Historical geography—Maps.   2. Soviet Union—
Historical geography—Maps.   I. Gilbert. Martin, 1936–   Russian
history atlas.
G2111.SIG52   1993   <G&M>
911.47—dc20

                     93–21920
                     CIP
                    MAP

Printing (last digit): 9 8 7 6 5 4 3 2

Printed in Great Britain

Preface

I have designed this Atlas in the hope that it is possible to present—within the span of 161 maps—a survey of Russian history from the earliest times to the present day. In drafting each map, I drew upon material from a wide range of published works—books, articles, atlases and single sheet maps—each of which I have listed in the bibliography.

On the maps themselves I have included much factual material not normally associated with historical geography, such as the text of one of Stalin's few surviving personal communications—the postcard to his sister-in-law (printed on map 54), and Lenin's telegram to the Bolsheviks in Sweden (printed on map 87). I have drafted each map individually, in such a way as to enable the maximum factual information to be included without making use of a separate page of text; and I have compiled the index in order that it may serve as a means of using the Atlas as if it were a volume of narrative.

I wish to acknowledge the help of many colleagues and friends. In 1962 I began research into Russian history under the supervision of Dr George Katkov, whose insatiable curiosity about elusive historical facts, and whose enthusiasm in tracking them down, have influenced all my subsequent work. I also benefitted from the teaching and encouragement of Mr David Footman, Mr Max Hayward, Dr Harry Willetts and the late Mr Guy Wint. When I was preparing the first sketches for this Atlas, the maps I had drawn and the facts I had incorporated on them were scrutinized by three friends—Mr Michael Glenny, Mr Dennis O'Flaherty and Dr Harry Shukman—to each of whom I am most grateful for many detailed suggestions, and for giving up much time to help me. At the outset of my research I received valuable bibliographical advice from Dr J. L. I. Simmons, and suggestions for specific maps from Mr Norman Davies, Dr Ronald Hingley, Mr John B. Kingston and Mr Ewald Uustalu. Jane Cousins helped me with bibliographical and historical research; Mr Arthur Banks transcribed my sketches into clear, printable maps, and Kate Fleming kept a vigilant eye on the cartography. Susie Sacher helped me to compile the index: Sarah Graham, as well as undertaking all the secretarial work, made many important suggestions, factual and cartographic.

The first 146 maps in this atlas were drawn by Arthur Banks and his team of expert cartographers, including the late Terry Bicknell, who subsequently drew more than six hundred historical maps for me. The last fifteen maps were drawn by Tim Aspden, who also drew the extra maps for several of my other books and historical atlases.

I am particularly grateful to Abe Eisenstat and Kay Thomson for their help over several months in enabling me to bring this atlas up to date for this new edition. The collapse of Soviet Communism and the disintegration of the Soviet Union before the end of its eighth decade, an event which was not conceivable (certainly not to this author) when the atlas was first published in 1972, has led me to prepare fifteen new maps. In designing them, I have tried to show in detail the sequence of events that shook both the Soviet Union and Eastern Europe within the space of a decade, creating new States and new perspectives as the territorial and ideological monolith dissolved.

MARTIN GILBERT
Merton College, Oxford

3 March 1993

Maps

SECTION FOUR: THE END OF THE SOVIET UNION

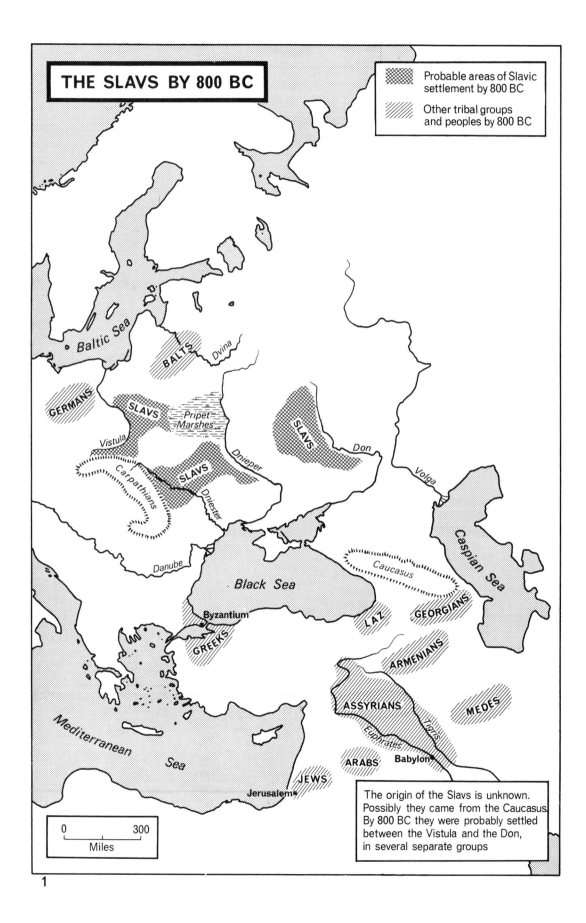

THE SLAVS BY 800 BC

Probable areas of Slavic settlement by 800 BC

Other tribal groups and peoples by 800 BC

Baltic Sea

BALTS

Dvina

GERMANS

SLAVS

Pripet Marshes

SLAVS

Don

Vistula

Carpathians

SLAVS

Dnieper

Dniester

Volga

Danube

Caspian Sea

Caucasus

Black Sea

Byzantium

LAZ

GEORGIANS

GREEKS

ARMENIANS

Mediterranean

ASSYRIANS

MEDES

Sea

Euphrates

Tigris

ARABS

Babylon

JEWS

Jerusalem

0   300
Miles

The origin of the Slavs is unknown.
Possibly they came from the Caucasus.
By 800 BC they were probably settled
between the Vistula and the Don,
in several separate groups

1

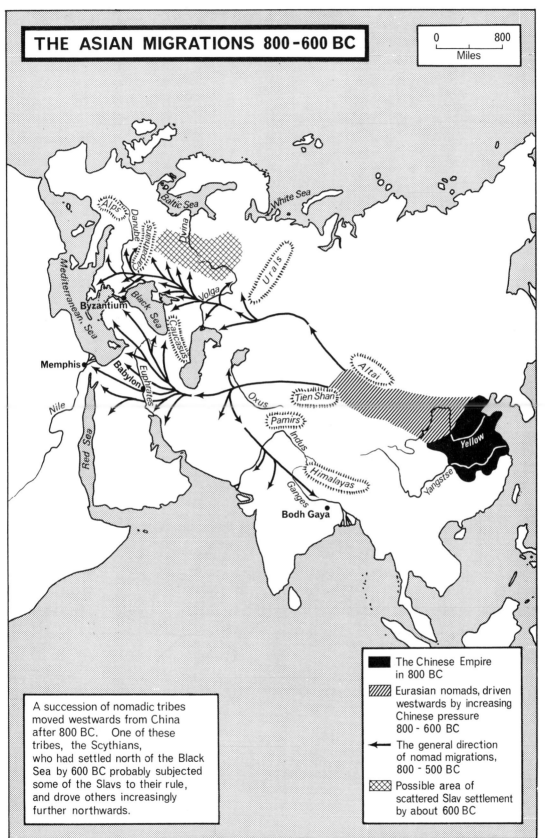

THE ASIAN MIGRATIONS 800–600 BC

0   800
Miles

Baltic Sea
White Sea
Alps
Danube
Dvina
Sudetenland
Carpathians
Volga
Urals
Mediterranean Sea
Byzantium
Black Sea
Caucasus
Altai
Memphis
Babylon
Euphrates
Oxus
Tien Shan
Nile
Red Sea
Pamirs
Yellow
Indus
Himalayas
Yangstse
Ganges
Bodh Gaya

A succession of nomadic tribes
moved westwards from China
after 800 BC. One of these
tribes, the Scythians,
who had settled north of the Black
Sea by 600 BC probably subjected
some of the Slavs to their rule,
and drove others increasingly
further northwards.

■ The Chinese Empire
in 800 BC

▨ Eurasian nomads, driven
westwards by increasing
Chinese pressure
800 - 600 BC

← The general direction
of nomad migrations,
800 - 500 BC

▨ Possible area of
scattered Slav settlement
by about 600 BC

2

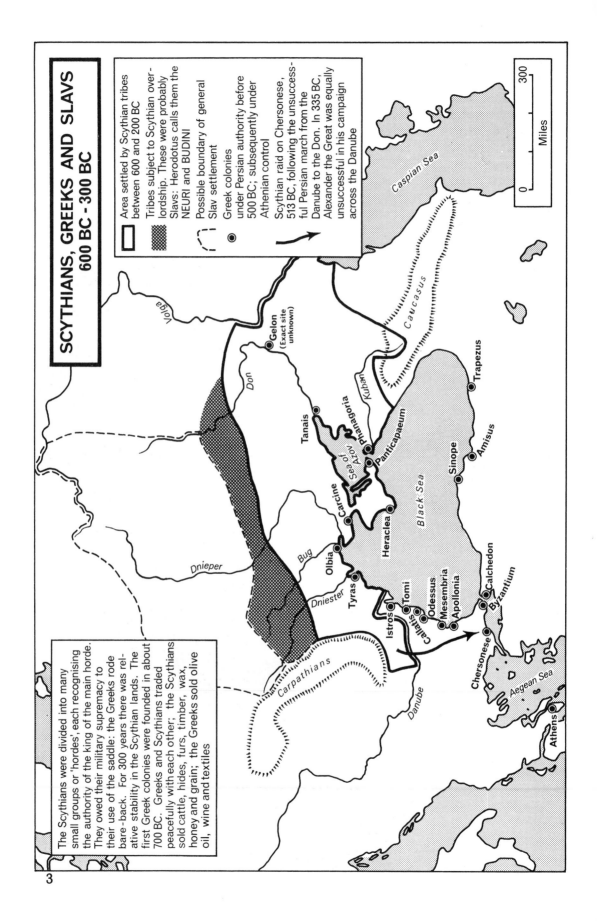

SCYTHIANS, GREEKS AND SLAVS
600 BC - 300 BC

Area settled by Scythian tribes between 600 and 200 BC

Tribes subject to Scythian over-lordship. These were probably Slavs; Herodotus calls them the NEURI and BUDINI

Possible boundary of general Slav settlement

Greek colonies under Persian authority before 500 BC; subsequently under Athenian control

Scythian raid on Chersonese, 513 BC, following the unsuccess-ful Persian march from the Danube to the Don. In 335 BC, Alexander the Great was equally unsuccessful in his campaign across the Danube

The Scythians were divided into many small groups or 'hordes', each recognising the authority of the king of the main horde. They owed their military supremacy to their use of the saddle: the Greeks rode bare-back. For 300 years there was rel-ative stability in the Scythian lands. The first Greek colonies were founded in about 700 BC. Greeks and Scythians traded peacefully with each other; the Scythians sold cattle, hides, furs, timber, wax, honey and grain; the Greeks sold olive oil, wine and textiles

Caspian Sea

Volga

Gelon
(Exact site unknown)

Don

Caucasus

Kuban

Tanais

Phanagoria

Sea of Azov

Panticapaeum

Trapezus

Carcine

Sinope

Amisus

Heraclea

Black Sea

Dnieper

Bug

Olbia

Tyras

Dniester

Istros

Tomi

Callatis

Odessus

Mesembria

Apollonia

Calchedon

Byzantium

Carpathians

Chersonese

Danube

Aegean Sea

Athens

300

0

Miles

3

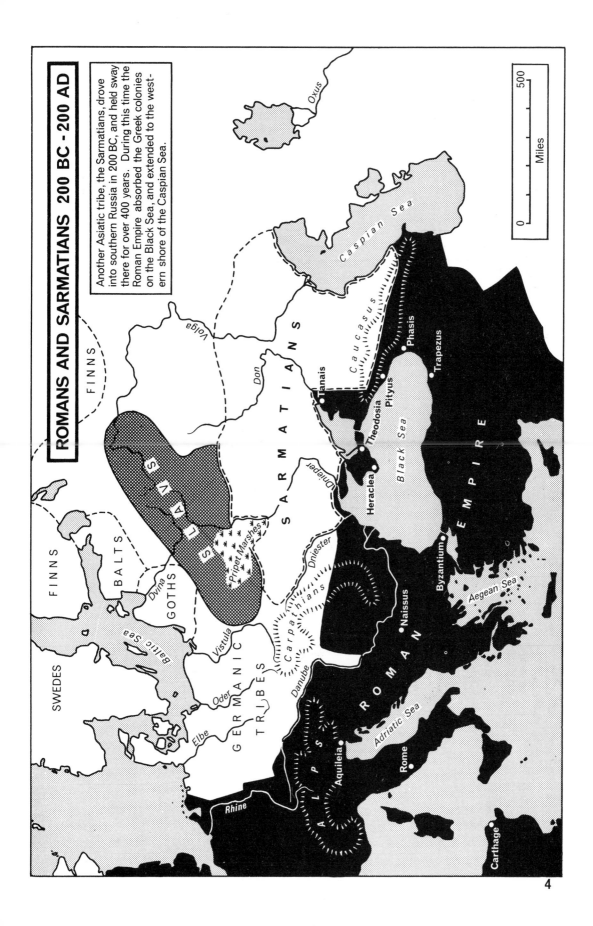

ROMANS AND SARMATIANS 200 BC - 200 AD

Another Asiatic tribe, the Sarmatians, drove into southern Russia in 200 BC, and held sway there for over 400 years. During this time the Roman Empire absorbed the Greek colonies on the Black Sea, and extended to the western shore of the Caspian Sea.

FINNS

FINNS

SWEDES

BALTS

GOTHS

SLAVS

Pripet Marshes

SARMATIANS

GERMANIC TRIBES

Carpathians

ROMAN EMPIRE

ALPS

Caspian Sea

Caucasus

Black Sea

Aegean Sea

Adriatic Sea

Oxus

Volga

Don

Dnieper

Dniester

Vistula

Oder

Elbe

Dvina

Danube

Rhine

Baltic Sea

Tanais

Phasis

Trapezus

Pityus

Theodosia

Heraclea

Byzantium

Naissus

Aquileia

Rome

Carthage

0   500
Miles

4

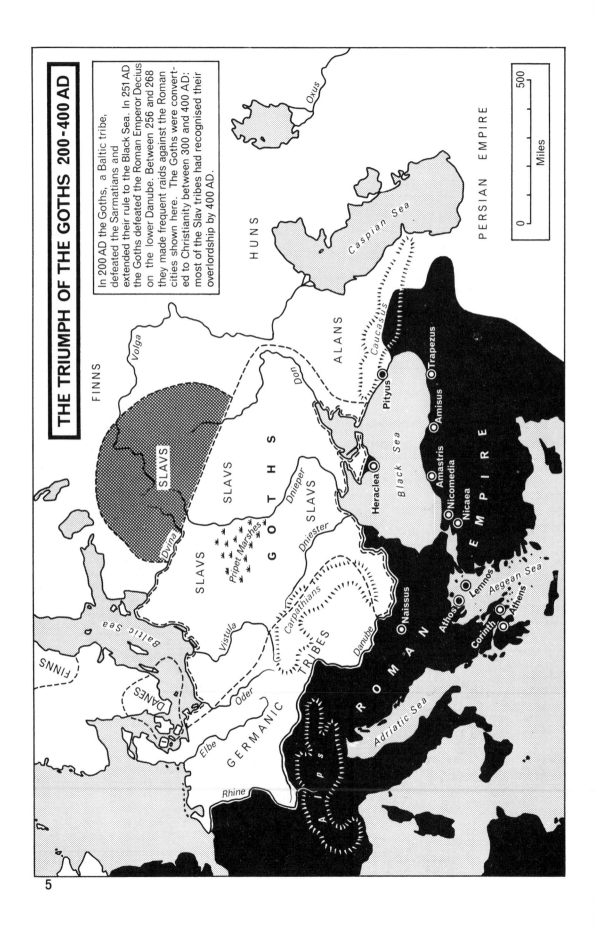

THE TRIUMPH OF THE GOTHS 200-400 AD

In 200 AD the Goths, a Baltic tribe, defeated the Sarmatians and extended their rule to the Black Sea. In 251 AD the Goths defeated the Roman Emperor Decius on the lower Danube. Between 256 and 268 they made frequent raids against the Roman cities shown here. The Goths were converted to Christianity between 300 and 400 AD: most of the Slav tribes had recognised their overlordship by 400 AD.

500

Miles

0

Oxus

PERSIAN EMPIRE

HUNS

Caspian Sea

Volga

FINNS

ALANS

Caucasus

Don

Trapezus

Amisus

Pityus

Anastris

Black Sea

Nicomedia

Heraclea

Nicaea

SLAVS

EMPIRE

Dnieper

SLAVS

G O T H S

SLAVS

Dniester

SLAVS

Lemnos

Aegean Sea

Pripet Marshes

Carpathians

Athos

Dvina

Naissus

Corinth

Athens

Baltic Sea

Vistula

TRIBES

R O M A N

FINNS

DANES

Oder

GERMANIC

Danube

Adriatic Sea

A L P S

Elbe

Rhine

5

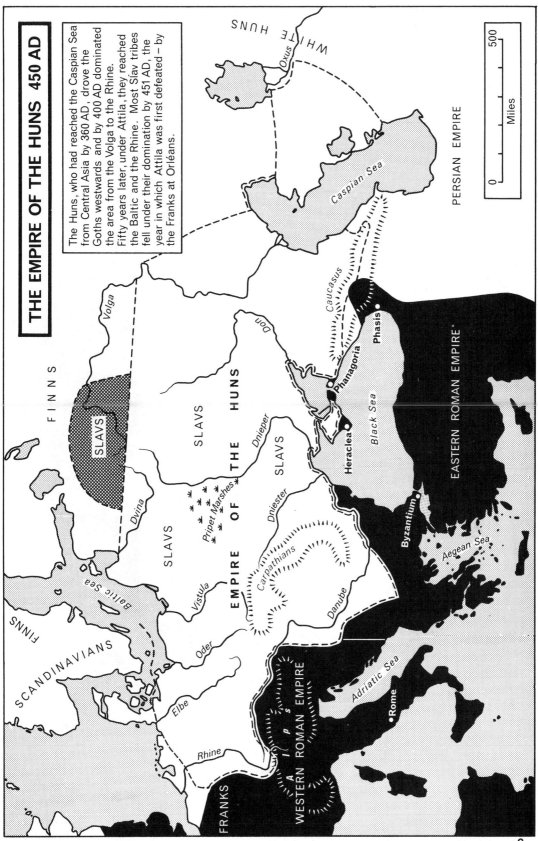

THE EMPIRE OF THE HUNS 450 AD

The Huns, who had reached the Caspian Sea from Central Asia by 360 AD, drove the Goths westwards and by 400 AD dominated the area from the Volga to the Rhine. Fifty years later, under Attila, they reached the Baltic and the Rhine. Most Slav tribes fell under their domination by 451 AD, the year in which Attila was first defeated – by the Franks at Orléans.

WHITE HUNS

Oxus

PERSIAN EMPIRE

Caspian Sea

Miles

0   500

Caucasus

Volga

Don

Phasis

FINNS

SLAVS

Phanagoria

SLAVS

Black Sea

EMPIRE OF THE HUNS

Dnieper

Heraclea

SLAVS

Pripet Marshes

Dniester

Byzantium

EASTERN ROMAN EMPIRE°

Aegean Sea

SLAVS

Carpathians

Dvina

Baltic Sea

Vistula

Danube

SCANDINAVIANS

Oder

FINNS

Adriatic Sea

Elbe

A l p s

Rome

Rhine

FRANKS

WESTERN ROMAN EMPIRE

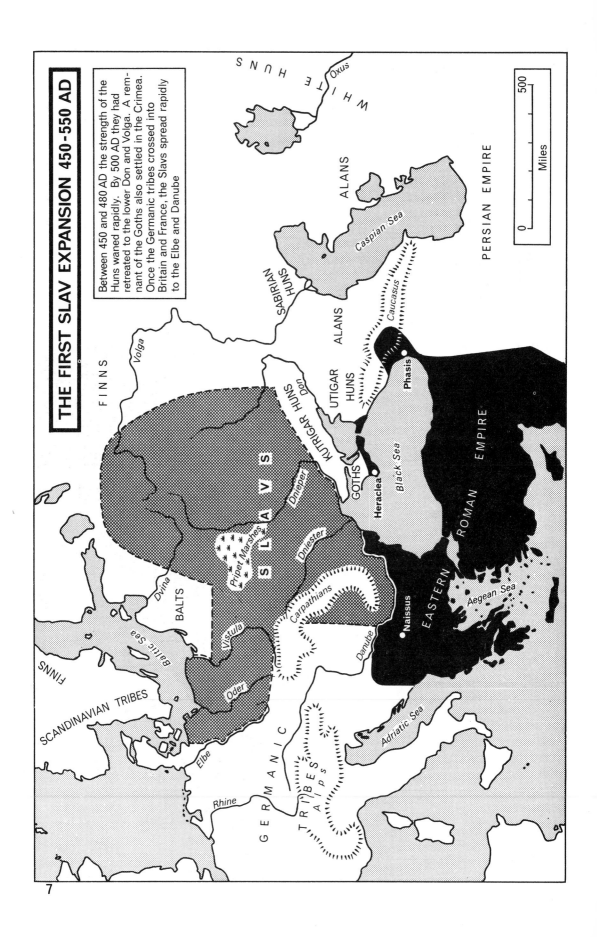

THE FIRST SLAV EXPANSION 450-550 AD

Between 450 and 480 AD the strength of the Huns waned rapidly. By 500 AD they had retreated to the lower Don and Volga. A remnant of the Goths also settled in the Crimea. Once the Germanic tribes crossed into Britain and France, the Slavs spread rapidly to the Elbe and Danube

WHITE HUNS

Oxus

ALANS

Caspian Sea

PERSIAN EMPIRE

500

Miles

0

FINNS

Volga

SABIRIAN HUNS

ALANS

UTIGAR HUNS

Caucasus

KUTRIGAR HUNS

Don

Phasis

GOTHS

Black Sea

Heraclea

EASTERN ROMAN EMPIRE

S L A V S

Dnieper

Pripet Marshes

Dniester

Carpathians

Naissus

FINNS

Dvina

BALTS

Baltic Sea

Vistula

Aegean Sea

Danube

Oder

SCANDINAVIAN TRIBES

Adriatic Sea

Elbe

G E R M A N I C   T R I B E S

Alps

Rhine

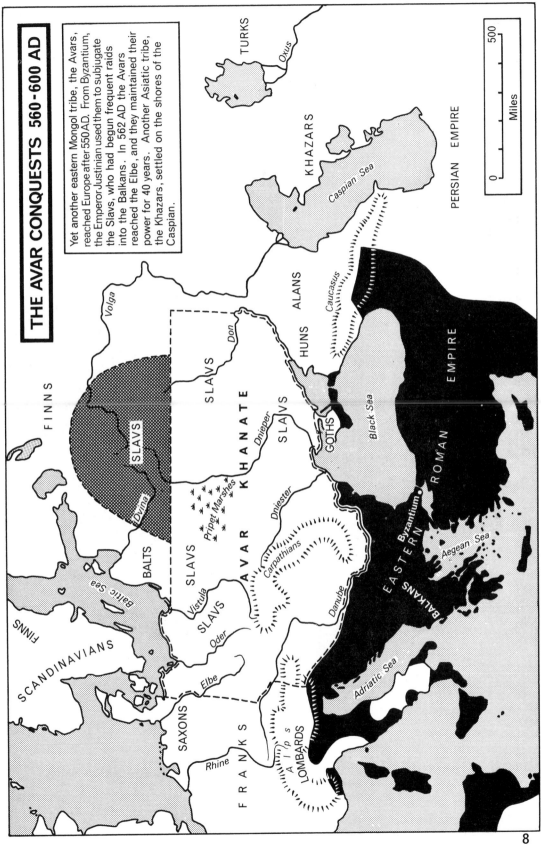

THE AVAR CONQUESTS 560-600 AD

Yet another eastern Mongol tribe, the Avars, reached Europe after 550AD. From Byzantium, the Emperor Justinian used them to subjugate the Slavs, who had begun frequent raids into the Balkans. In 562 AD the Avars reached the Elbe, and they maintained their power for 40 years. Another Asiatic tribe, the Khazars, settled on the shores of the Caspian.

TURKS

Oxus

KHAZARS

Caspian Sea

PERSIAN EMPIRE

500

0

Miles

FINNS

Volga

SLAVS

Don

SLAVS

HUNS ALANS

Caucasus

SLAVS

SLAVS

Dnieper

EMPIRE

Black Sea

ROMAN

GOTHS

Byzantium

FINNS

Dvina

SLAVS

BALTS

Baltic Sea

SLAVS

Vistula

Pripet Marshes

A V A R   K H A N A T E

Dniester

Carpathians

Danube

EASTERN

Aegean Sea

BALKANS

SCANDINAVIANS

SLAVS

Oder

SLAVS

Elbe

SAXONS

Adriatic Sea

F R A N K S

Rhine

A l p s

LOMBARDS

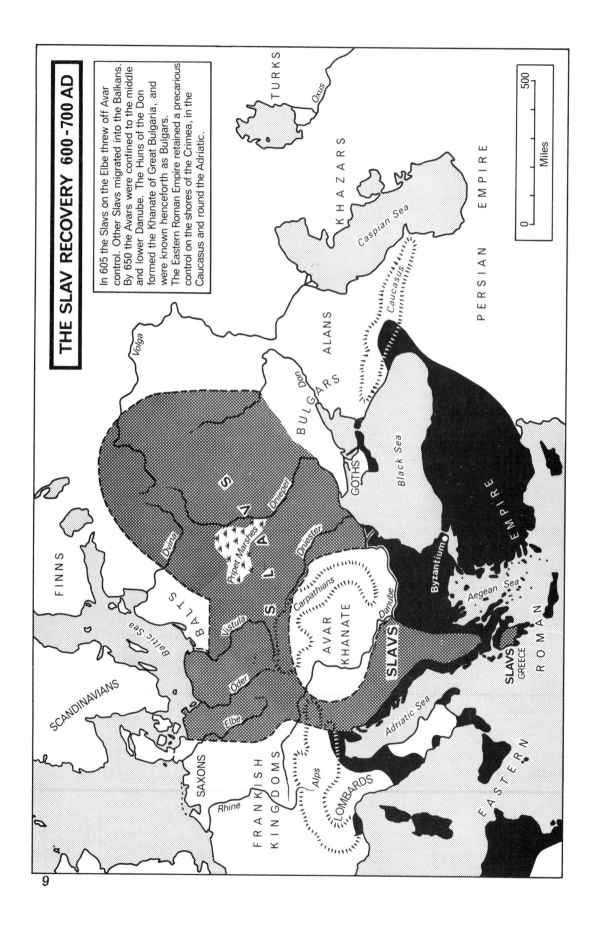

THE SLAV RECOVERY 600-700 AD

In 605 the Slavs on the Elbe threw off Avar control. Other Slavs migrated into the Balkans. By 650 the Avars were confined to the middle and lower Danube. The Huns of the Don formed the Khanate of Great Bulgaria, and were known henceforth as Bulgars. The Eastern Roman Empire retained a precarious control on the shores of the Crimea, in the Caucasus and round the Adriatic.

500

0

Miles

TURKS

Oxus

KHAZARS

Caspian Sea

PERSIAN EMPIRE

Volga

BULGARS

ALANS

Don

GOTHS

Black Sea

FINNS

S

L

A

V

Dnieper

Dvina

Pripet Marshes

Dniester

Caucasus

BALTS

Vistula

Carpathians

AVAR KHANATE

Danube

SLAVS

Byzantium

EMPIRE

Aegean Sea

SCANDINAVIANS

Baltic Sea

Oder

SLAVS

GREECE

ROMAN

SAXONS

Elbe

FRANKISH KINGDOMS

Alps

LOMBARDS

Adriatic Sea

EASTERN

Rhine

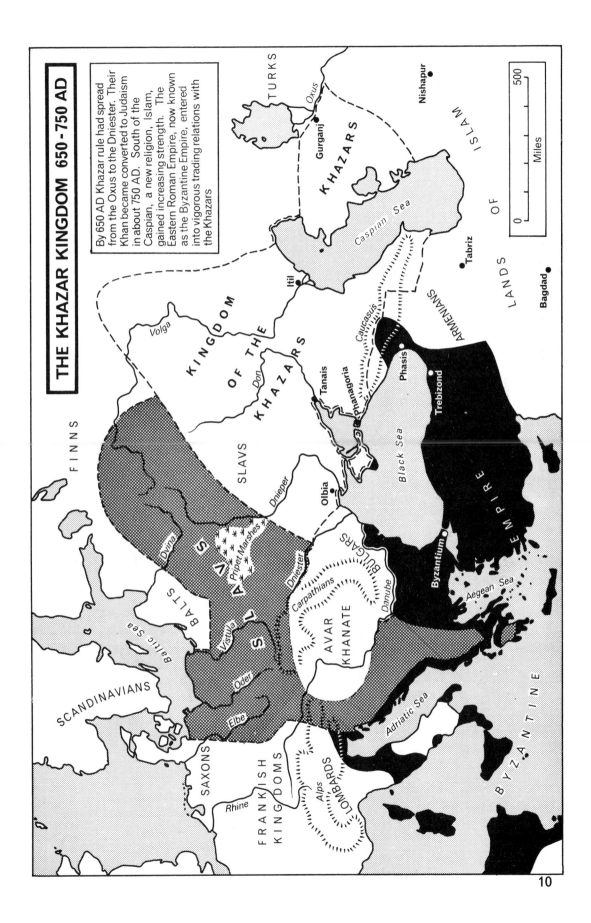

THE KHAZAR KINGDOM 650 - 750 AD

By 650 AD Khazar rule had spread from the Oxus to the Dniester. Their Khan became converted to Judaism in about 750 AD. South of the Caspian, a new religion, Islam, gained increasing strength. The Eastern Roman Empire, now known as the Byzantine Empire, entered into vigorous trading relations with the Khazars

500

Miles

0

TURKS

Oxus

Gurganj

KHAZARS

Nishapur

ISLAM

Caspian Sea

Tabriz

Bagdad

OF

LANDS

Itil

KINGDOM

OF

THE

Volga

KHAZARS

Don

Tanais

Phanagoria

Caucasus

Phasis

ARMENIANS

Trebizond

FINNS

SLAVS

Dnieper

Black Sea

Olbia

Byzantium

S
L
A
V
S

Pripet Marshes

Dniester

BULGARS

Aegean Sea

Duna

Carpathians

AVAR

Danube

EMPIRE

BALTS

Vistula

S
L
A
V
S

KHANATE

Adriatic Sea

Baltic Sea

Oder

BYZANTINE

SCANDINAVIANS

Elbe

SAXONS

FRANKISH
KINGDOMS

Alps

LOMBARDS

Rhine

10

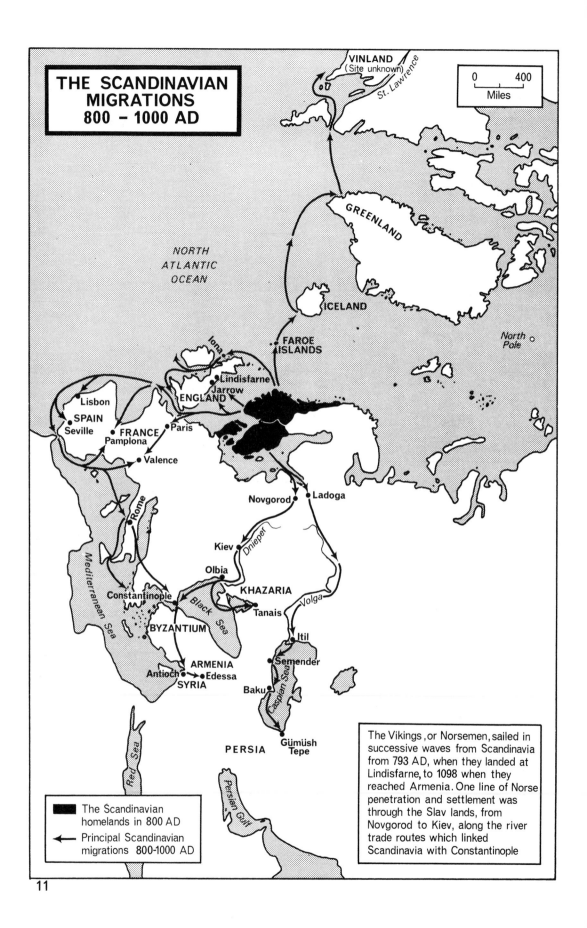

THE SCANDINAVIAN MIGRATIONS 800 – 1000 AD

VINLAND
(Site unknown)

St. Lawrence

0   400
Miles

GREENLAND

NORTH
ATLANTIC
OCEAN

ICELAND

North
Pole

FAROE
ISLANDS

Iona

Lindisfarne
Jarrow
ENGLAND

Lisbon
SPAIN
Seville   FRANCE   Paris
Pamplona
Valence

Rome

Novgorod   Ladoga

Mediterranean Sea

Kiev   Dnieper

Olbia

Constantinople   Black Sea   KHAZARIA

BYZANTIUM   Tanais

Volga

Itil

ARMENIA   Semender
Antioch   Edessa
SYRIA   Baku
Caspian Sea

Red Sea

PERSIA   Gümüsh
Tepe

Persian Gulf

⬛ The Scandinavian
homelands in 800 AD
⬅ Principal Scandinavian
migrations 800-1000 AD

The Vikings, or Norsemen, sailed in
successive waves from Scandinavia
from 793 AD, when they landed at
Lindisfarne, to 1098 when they
reached Armenia. One line of Norse
penetration and settlement was
through the Slav lands, from
Novgorod to Kiev, along the river
trade routes which linked
Scandinavia with Constantinople

THE SLAVS AND THE NORSEMEN BY 880 AD

FINNS

SLOVIANIANS

• Novgorod

CHEREMESIANS

NORSE

SWEDES

• Visby

DANES

OBODRICHI

Baltic Sea

BALTS

VIATCHIANS

Volga

• Smolensk

MORDVINS

POLOCHANE

GERMANS

POLES

MAZOVIANS

Elbe

Pripet Marshes

KRIVICHIANS

SILESIANS

RADIMICHIANS

CZECHS

DEREVLIANS

MORAVIANS

SEVERIANS

SLOVAKS

VOLHYNIANS

POLIANIANS

• Kiev

Don

KHAZARS

Danube

SLOVENES

MAGYARS

VLACHS

PECHENEGS

Venice •

CROATS

Adriatic Sea

SERBS

Tmutorokan

Caucasus

Preslav •

Black Sea

BULGARS

Constantinople

ARMENIANS

Egean Sea

• Athens

GREEKS

The Norse settlers between Novgorod and Kiev quickly dominated the local Slavs, over whom they established political control. Known as "Varangarians", these Norse overlords moulded the Slavs into a coherent federation, "Kievan Rus". Originally Norse speaking, Kievan Rus, or Russia, saw a close mingling of Scandinavian and Slav culture; and the emergence of a strong Kievan, or Russian national consciousness. The first Varangarian ruler, Rurik, led an expedition against Constantinople in 860 AD. His successor Oleg established his capital at Kiev in about 880 AD.

0   300
Miles

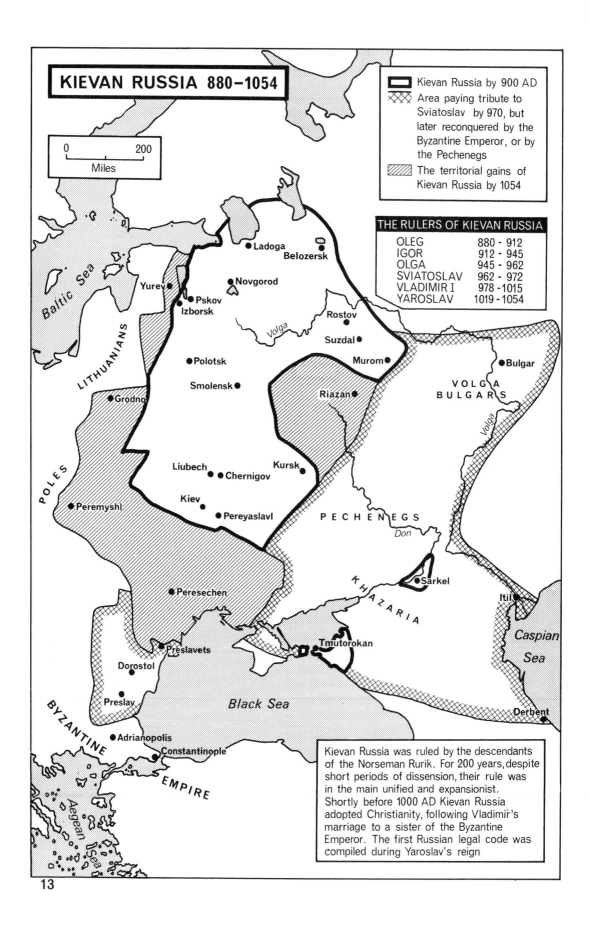

KIEVAN RUSSIA 880–1054

0   200
Miles

Kievan Russia by 900 AD

Area paying tribute to Sviatoslav by 970, but later reconquered by the Byzantine Emperor, or by the Pechenegs

The territorial gains of Kievan Russia by 1054

THE RULERS OF KIEVAN RUSSIA

OLEG	880 - 912
IGOR	912 - 945
OLGA	945 - 962
SVIATOSLAV	962 - 972
VLADIMIR I	978 -1015
YAROSLAV	1019 -1054

Baltic Sea

Ladoga

Belozersk

Yurev

Novgorod

Pskov

Izborsk

Rostov

Volga

Suzdal

LITHUANIANS

Murom

Bulgar

Polotsk

VOLGA
BULGARS

Smolensk

Riazan

Volga

Grodno

POLES

Liubech

Kursk

Chernigov

Kiev

Peremyshl

Pereyaslavl

PECHENEGS

Don

Peresechen

KHAZARIA

Sarkel

Itil

Caspian
Sea

Preslavets

Tmutorokan

Dorostol

Derbent

Preslav

Black Sea

BYZANTINE

Adrianopolis

Constantinople

EMPIRE

Aegean Sea

Kievan Russia was ruled by the descendants of the Norseman Rurik. For 200 years, despite short periods of dissension, their rule was in the main unified and expansionist. Shortly before 1000 AD Kievan Russia adopted Christianity, following Vladimir's marriage to a sister of the Byzantine Emperor. The first Russian legal code was compiled during Yaroslav's reign

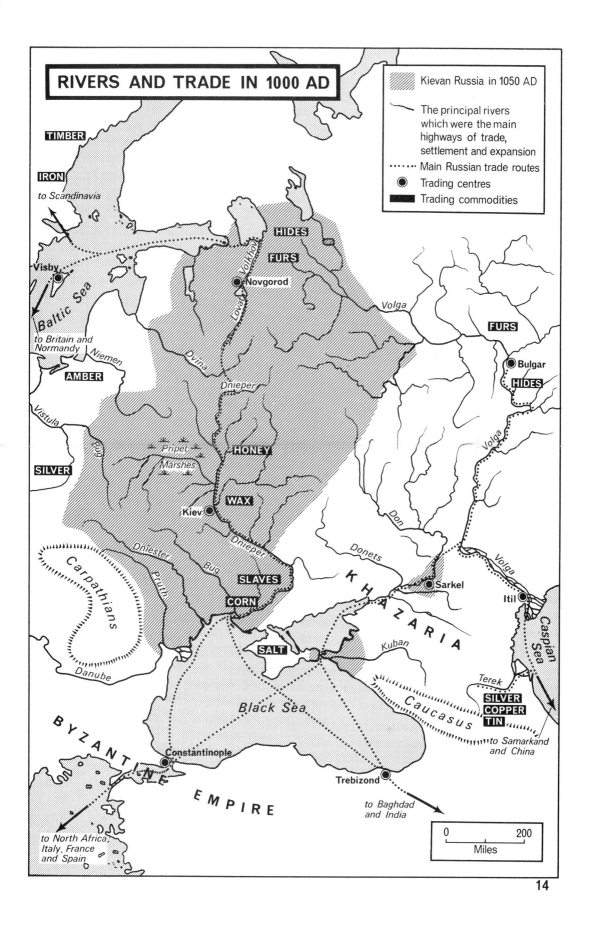

RIVERS AND TRADE IN 1000 AD

Kievan Russia in 1050 AD

The principal rivers which were the main highways of trade, settlement and expansion

Main Russian trade routes

Trading centres

Trading commodities

TIMBER

IRON

to Scandinavia

Visby

Baltic Sea

to Britain and Normandy

Niemen

AMBER

Vistula

Bug

SILVER

Carpathians

Danube

HIDES

FURS

Novgorod

Volkhov

Lovat

Dvina

Dnieper

Pripet Marshes

HONEY

WAX

Kiev

Dnieper

Dniester

Pruth

Bug

SLAVES

CORN

SALT

Black Sea

Constantinople

B Y Z A N T I N E   E M P I R E

to North Africa, Italy, France and Spain

Volga

FURS

Bulgar

HIDES

Volga

Don

Donets

K H A Z A R I A

Sarkel

Kuban

C a u c a s u s

Terek

Volga

Itil

Caspian Sea

SILVER COPPER TIN

to Samarkand and China

Trebizond

to Baghdad and India

0   200
Miles

14

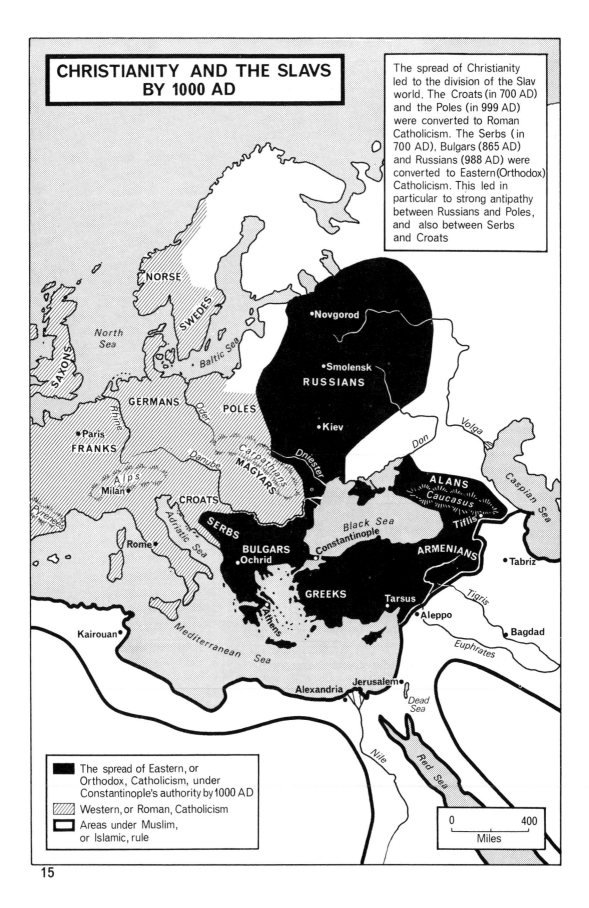

CHRISTIANITY AND THE SLAVS BY 1000 AD

The spread of Christianity led to the division of the Slav world. The Croats (in 700 AD) and the Poles (in 999 AD) were converted to Roman Catholicism. The Serbs (in 700 AD), Bulgars (865 AD) and Russians (988 AD) were converted to Eastern (Orthodox) Catholicism. This led in particular to strong antipathy between Russians and Poles, and also between Serbs and Croats

NORSE

SWEDES

North Sea

Baltic Sea

SAXONS

•Novgorod

•Smolensk

RUSSIANS

GERMANS

Rhine

Oder

POLES

Paris
FRANKS

•Kiev

Volga

Don

Danube

Carpathians

Dniester

MAGYARS

ALANS
Caucasus

Alps

Milan

CROATS

Caspian Sea

Adriatic Sea

Tiflis

SERBS

Black Sea

Constantinople

ARMENIANS

Rome

BULGARS
•Ochrid

•Tabriz

Pyrenees

Provence

GREEKS

Tarsus

Tigris

Athens

•Aleppo

Kairouan•

Mediterranean Sea

•Bagdad

Euphrates

Jerusalem•

Alexandria

Dead
Sea

Nile

Red Sea

■ The spread of Eastern, or
Orthodox, Catholicism, under
Constantinople's authority by 1000 AD

▨ Western, or Roman, Catholicism

▢ Areas under Muslim,
or Islamic, rule

0   400
Miles

THE FLOURISHING OF RUSSIAN MONASTICISM 1200-1600

White Sea

KINGDOM OF SWEDEN

Urals

Solovetski monastery

ZIRIANS

Siskoi monastery

Valaam

Ustiug

PERMIAKS

Baltic Sea

Belozersk

Ladoga

Spaso-Kamenni monastery

Novgorod

Galich

TEUTONIC KNIGHTS

Pskov

Kostroma

Tver

Rostov
Pereyaslavl

Nizhni Novgorod

Suzdal

Volga

Troitski-Sergievski monastery

Vladimir

Volokolamsk

Moscow

Polotsk

Smolensk

GRAND DUCHY OF LITHUANIA

Chernigov

MONGOL KHANATES

Kiev

Volga

Caspian Sea

The foundation of urban monasteries was most intense between 1200 and 1350. By 1400 the majority of monasteries being founded were rural or "desert" monasteries. Between 1350 and 1450 over 150 new monasteries were established, and by 1500 many monastic colonies had been set up in the predominantly pagan areas between Galich and the Urals. In 1588 the English Ambassador to Moscow wrote of the monasteries owning all the best land in Russia and being among the principal landowners

◉ Principal Orthodox monasteries established by 1500
▨ Area of most active monastic colonization before 1500
■ Nomadic and heathen tribes among whom monastic missionary work was most active 1400-1500
–·–·– National frontiers in 1500

0   200
Miles

THE FRAGMENTATION OF KIEVAN RUSSIA 1054–1238

0   200
Miles

DEPENDENCIES OF NOVGOROD

FINNS

Ladoga

Belozersk

Ustiug

REPUBLIC
OF NOVGOROD
Novgorod

VLADIMIR–SUZDAL

Reval

Kostroma
Yaroslavl
Rostov

Pskov

Torzhok

VOLGA
BULGARS

Izborsk

Tver

Suzdal

Riga

Moscow

Vladimir

LITHUANIA

Polotsk

SMOLENSK

Murom
Riazan

Kovno

Vitebsk

Viazma

Smolensk

MUROM-
RIAZAN

POLOTSK
Minsk

CHERNIGOV

Białystok

TUROV

NOVGOROD-
SEVERSK

Pinsk

Turov

Chernigov

POLAND

VOLHYNIA

KIEV
Kiev

PEREYASLAVL
Pereyaslavl

Cracow

Zhitomir

GALICIA
Galich

Carpathians

Dniester

Don

HUNGARY

CUMANS or POLOVTSI

Black
Sea

Constantinople

The twelve Principalities
of Russia in 1100

On the death of Yaroslav in 1054, Kievan Russia
was divided among his sons. Their constant
feuds led to the fragmentation of the once
powerful kingdom. United briefly from 1113 to 1125
by Vladimir Monomakh, the Russian lands were again
divided and in conflict during the hundred years
before the Mongol invasion of 1238. In 1199 Galicia
and Volhynia were united, and in 1254 recognised
by the Pope as an independent kingdom. In
1307 Polotsk came under Lithuanian suzerainty

Baltic Sea

Dvina

Vistula

17

THE REPUBLIC OF NOVGOROD
997 – 1478

The Republic of Novgorod obtained self-government from Kievan Russia in 997, and complete independence in 1136. The Republic styled itself "Sovereign Great Novgorod" and was governed by a Grand Prince and an Assembly of citizens. Novgorod was for over three hundred years a flourishing trading and cultural centre, and successfully fought off attacks by the Teutonic Knights, the Swedes, the Lithuanians and the Mongols. In 1478 it was finally crushed into complete submission by Ivan the Terrible, and annexed to Moscow. The town itself was largely destroyed by fire in 1695.

Ponoy

White Sea

FINNS

SWEDES

Baltic Sea

Pogost-na-more

Spasskoi

Ilomanets

Pudozhskoi

Lake Onega

Onega

Olonets

Lake Ladoga

1396

1295

1284

1313

Vyborg

1240, 1348
Gulf of Finland

Ladoga

Kopore

Oreshek

Vologda

Reval

Yama

Volkhov

Nebolchi

1223

Dorpat

TEUTONIC KNIGHTS

1242

NOVGOROD

1253

Pskov

Staraya Rusa

Izborsk

Porkhov

1269

1298

1323

Opochka

Riga

Velikie Luki

Dvina

1213

Torzhok

Tver

Volga

1238

MONGOLS

Polotsk

1245

1253

Volokolamsk

1238

Moscow

LITHUANIANS

Territory of the Republic of Novgorod 1136–1478

Province of Pskov, gaining its independence from Novgorod in 1348

Principal military attacks on the Republic by the Swedes, the Teutonic Knights, the Lithuanians and the Mongols; with dates

0   100
Miles

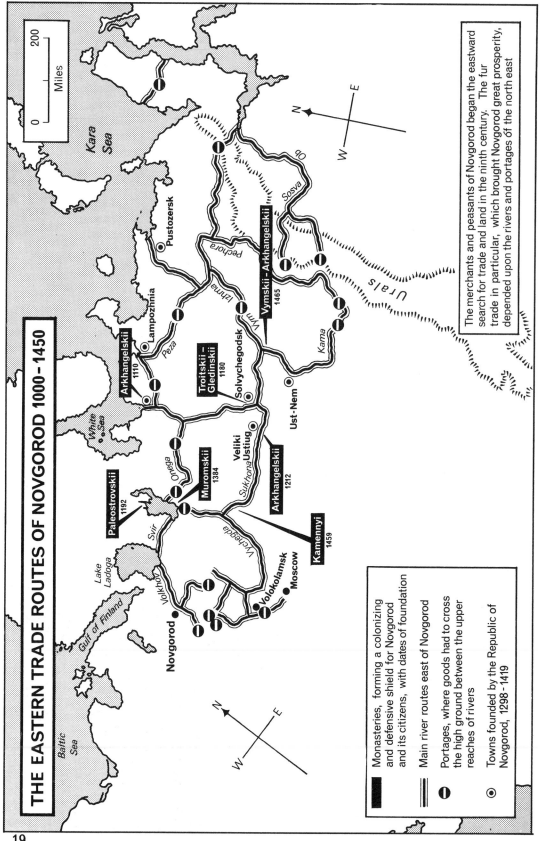

THE EASTERN TRADE ROUTES OF NOVGOROD 1000–1450

The merchants and peasants of Novgorod began the eastward search for trade and land in the ninth century. The fur trade in particular, which brought Novgorod great prosperity, depended upon the rivers and portages of the north east

Monasteries, forming a colonizing and defensive shield for Novgorod and its citizens, with dates of foundation

Main river routes east of Novgorod

Portages, where goods had to cross the high ground between the upper reaches of rivers

Towns founded by the Republic of Novgorod, 1298–1419

Kara Sea

Pustozersk

Lampozhnia

Arkhangelskii 1110

Troitskii–Gledinskii 1180

Solvychegodsk

Vymskii–Arkhangelskii 1465

Vym

Izhma

Pechora

Sosva

Ob

Urals

Kama

Ust-Nem

Peza

White Sea

Onega

Muromskii 1384

Veliki Ustiug

Sukhona

Arkhangelskii 1212

Paleostrovskii 1192

Svir

Lake Ladoga

Volkhov

Vchegda

Kamennyi 1459

Volokolamsk

Moscow

Novgorod

Gulf of Finland

Baltic Sea

0 200 Miles

19

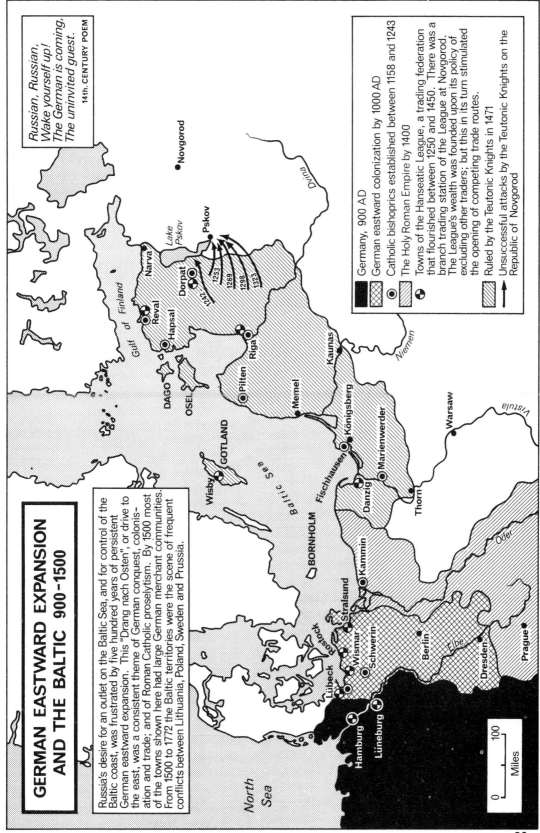

GERMAN EASTWARD EXPANSION
AND THE BALTIC 900–1500

Russia's desire for an outlet on the Baltic Sea, and for control of the Baltic coast, was frustrated by five hundred years of persistent German eastward expansion. This "Drang nach Osten", or drive to the east, was a consistent theme of German conquest, colonisation and trade; and of Roman Catholic proselytism. By 1500 most of the towns shown here had large German merchant communities. From 1500 to 1772 the Baltic territories were the scene of frequent conflicts between Lithuania, Poland, Sweden and Prussia.

Russian, Russian,
Wake yourself up!
The German is coming,
The uninvited guest.
14th. CENTURY POEM

Germany, 900 AD

German eastward colonization by 1000 AD

Catholic bishoprics established between 1158 and 1243

The Holy Roman Empire by 1400

Towns of the Hanseatic League, a trading federation that flourished between 1250 and 1450. There was a branch trading station of the League at Novgorod. The League's wealth was founded upon its policy of excluding other traders; but this in its turn stimulated the opening of competing trade routes.

Ruled by the Teutonic Knights in 1471

Unsuccessful attacks by the Teutonic Knights on the Republic of Novgorod

Novgorod

North
Sea

Hamburg
Lüneburg
Lübeck
Wismar
Schwerin
Berlin
Dresden
Prague
Elbe
Oder
Vistula
Warsaw
Thorn
Danzig
Kammin
Stralsund
Rostock
BORNHOLM
Marienwerder
Königsberg
Fischhausen
Memel
Kaunas
Niemen
GOTLAND
Wisby
Baltic Sea
DAGO
OSEL
Pilten
Riga
Hapsal
Reval
Narva
Gulf of Finland
Lake
Pskov
Pskov
Dorpat
1242
1253
1269
1298
1323
Dvina

0   100
Miles

20

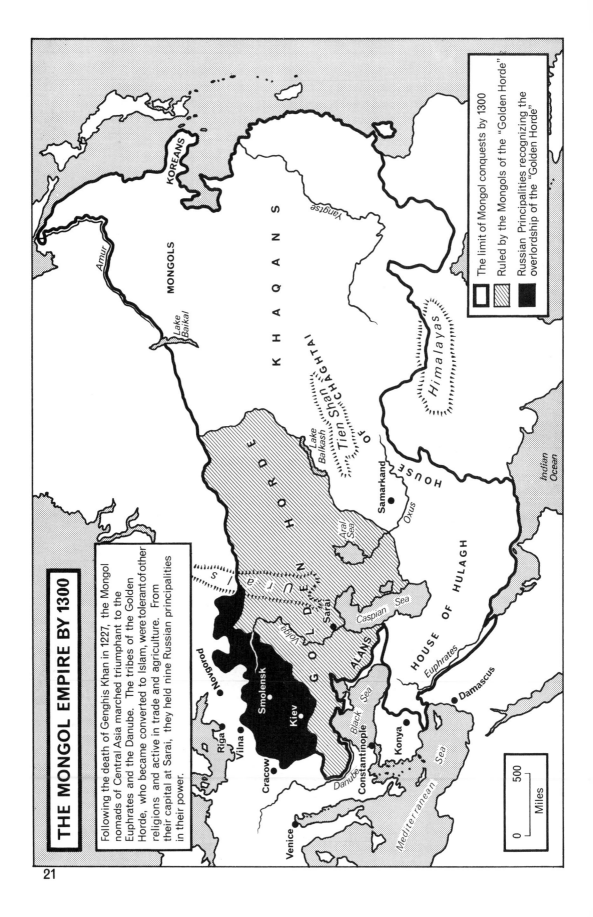

THE MONGOL EMPIRE BY 1300

Following the death of Genghis Khan in 1227, the Mongol nomads of Central Asia marched triumphant to the Euphrates and the Danube. The tribes of the Golden Horde, who became converted to Islam, were tolerant of other religions and active in trade and agriculture. From their capital at Sarai, they held nine Russian principalities in their power.

The limit of Mongol conquests by 1300

Ruled by the Mongols of the "Golden Horde"

Russian Principalities recognizing the overlordship of the "Golden Horde"

KOREANS

MONGOLS

Amur

Lake Baikal

Yangtse

K H A Q A N S

Tien Shan

CHAGHTAI

Lake Balkash

Himalayas

O F

H O U S E

Indian Ocean

Samarkand

Oxus

Aral Sea

S I B E R I A N S

G O L D E N   H O R D E

HOUSE OF HULAGH

Caspian Sea

Sarai

Volga

Euphrates

ALANS

Damascus

Novgorod

Smolensk

Kiev

Black Sea

Konya

Riga

Vilna

Cracow

Danube

Constantinople

Mediterranean Sea

Venice

0   500

Miles

21

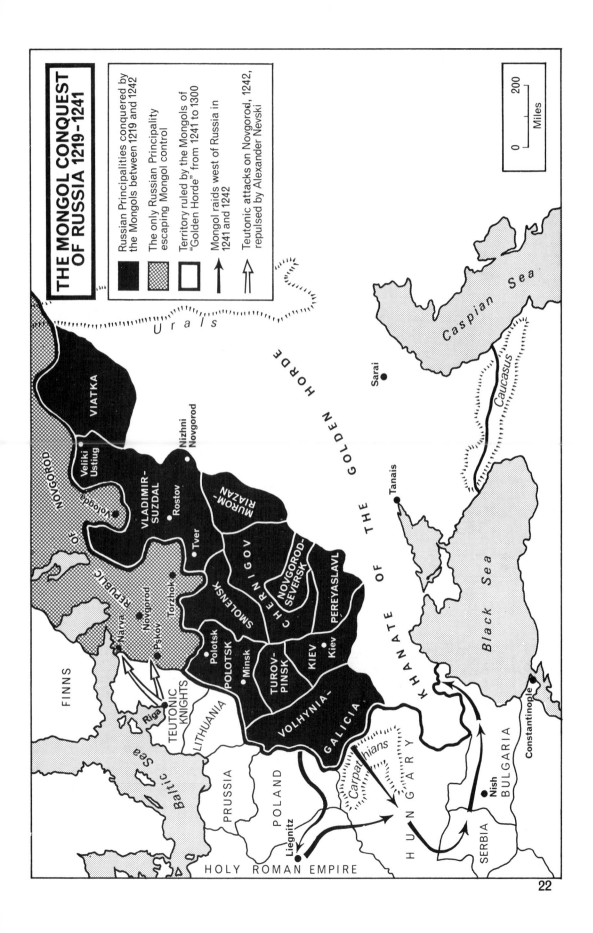

THE MONGOL CONQUEST OF RUSSIA 1219–1241

Russian Principalities conquered by the Mongols between 1219 and 1242

The only Russian Principality escaping Mongol control

Territory ruled by the Mongols of "Golden Horde" from 1241 to 1300

Mongol raids west of Russia in 1241 and 1242

Teutonic attacks on Novgorod, 1242, repulsed by Alexander Nevski

Caspian Sea

Caucasus

Sarai

U r a l s

VIATKA

Tanais

Nizhni Novgorod

Veliki Ustiug

NOVGOROD

VLADIMIR-SUZDAL

Rostov

MUROM-RIAZAN

Black Sea

Vologda

REPUBLIC OF

Tver

CHERNIGOV

NOVGOROD-SEVERSK

SMOLENSK

PEREYASLAVL

Narva

Novgorod

Torzhok

Pskov

Polotsk

Minsk

POLOTSK

TUROV-PINSK

KIEV

Kiev

FINNS

RIGA

Riga

TEUTONIC KNIGHTS

LITHUANIA

VOLHYNIA-GALICIA

Constantinople

Baltic Sea

PRUSSIA

POLAND

Liegnitz

Carpathians

H U N G A R Y

SERBIA

Nish

BULGARIA

K H A N A T E   O F   T H E   G O L D E N   H O R D E

HOLY ROMAN EMPIRE

200

0

Miles

22

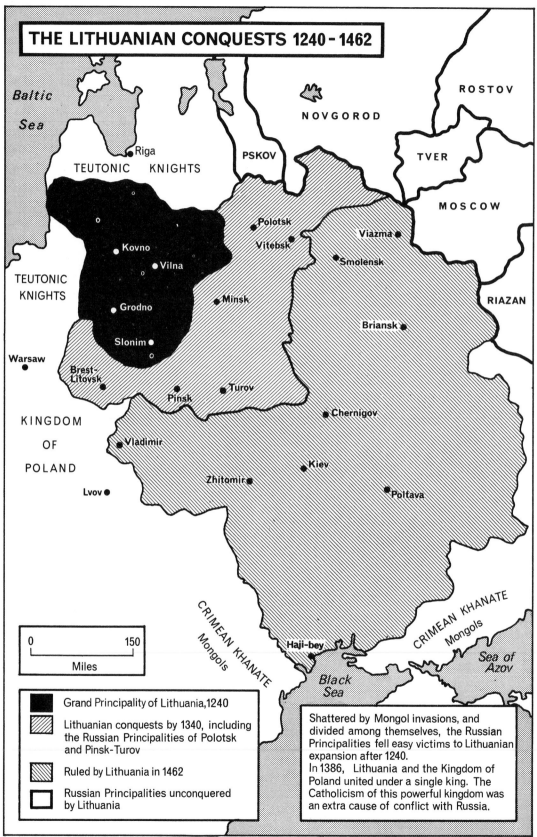

THE LITHUANIAN CONQUESTS 1240 - 1462

Baltic Sea

ROSTOV

NOVGOROD

TVER

PSKOV

• Riga

TEUTONIC KNIGHTS

MOSCOW

• Polotsk

• Viazma

Vitebsk •

• Smolensk

TEUTONIC KNIGHTS

○ Kovno

• Vilna

RIAZAN

• Minsk

Grodno •

• Briansk

Slonim •

Warsaw •

Brest-Litovsk •

• Turov

Pinsk •

KINGDOM OF POLAND

• Chernigov

Vladimir •

• Kiev

Zhitomir •

Lvov •

• Poltava

CRIMEAN KHANATE Mongols

Haji-bey •

CRIMEAN KHANATE Mongols

Black Sea

Sea of Azov

| 0 | 150 |

Miles

Legend:

- ■ Grand Principality of Lithuania, 1240
- ▨ Lithuanian conquests by 1340, including the Russian Principalities of Polotsk and Pinsk-Turov
- ▨ Ruled by Lithuania in 1462
- □ Russian Principalities unconquered by Lithuania

Shattered by Mongol invasions, and divided among themselves, the Russian Principalities fell easy victims to Lithuanian expansion after 1240.

In 1386, Lithuania and the Kingdom of Poland united under a single king. The Catholicism of this powerful kingdom was an extra cause of conflict with Russia.

THE EASTWARD SPREAD OF CATHOLICISM BY 1462

Simultaneously with the Mongol invasions from the east, Russia was subjected to the continual westward movement of Roman Catholicism. Under Swedish and Lithuanian pressure, Russian Orthodoxy was pushed back almost to Moscow. Roman Catholicism also made advances against the Orthodox Bulgars in the Balkans, and against the Muslim lands in the eastern Mediterranean.

LAPLAND
1300

NORWAY

SWEDEN

DENMARK

Baltic Sea

RUSSIA

Vyborg
1293

Reval
1219

Novgorod

Pskov

Tver

Moscow

Mitava
1271

Kaluga

Danzig
1200

Vilna
1386

Smolensk
1450

PRUSSIA

Warsaw

LITHUANIA

THE

POLAND

Prague

Kiev
1385

HOLY

BOHEMIA

GALICIA

ROMAN

Vienna

Lvov
1340

UKRAINE

Tana
1261

EMPIRE

HUNGARY

CROATIA

TRANSYLVANIA

Kaffa
1261

Black   Sea

Rome

BALKANS

Constantinople
1261

Amastris
1310

Samsun
1310

Athens
1305

Aegean Sea

Edessa
1098

Antioch
1098

■ The Roman Catholic world in 1000 AD

▨ Conquered between 1000 and 1462 AD by Roman Catholic rulers, and forming part of Catholic kingdoms

0   300

Miles

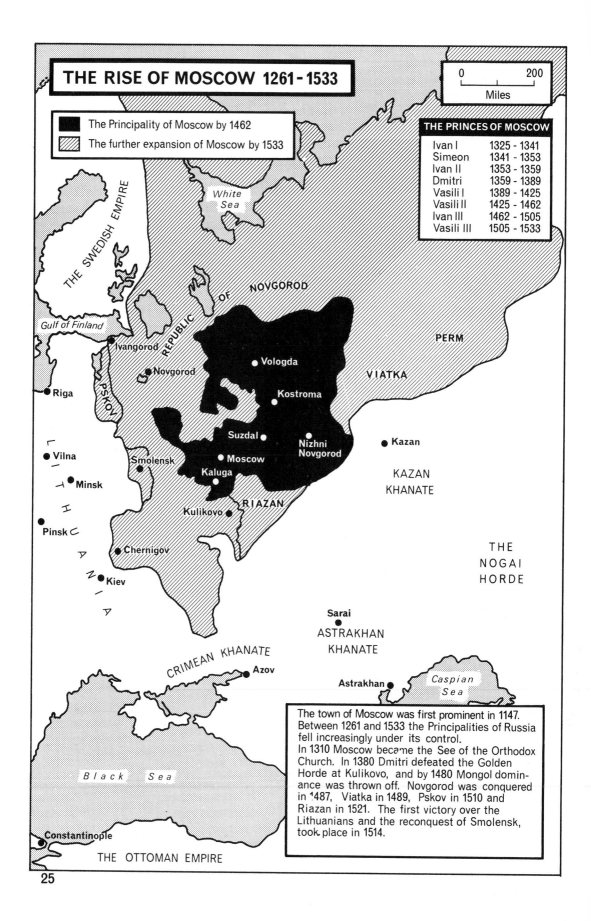

THE RISE OF MOSCOW 1261-1533

0   200
Miles

■ The Principality of Moscow by 1462
▨ The further expansion of Moscow by 1533

THE PRINCES OF MOSCOW	
Ivan I	1325 - 1341
Simeon	1341 - 1353
Ivan II	1353 - 1359
Dmitri	1359 - 1389
Vasili I	1389 - 1425
Vasili II	1425 - 1462
Ivan III	1462 - 1505
Vasili III	1505 - 1533

THE SWEDISH EMPIRE

White Sea

Gulf of Finland

REPUBLIC OF NOVGOROD

PERM

Ivangorod

● Novgorod

● Vologda

VIATKA

PSKOV

● Riga

● Kostroma

Suzdal ●

● Nizhni Novgorod

● Kazan

● Vilna

Smolensk ●

● Moscow

KAZAN KHANATE

L I T H U A N I A

● Minsk

Kaluga ●

R I A Z A N

Kulikovo ●

● Pinsk

THE NOGAI HORDE

● Chernigov

● Kiev

Sarai
●
ASTRAKHAN KHANATE

CRIMEAN KHANATE

● Azov

Astrakhan ●

Caspian Sea

Black Sea

The town of Moscow was first prominent in 1147. Between 1261 and 1533 the Principalities of Russia fell increasingly under its control.
In 1310 Moscow became the See of the Orthodox Church. In 1380 Dmitri defeated the Golden Horde at Kulikovo, and by 1480 Mongol dominance was thrown off. Novgorod was conquered in 1487, Viatka in 1489, Pskov in 1510 and Riazan in 1521. The first victory over the Lithuanians and the reconquest of Smolensk, took place in 1514.

● Constantinople

THE OTTOMAN EMPIRE

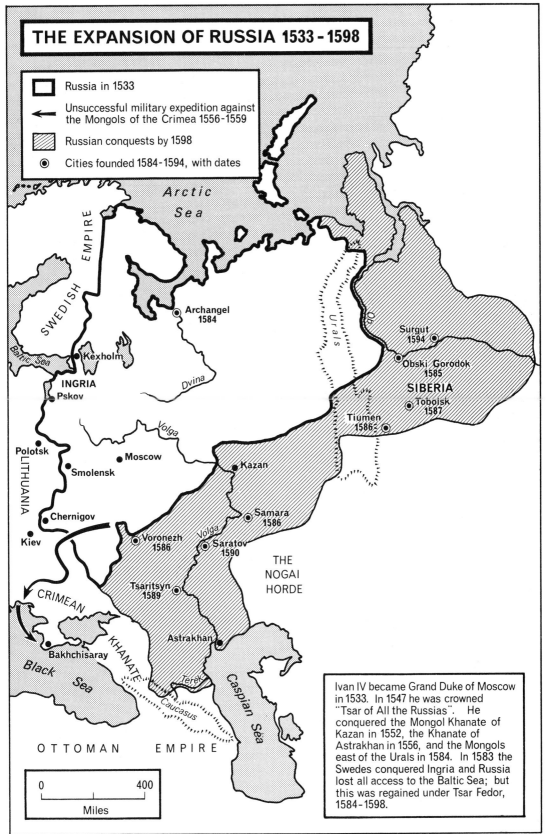

THE EXPANSION OF RUSSIA 1533-1598

☐ Russia in 1533

← Unsuccessful military expedition against
   the Mongols of the Crimea 1556-1559

▨ Russian conquests by 1598

◉ Cities founded 1584-1594, with dates

Arctic Sea

SWEDISH EMPIRE

Baltic Sea

Archangel
1584

Kexholm

Dvina

INGRIA

Pskov

Urals

Ob

Surgut
1594

Obski Gorodok
1885

SIBERIA

Tobolsk
1587

Tiumen
1586

Volga

Polotsk

Moscow

LITHUANIA

Smolensk

Kazan

Chernigov

Samara
1586

Kiev

Voronezh
1586

Volga

Saratov
1590

THE
NOGAI
HORDE

CRIMEAN

Tsaritsyn
1589

KHANATE

Astrakhan

Bakhchisaray

Black Sea

Terek

Caucasus

Caspian Sea

OTTOMAN EMPIRE

0	400

Miles

Ivan IV became Grand Duke of Moscow
in 1533. In 1547 he was crowned
"Tsar of All the Russias". He
conquered the Mongol Khanate of
Kazan in 1552, the Khanate of
Astrakhan in 1556, and the Mongols
east of the Urals in 1584. In 1583 the
Swedes conquered Ingria and Russia
lost all access to the Baltic Sea; but
this was regained under Tsar Fedor,
1584-1598.

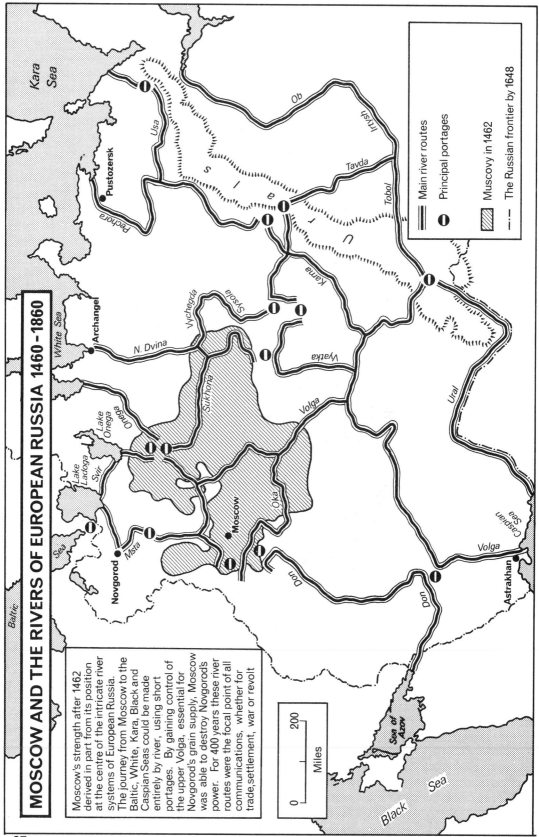

MOSCOW AND THE RIVERS OF EUROPEAN RUSSIA 1460–1860

Moscow's strength after 1462 derived in part from its position at the centre of the intricate river systems of European Russia. The journey from Moscow to the Baltic, White, Kara, Black and Caspian Seas could be made entirely by river, using short portages. By gaining control of the upper Volga, essential for Novgorod's grain supply, Moscow was able to destroy Novgorod's power. For 400 years these river routes were the focal point of all communications, whether for trade, settlement, war or revolt

Legend:
- Main river routes
- **0** Principal portages
- Muscovy in 1462
- – · – The Russian frontier by 1648

Scale: 0 — 200 Miles

Kara Sea

Pustozersk

Archangel

White Sea

Baltic Sea

Lake Ladoga

Lake Onega

Novgorod

Moscow

Astrakhan

Black Sea

Sea of Azov

Caspian Sea

Pechora

Usa

Ob

Irtysh

Tavda

Tobol

Ural

Kama

Vychegda

Sysola

N. Dvina

Vyatka

Volga

Sukhona

Onega

Svir

Msta

Oka

Don

Volga

Siberia

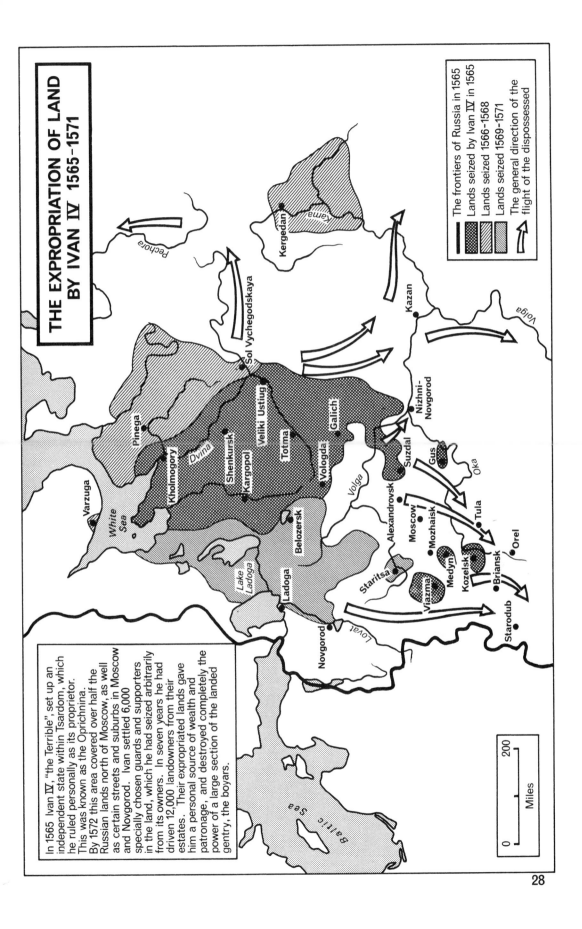

THE EXPROPRIATION OF LAND
BY IVAN IV 1565-1571

In 1565 Ivan IV, "the Terrible", set up an independent state within Tsardom, which he ruled personally as its proprietor. This was known as the Oprichnina. By 1572 this area covered over half the Russian lands north of Moscow, as well as certain streets and suburbs in Moscow and Novgorod. Ivan settled 6,000 specially chosen guards and supporters in the land, which he had seized arbitrarily from its owners. In seven years he had driven 12,000 landowners from their estates. Their expropriated lands gave him a personal source of wealth and patronage, and destroyed completely the power of a large section of the landed gentry, the boyars.

The frontiers of Russia in 1565
Lands seized by Ivan IV in 1565
Lands seized 1566-1568
Lands seized 1569-1571
The general direction of the flight of the dispossessed

Kergedan

Kama

Pechora

Sol Vychegodskaya

Kazan

Volga

Nizhni-Novgorod

Pinega

Dvina

Kholmogory

Shenkursk

Kargopol

Veliki Ustiug

Totma

Vologda

Galich

Suzdal

Gus

Oka

Varzuga

White Sea

Belozersk

Alexandrovsk

Moscow

Mozhaisk

Tula

Orel

Lake Ladoga

Ladoga

Volga

Staritsa

Viazma

Medyn

Kozelsk

Briansk

Starodub

Novgorod

Lovat

Baltic Sea

0   200
Miles

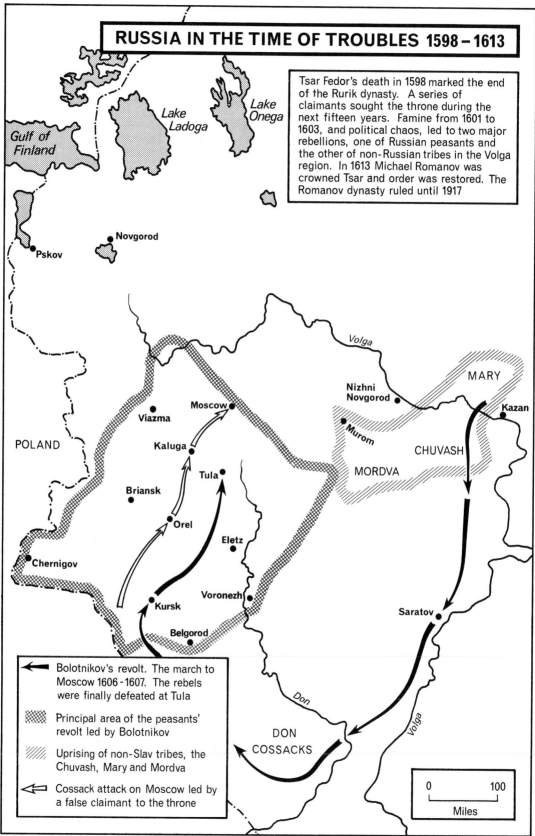

RUSSIA IN THE TIME OF TROUBLES 1598–1613

Tsar Fedor's death in 1598 marked the end of the Rurik dynasty. A series of claimants sought the throne during the next fifteen years. Famine from 1601 to 1603, and political chaos, led to two major rebellions, one of Russian peasants and the other of non-Russian tribes in the Volga region. In 1613 Michael Romanov was crowned Tsar and order was restored. The Romanov dynasty ruled until 1917

Gulf of Finland

Lake Ladoga

Lake Onega

Novgorod

Pskov

Volga

MARY

Nizhni Novgorod

Kazan

Moscow

Viazma

Murom

CHUVASH

POLAND

Kaluga

MORDVA

Tula

Brianski

Orel

Eletz

Chernigov

Voronezh

Kursk

Saratov

Belgorod

Don

Volga

DON COSSACKS

Bolotnikov's revolt. The march to Moscow 1606–1607. The rebels were finally defeated at Tula

Principal area of the peasants' revolt led by Bolotnikov

Uprising of non-Slav tribes, the Chuvash, Mary and Mordva

Cossack attack on Moscow led by a false claimant to the throne

0   100
Miles

29

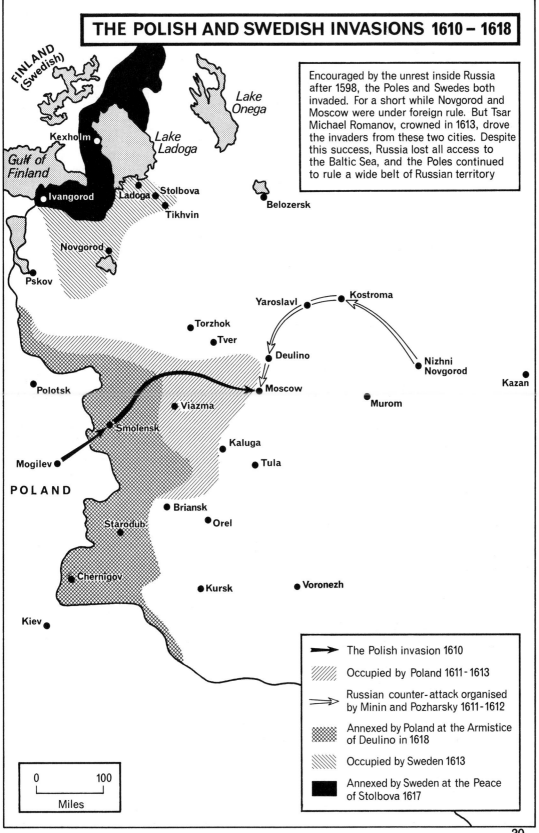

THE POLISH AND SWEDISH INVASIONS 1610 – 1618

Encouraged by the unrest inside Russia after 1598, the Poles and Swedes both invaded. For a short while Novgorod and Moscow were under foreign rule. But Tsar Michael Romanov, crowned in 1613, drove the invaders from these two cities. Despite this success, Russia lost all access to the Baltic Sea, and the Poles continued to rule a wide belt of Russian territory

FINLAND (Swedish)

Lake Onega

Lake Ladoga

Gulf of Finland

Kexholm

Ivangorod

Ladoga

Stolbova

Tikhvin

Belozersk

Novgorod

Pskov

Yaroslavl

Kostroma

Torzhok

Tver

Deulino

Nizhni Novgorod

Kazan

Polotsk

Moscow

Murom

Viazma

Smolensk

Kaluga

Mogilev

Tula

POLAND

Briansk

Orel

Starodub

Chernigov

Kursk

Voronezh

Kiev

	The Polish invasion 1610
	Occupied by Poland 1611 - 1613
	Russian counter-attack organised by Minin and Pozharsky 1611-1612
	Annexed by Poland at the Armistice of Deulino in 1618
	Occupied by Sweden 1613
	Annexed by Sweden at the Peace of Stolbova 1617

0   100

Miles

THE WESTWARD EXPANSION
OF RUSSIA 1640-1667

Western Russia in 1640

Cossack revolt of 1648 against Polish landowners and gentry. The revolt was led by Bogdan Khmelnitski. After defeating the Polish army, the Cossacks joined with the Polish peasantry, murdering over 100,000 Jews

Towns in which Jews were murdered by Cossacks and Poles 1648-1652

Advance of Russian and Ukrainian forces against the Poles 1654-1655

Polish territory ceded to Russia at the Armistice of Andrusovo in 1667

Baltic Sea

LITHUANIA

Nevel

Moscow

Polotsk

Viazma

Kovno

Vilna

Vitebsk

Smolensk

Königsberg

Orsha

Andrusovo

Borisov

P R U S S I A

Grodno

Minsk

Mogilev

Briansk

WHITE RUSSIA

Wa saw

Orel

Gomel

POLAND

Starodub

Brest-Litovsk

Pinsk

Mozyr

Kursk

Lublin

Turov

Pripet Marshes

Kovel

WESTERN UKRAINE

Chernigov

EASTERN UKRAINE

Belgorod

Zamosc

Lutsk

Berestechke

Rovno

Przemysl

Belz

Kiev

Kharkov

Lvov

Zhitomir

Pereyaslavl

Zbarazh

C a r p a t h i a n s

Poltava

Kamenets

Bar

Vinnitsa

Korsun

H U N G A R Y

Kodak

ZAPOROZHE

0   100

Miles

OTTOMAN
EMPIRE

Sech

CRIMEAN
KHANATE

Haji-bey

SOCIAL UNREST 1648 and 1670

In 1648 uprisings took place in many of the principal Russian towns. As a result, a new code of laws was drawn up, protecting the rights of traders and town-dwellers. In 1670 a Don Cossack, Stenka Razin, led a widespread revolt of Cossacks, peasants, small traders, minor officials and the dispossessed of the Volga, Don and Donets river valleys. The revolt was crushed in 1671 and Razin broken on the wheel in Moscow.

Kargopol

Solvychegodsk

Olonets

Veliki Ustiug

Cherdin

Totma

Solikamsk

Gdov

Novgorod

Romanov

Pskov

Volga

Ostrov

Vladimir

Ruza

Yadrin

Moscow

Simbirsk

Koslov

Penza

Samara

Tambov

Donets

Kursk

Voronezh

Saratov

Don

Tsaritsyn

DON
COSSACKS

Gurev

*Sea of
Azov*

Astrakhan

*Caspian
Sea*

Black Sea

Terski
Gorodok

- ◉ Urban uprisings of 1648-1650
- ■ The peasants' revolt led by Stenka Razin 1670-1671
- — The Russian frontier in 1670

0   500

Miles

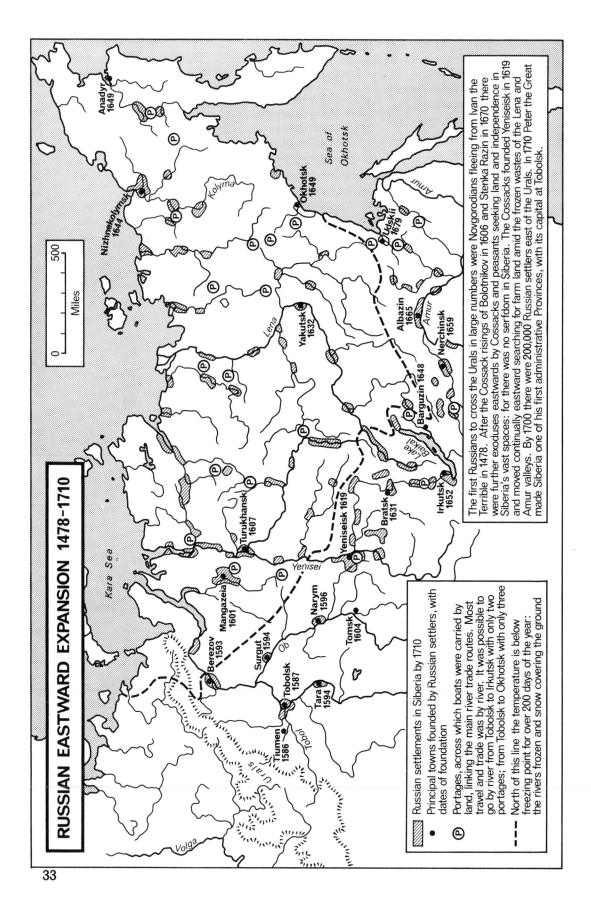

RUSSIAN EASTWARD EXPANSION 1478–1710

The first Russians to cross the Urals in large numbers were Novgorodians fleeing from Ivan the Terrible in 1478. After the Cossack risings of Bolotnikov in 1606 and Stenka Razin in 1670 there were further exoduses eastwards by Cossacks and peasants seeking land and independence in Siberia's vast spaces: for there was no serfdom in Siberia. The Cossacks founded Yeniseisk in 1619 and moved continually eastward searching for farm land amid the frozen wastes of the Lena and Amur valleys. By 1700 there were 200,000 Russian settlers east of the Urals. In 1710 Peter the Great made Siberia one of his first administrative Provinces, with its capital at Tobolsk.

◫ Russian settlements in Siberia by 1710

● Principal towns founded by Russian settlers, with dates of foundation

Ⓟ Portages, across which boats were carried by land, linking the main river trade routes. Most travel and trade was by river. It was possible to go by river from Tobolsk to Irkutsk with only two portages; from Tobolsk to Okhotsk with only three

--- North of this line the temperature is below freezing point for over 200 days of the year: the rivers frozen and snow covering the ground

500

Miles

0

Anadyr 1649

Nizhnekolymsk 1644

Okhotsk 1649

Udskii 1679

Albazin 1665

Nerchinsk 1659

Barguzin 1648

Yakutsk 1632

Irkutsk 1652

Bratsk 1631

Turukhansk 1607

Yeniseisk 1619

Mangazeia 1601

Narym 1596

Surgut 1594

Tomsk 1604

Berezov 1593

Tobolsk 1587

Tara 1594

Tiumen 1586

Sea of Okhotsk

Kolyma

Lena

Amur

Lake Baikal

Yenisei

Ob

Tobol

Kara Sea

Urals

Volga

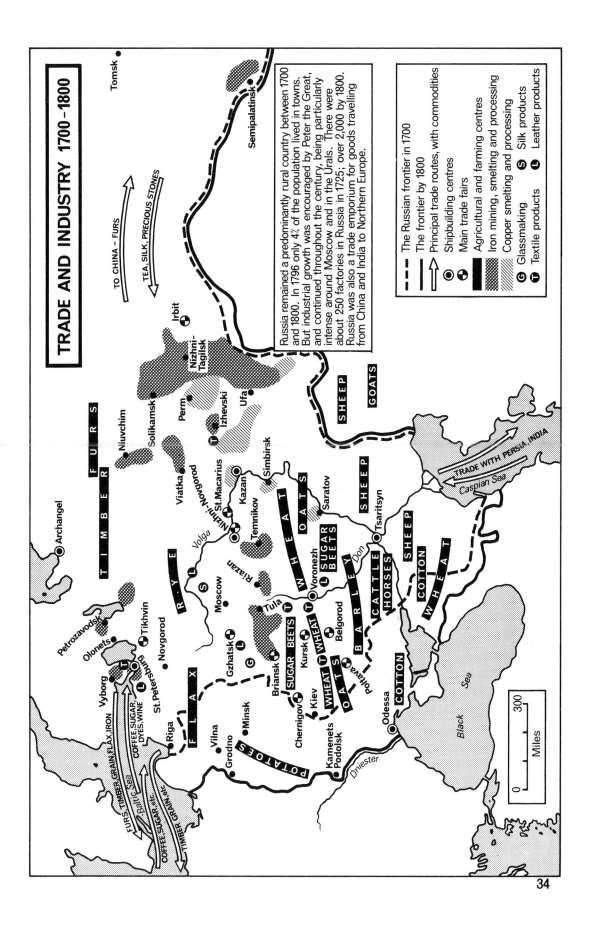

TRADE AND INDUSTRY 1700–1800

Russia remained a predominantly rural country between 1700 and 1800. In 1796 only 4% of the population lived in towns. But industrial growth was encouraged by Peter the Great, and continued throughout the century, being particularly intense around Moscow and in the Urals. There were about 250 factories in Russia in 1725; over 2,000 by 1800. Russia was also a trade emporium for goods travelling from China and India to Northern Europe.

Legend:
- — — — The Russian frontier in 1700
- ——— The frontier by 1800
- ⟶ Principal trade routes, with commodities
- ◉ Shipbuilding centres
- ⦿ Main trade fairs
- ◕ Agricultural and farming centres
- ■ Iron mining, smelting and processing
- ▦ Copper smelting and processing
- Ⓖ Glassmaking
- Ⓣ Textile products
- Ⓢ Silk products
- Ⓛ Leather products

TO CHINA – FURS

TEA, SILK, PRECIOUS STONES

Tomsk

Semipalatinsk

Irbit

Nizhni-Tagilsk

Niuvchim

Solikamsk

Perm

Izhevski

Ufa

SHEEP

GOATS

FURS

TIMBER

Viatka

Simbirsk

St.Macarius

Nizhni-Novgorod

Kazan

Temnikov

Saratov

SHEEP

TRADE WITH PERSIA, INDIA

Caspian Sea

Archangel

Volga

Riazan

WHEAT

OATS

SUGAR BEETS

Voronezh

Don

Tsaritsyn

SHEEP

Petrozavodsk

Olonets

Novgorod

Moscow

Tula

BARLEY

CATTLE

HORSES

SHEEP

COTTON

WHEAT

RYE

Tikhvin

Vyborg

St. Petersburg

Gzhatsk

Briansk

SUGAR BEETS

Kursk

WHEAT

Belgrod

FURS, TIMBER, GRAIN, FLAX, IRON

COFFEE, SUGAR, DYES, WINE

Baltic Sea

Riga

FLAX

Vilna

Minsk

Chernigov

Kiev

WHEAT

OATS

Poltava

COFFEE, SUGAR, etc.

TIMBER, GRAIN, etc.

Grodno

Kamenets Podolsk

POTATOES

Dniester

Odessa

COTTON

Black Sea

0   300
Miles

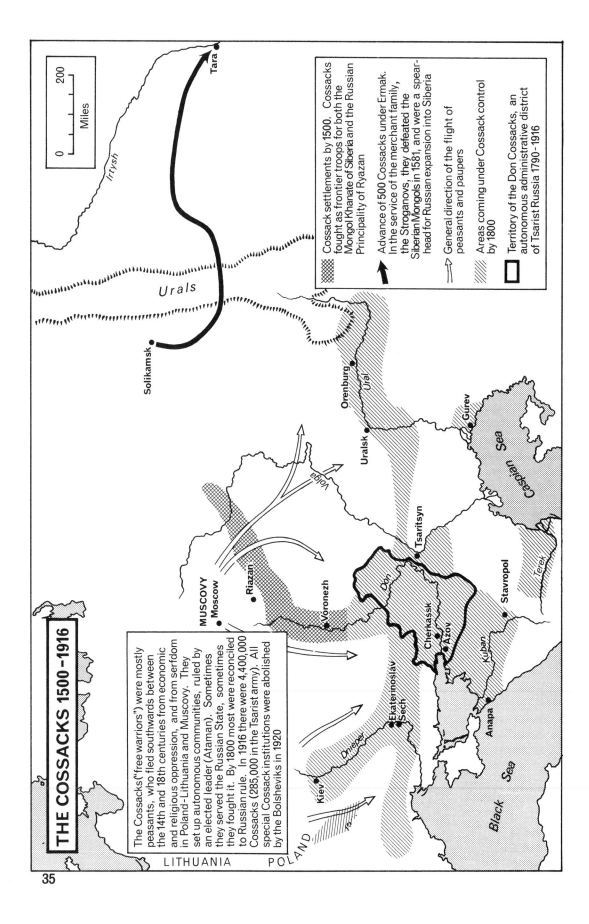

THE COSSACKS 1500–1916

The Cossacks("free warriors") were mostly peasants, who fled southwards between the 14th and 18th centuries from economic and religious oppression, and from serfdom in Poland-Lithuania and Muscovy. They set up autonomous communities, ruled by an elected leader (Ataman). Sometimes they served the Russian State, sometimes they fought it. By 1800 most were reconciled to Russian rule. In 1916 there were 4,400,000 Cossacks (285,000 in the Tsarist army). All special Cossack institutions were abolished by the Bolsheviks in 1920

Cossack settlements by 1500. Cossacks fought as frontier troops for both the Mongol Khanate of Siberia and the Russian Principality of Ryazan

Advance of 500 Cossacks under Ermak. In the service of the merchant family, the Stroganovs, they defeated the Siberian Mongols in 1581, and were a spearhead for Russian expansion into Siberia

General direction of the flight of peasants and paupers

Areas coming under Cossack control by 1800

Territory of the Don Cossacks, an autonomous administrative district of Tsarist Russia 1790-1916

Tara

Irtysh

200

Miles

0

Urals

Solikamsk

Orenburg

Ural

Uralsk

Gurev

Caspian Sea

Volga

Tsaritsyn

Don

Cherkassk

Azov

Stavropol

Terek

Kuban

MUSCOVY
Moscow

Riazan

Voronezh

Ekaterinoslav
Sech

Dnieper

Kiev

Anapa

Black Sea

LITHUANIA

POLAND

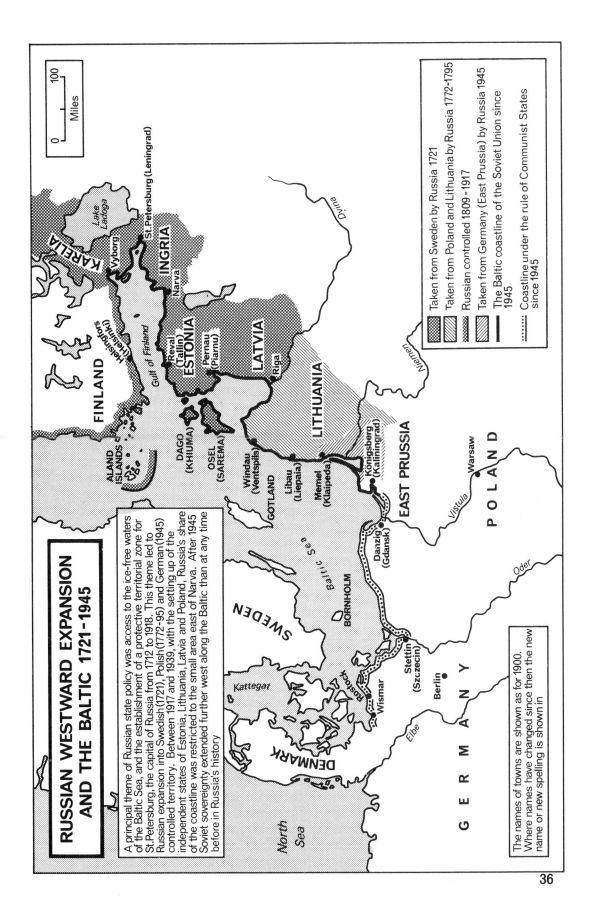

RUSSIAN WESTWARD EXPANSION AND THE BALTIC 1721-1945

A principal theme of Russian state policy was access to the ice-free waters of the Baltic Sea, and the establishment of a protective territorial zone for St.Petersburg, the capital of Russia from 1712 to 1918. This theme led to Russian expansion into Swedish (1721), Polish (1772-95) and German (1945) controlled territory. Between 1917 and 1939, with the setting up of the independent states of Estonia, Lithuania, Latvia and Poland, Russia's share of the coastline was restricted to the small area east of Narva. After 1945 Soviet sovereignty extended further west along the Baltic than at any time before in Russia's history

The names of towns are shown as for 1900. Where names have changed since then the new name or new spelling is shown in

Taken from Sweden by Russia 1721

Taken from Poland and Lithuania by Russia 1772-1795

Russian controlled 1809 - 1917

Taken from Germany (East Prussia) by Russia 1945

The Baltic coastline of the Soviet Union since 1945

Coastline under the rule of Communist States since 1945

KARELIA

INGRIA

Lake Ladoga

Vyborg

St.Petersburg (Leningrad)

Narva

ESTONIA

Reval (Tallin)

Pernau (Piarnu)

LATVIA

Riga

Dvina

LITHUANIA

Niemen

FINLAND

Helsingfors (Helsinki)

Gulf of Finland

ÅLAND ISLANDS

DAGO (KHIUMA)

OSEL (SAREMA)

Windau (Ventspils)

Libau (Liepaia)

Memel (Klaipeda)

Königsberg (Kaliningrad)

EAST PRUSSIA

Vistula

POLAND

Warsaw

GOTLAND

Baltic Sea

BORNHOLM

Danzig (Gdansk)

Oder

SWEDEN

Kattegat

Rostock

Wismar

Stettin (Szczecin)

Berlin

G E R M A N Y

DENMARK

North Sea

Elbe

0 100 Miles

36

WAR AND REVOLT UNDER PETER THE GREAT
1695 – 1723

Peter the Great's reign saw a series of widespread revolts ruthlessly crushed, the successful conquest of Swedish land, and Russian access to the ice-free waters of the Baltic Sea. But Peter was unable to drive the Turk from the Crimea, or to reach the Black Sea.

1695	Unsuccessful attack on the Turks at Azov
1696	Azov captured from the Turks. Taganrog founded as a new naval base
1700	Russians defeated by the Swedes at Narva
1709	Swedes defeated by the Russians at Poltava
1710	First Russian attacks against the Swedes, leading to Baltic annexations from Sweden in 1721
1711	Unsuccessful attack against the Turks at Jassy and Braila. Azov and Taganrog returned to Turkey
1722	Successful attack against Persia largely to forestall a Turkish advance to the Persian shore of the Caspian Sea

The privileged Moscow garrison, or Streltsy, who had helped Peter's half-sister Sophia seize power in 1682, had been exiled by him to Astrakhan in 1698. They opposed his increasingly heavy taxation and in 1705 set up a Cossack-style Government and elected an Ataman. Peter refused all pleas for mercy; the revolt was crushed and its leaders were executed with great cruelty, 1706-1708.

The Bashkirs, a Muslim nomad people subject to Russia since 1557, resented Russian colonization and sought Crimean and Turkish help to assert their independence. In 1708 they attacked Russian colonists and destroyed over 300 villages from the Ural river to the Volga, killing or capturing 13,000 settlers. The revolt was not finally crushed until 1711.

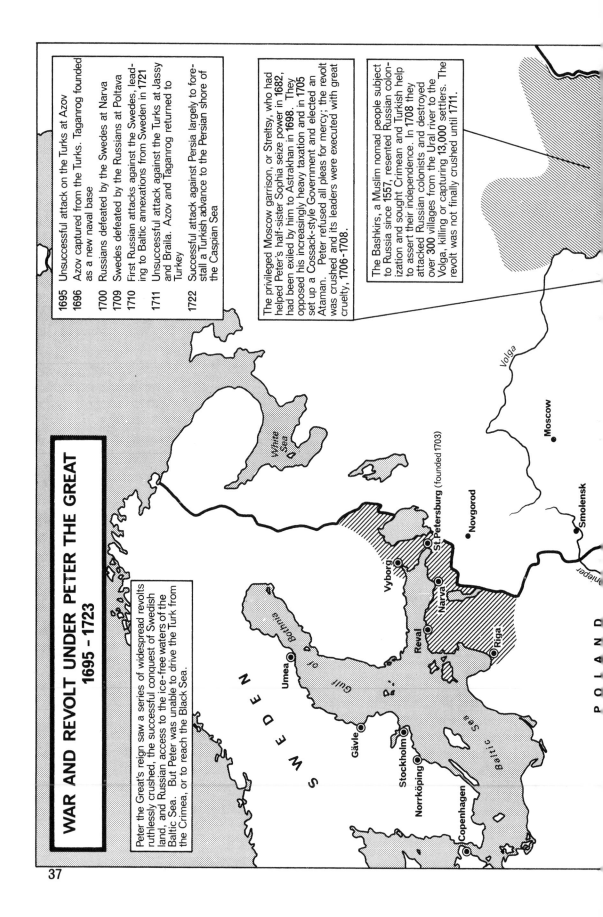

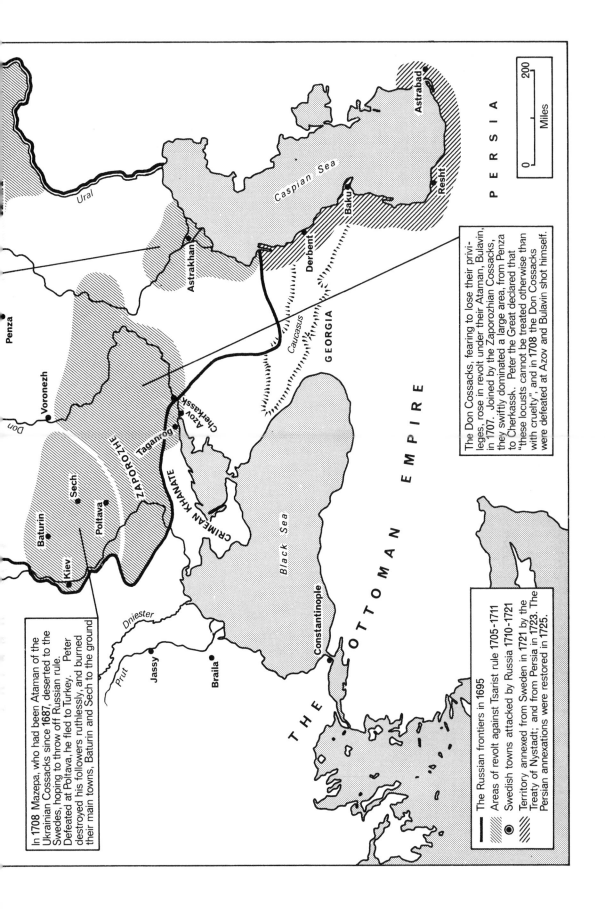

In 1708 Mazepa, who had been Ataman of the Ukrainian Cossacks since 1687, deserted to the Swedes, hoping to throw off Russian rule. Defeated at Poltava, he fled to Turkey. Peter destroyed his followers ruthlessly, and burned their main towns, Baturin and Sech to the ground.

The Don Cossacks, fearing to lose their privileges, rose in revolt under their Ataman, Bulavin, in 1707. Joined by the Zaporozhian Cossacks, they swiftly dominated a large area, from Penza to Cherkassk. Peter the Great declared that "these locusts cannot be treated otherwise than with cruelty", and in 1708 the Don Cossacks were defeated at Azov and Bulavin shot himself.

The Russian frontiers in 1695

Areas of revolt against Tsarist rule 1705-1711

⊙ Swedish towns attacked by Russia 1710-1721

Territory annexed from Sweden in 1721 by the Treaty of Nystadt; and from Persia in 1723. The Persian annexations were restored in 1725.

PERSIA

Miles
0   200

Astrabad

Resht

Baku

Derbent

Caspian Sea

Astrakhan

Penza

Voronezh

GEORGIA

Caucasus

Don

Ural

ZAPOROZHE

Sech

Baturin

Poltava

Kiev

Taganrog

Cherkassk

Azov

CRIMEAN KHANATE

Black Sea

Constantinople

THE   OTTOMAN   EMPIRE

Dniester

Prut

Jassy

Braila

THE PROVINCES AND POPULATION OF RUSSIA IN 1724

0   300
Miles

St. Petersburg

Selected as the site of a new town by Peter the Great in 1703, and built at great cost in human life by serf labour, St. Petersburg became the seat of the Russian Government in 1712. Courtiers and noble families were compelled by law to live there from 1725. The city had a population of 200,000 by 1788.

White Sea

Archangel

A R C H A N G E L

Dvina

S I B E R I A

Gulf of Finland

St. Petersburg

Novgorod

Pskov

Viatka

Perm

Vologda

Kostroma

S T.   P E T E R S B U R G

Tver

Volga

Kazan

Moscow

Nizhni Novgorod

K A Z A N

Smolensk

MOSCOW

Simbirsk

Mogilev

SMOLENSK

Riazan

Tula

Samara

Orel

Tambov

Penza

Orenburg

Chernigov

A Z O V

Saratov

Ural

Dnieper

K I E V

Voronezh

C O S S A C K S

Kiev

Poltava

Kharkov

Don

Volga

Dniester

C O S S A C K S

Azov

Caspian Sea

C O S S A C K S

Black Sea

COSSACKS

It was Peter the Great who first divided Russia into Provinces (known as "Gubernii" or "Governments"). These administrative divisions served a military, financial and judicial purpose. They enabled Peter to supervise the whole kingdom by means of Governors responsible directly to himself. Catherine the Great later divided these Provinces into smaller units. The establishment of Provincial administrations led to a rapid growth of bureaucracy, and a complex hierarchy of local seniority. The population of Russia in 1724 was just over 15 million, of whom only ½ million lived in towns.

—·—·— Russia's frontiers by 1725

▬▬▬▬ Provinces established by Peter the Great

Area with over 20 inhabitants in every square verst. (One verst = two-thirds of a mile)

Area with between 10 and 20 inhabitants per square verst

Russian territory with less than 10 inhabitants per square verst is not shaded

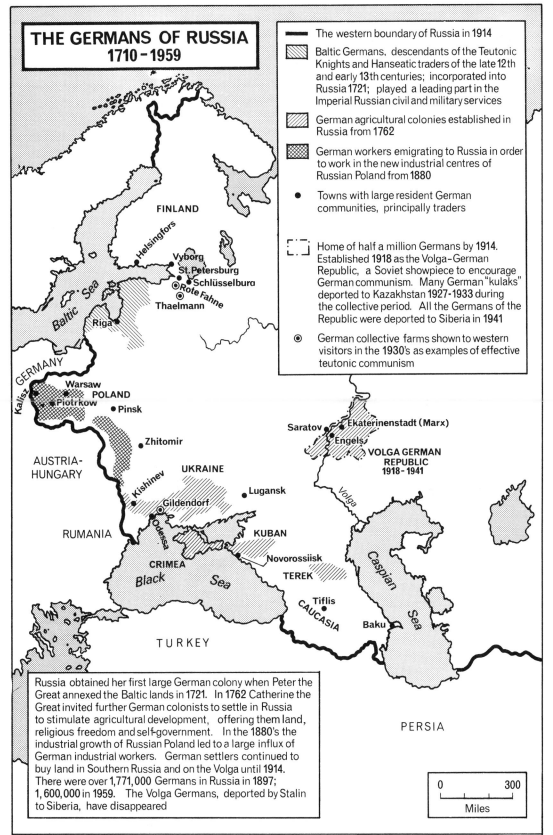

THE GERMANS OF RUSSIA 1710 – 1959

━━━ The western boundary of Russia in 1914

Baltic Germans, descendants of the Teutonic Knights and Hanseatic traders of the late 12th and early 13th centuries; incorporated into Russia 1721; played a leading part in the Imperial Russian civil and military services

German agricultural colonies established in Russia from 1762

German workers emigrating to Russia in order to work in the new industrial centres of Russian Poland from 1880

● Towns with large resident German communities, principally traders

⌐ ¬
⌊ ⌋ Home of half a million Germans by 1914. Established 1918 as the Volga-German Republic, a Soviet showpiece to encourage German communism. Many German "kulaks" deported to Kazakhstan 1927-1933 during the collective period. All the Germans of the Republic were deported to Siberia in 1941

◉ German collective farms shown to western visitors in the 1930's as examples of effective teutonic communism

FINLAND

Helsingfors

Vyborg
St.Petersburg
Schlüsselburg
◉ Rote Fahne
Thaelmann

Riga ●

Baltic Sea

GERMANY

Kalisz
Warsaw ●
POLAND
Piotrkow ●
● Pinsk

● Zhitomir

AUSTRIA-
HUNGARY

Kishinev ●
UKRAINE
Gildendorf ◉
● Lugansk

Odessa

RUMANIA

CRIMEA
Black   Sea

KUBAN
Novorossiisk
TEREK

Tiflis ●
CAUCASIA

Baku ●

Saratov ●
● Ekaterinenstadt (Marx)
Engels ●
VOLGA GERMAN REPUBLIC 1918-1941

Volga

Caspian   Sea

TURKEY

PERSIA

Russia obtained her first large German colony when Peter the Great annexed the Baltic lands in 1721. In 1762 Catherine the Great invited further German colonists to settle in Russia to stimulate agricultural development, offering them land, religious freedom and self-government. In the 1880's the industrial growth of Russian Poland led to a large influx of German industrial workers. German settlers continued to buy land in Southern Russia and on the Volga until 1914. There were over 1,771,000 Germans in Russia in 1897; 1,600,000 in 1959. The Volga Germans, deported by Stalin to Siberia, have disappeared

0   300
� Miles

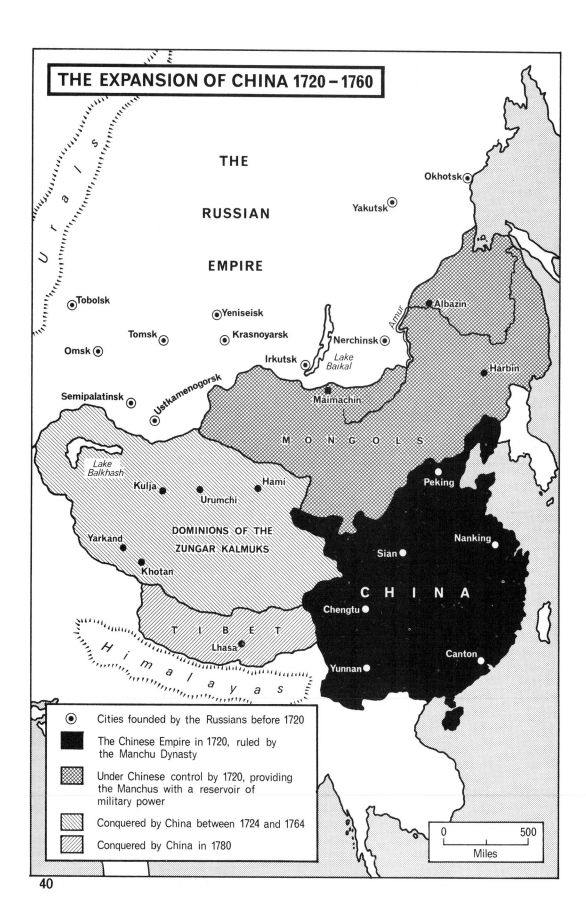

THE EXPANSION OF CHINA 1720–1760

THE

RUSSIAN

EMPIRE

Okhotsk

Yakutsk

U r a l s

Tobolsk

Yeniseisk

Omsk

Tomsk

Krasnoyarsk

Semipalatinsk

Ustkamenogorsk

Nerchinsk

Albazin

Amur

Irkutsk

Lake Baikal

Harbin

Maimachin

M O N G O L S

Lake Balkhash

Kulja

Hami

Peking

Urumchi

Nanking

DOMINIONS OF THE
ZUNGAR KALMUKS

Sian

Yarkand

C H I N A

Khotan

Chengtu

Canton

T I B E T

Lhasa

Yunnan

H i m a l a y a s

⊙   Cities founded by the Russians before 1720

■   The Chinese Empire in 1720, ruled by
the Manchu Dynasty

▦   Under Chinese control by 1720, providing
the Manchus with a reservoir of
military power

▨   Conquered by China between 1724 and 1764

▨   Conquered by China in 1780

0   500

Miles

40

RUSSIAN EXPANSION UNDER CATHERINE THE GREAT 1762-1796

The Provinces of Russia in 1750

Territory annexed by Russia 1762-1796, giving Russia an outlet on the Black Sea, and a common frontier with Prussia and Austria

White Sea

Archangel

ARCHANGEL

FINLAND

Helsingfors

ST. PETERSBURG

Baltic Sea

ESTONIA

LIVONIA

Novgorod

NOVGOROD

Vologda

Viatka

Perm

KURLAND

Pskov

Tver

MOSCOW

Moscow

KAZAN

Kazan

Ufa

UFA

Vilna

LITHUANIA

Minsk

SMOLENSK

NIZHNI NOVGOROD

PRUSSIA

Niemen

WHITE RUSSIA

Pinsk

Orel

BELGOROD

Stavropol

Samara

Warsaw

PODLESIA

Lutsk

KIEV

Kiev

VORONEZH

AUSTRIA

Belgorod

ASTRAKHAN

Dniester

Dnieper

PODOLIA

ZAPOROZHE

Jassy

Odessa

Taganrog

Astrakhan

CRIMEA

KUBAN

Caspian Sea

Kutchuk Kainardji

Sebastopol

KABARDA

Tarki

Black Sea

Constantinople

THE OTTOMAN EMPIRE

Kars

0   200
Miles

PERSIA

41

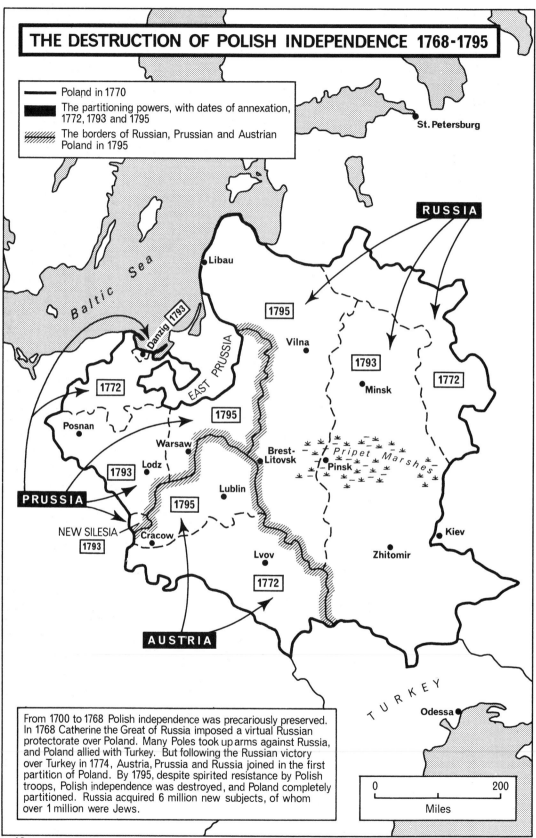

THE DESTRUCTION OF POLISH INDEPENDENCE 1768-1795

— Poland in 1770

▬ The partitioning powers, with dates of annexation, 1772, 1793 and 1795

▨ The borders of Russian, Prussian and Austrian Poland in 1795

St. Petersburg

RUSSIA

Baltic Sea

Libau

1795

Danzig 1793

Vilna

1772

EAST PRUSSIA

Posnan

1795

Warsaw

1793

Minsk

1772

Brest-Litovsk

Pripet Marshes

Lodz

Pinsk

PRUSSIA

Lublin

1795

NEW SILESIA
1793

Cracow

Kiev

Lvov

Zhitomir

1772

AUSTRIA

T U R K E Y

Odessa

From 1700 to 1768 Polish independence was precariously preserved. In 1768 Catherine the Great of Russia imposed a virtual Russian protectorate over Poland. Many Poles took up arms against Russia, and Poland allied with Turkey. But following the Russian victory over Turkey in 1774, Austria, Prussia and Russia joined in the first partition of Poland. By 1795, despite spirited resistance by Polish troops, Polish independence was destroyed, and Poland completely partitioned. Russia acquired 6 million new subjects, of whom over 1 million were Jews.

0   200

Miles

THE RUSSIAN ANNEXATIONS OF POLAND 1772-1795

0 ——————— 150
Miles

Baltic Sea

LATVIA
Pskov

Windau
Riga

Libau
Mitau

Palanga
Dvinsk
Nevel

Memel
Polotsk

LITHUANIA
1795

Kovno
Vitebsk
Smolensk

Königsberg
Vilna
1793
1772

EAST
PRUSSIA
Troki
Borisov
Orsha
Mogilev
Mstislav

Suvalki
Lida

Grodno
Minsk

Novogrudok
WHITE
RUSSIA

Vilkoviski
Mir
Bobruisk

Bialystok
Baranovichi
Starodub

Warsaw
Slutsk

Brest-Litovsk
Gomel

Pinsk
Pripet
Marshes

Pripet
Turov
Mozyr

Lublin
Kovel
Olevsk
Chernigov

AUSTRIAN-ANNEXED
POLAND
VOLHYNIA
Lutsk
WESTERN
UKRAINE

UKRAINE

Rovno
Kiev

Lvov
Dubno
Zhitomir
Pereyaslavl

Przemysl
Staro-
Konstantinov
Berdychev

GALICIA
Tarnopol
Boguslav

Stanislavov
Vinnitsa
PODOLIA

Kamenets-
Podolsk
Bug

BESSARABIA
Dniester
Balta

AUSTRIA
RUSSIAN-
ANNEXED
TURKEY

TURKEY
1791
Odessa
Kherson
1774

Black
Sea

Dvina
Dnieper
Dnieper

PRUSSIAN-ANNEXED POLAND

	The western part of Russia in 1770
- - -	Partition lines
⊙	Principal Polish military resistance to the Russians
▬▬	The western frontier of Russia 1795

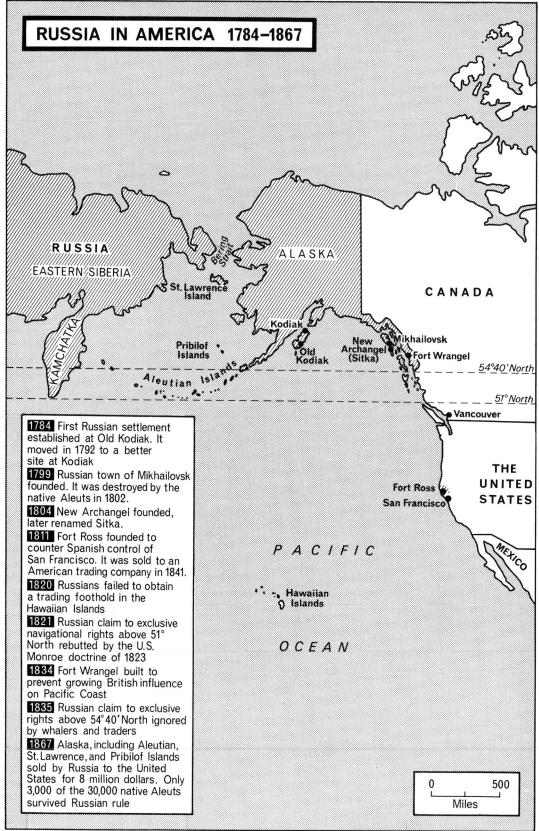

RUSSIA IN AMERICA 1784–1867

RUSSIA

EASTERN SIBERIA

KAMCHATKA

St. Lawrence Island

Bering Strait

ALASKA

CANADA

Pribilof Islands

Aleutian Islands

Kodiak

Old Kodiak

New Archangel (Sitka)

Mikhailovsk

Fort Wrangel

54°40' North

51° North

Vancouver

THE UNITED STATES

Fort Ross

San Francisco

PACIFIC

Hawaiian Islands

OCEAN

MEXICO

1784 First Russian settlement established at Old Kodiak. It moved in 1792 to a better site at Kodiak

1799 Russian town of Mikhailovsk founded. It was destroyed by the native Aleuts in 1802.

1804 New Archangel founded, later renamed Sitka.

1811 Fort Ross founded to counter Spanish control of San Francisco. It was sold to an American trading company in 1841.

1820 Russians failed to obtain a trading foothold in the Hawaiian Islands

1821 Russian claim to exclusive navigational rights above 51° North rebutted by the U.S. Monroe doctrine of 1823

1834 Fort Wrangel built to prevent growing British influence on Pacific Coast

1835 Russian claim to exclusive rights above 54°40' North ignored by whalers and traders

1867 Alaska, including Aleutian, St. Lawrence, and Pribilof Islands sold by Russia to the United States for 8 million dollars. Only 3,000 of the 30,000 native Aleuts survived Russian rule

0   500
Miles

RUSSIA IN THE MEDITERRANEAN 1798–1807

RUSSIA

Vienna

AUSTRIA

Dniester

Odessa

Sébastopol

Venice

Belgrade

Bucharest

Black Sea

Danube

Fano
Senigallia
ROMAN
REPUBLIC
(French)
Ancona

MONTENEGRO
Cattaro
(Kotor)

OTTOMAN

Constantinople

Rome

Adriatic Sea

Manfredonia
Bari

Salonika

Dardanelles

EMPIRE

Naples

PARTHENOPAEAN
REPUBLIC
(French)

Ægean
Sea

Palermo

CORFU
PAXO
LEUCAS
CEPHALONIA
ZANTE
ITHACA
Athens

Messina

CYTHERA

Mediterranean Sea

Aboukir
Alexandria

Cairo

EGYPT
(French)

Nile

Route of the principal Russian naval squadron
in the war against France, 1798–1800

⊙ Ports controlled by France, and bombarded by a
joint Russian-Turkish naval squadron, 1798–1800

▬ Islands seized by France from Venice in 1797,
and occupied by Russian forces 1800–1807.
The islands were transferred to France
in 1807 by the Treaty of Tilsit

▨ Acquired by France from Austria in 1806,
and occupied by Russia 1806–1807

0   200
Miles

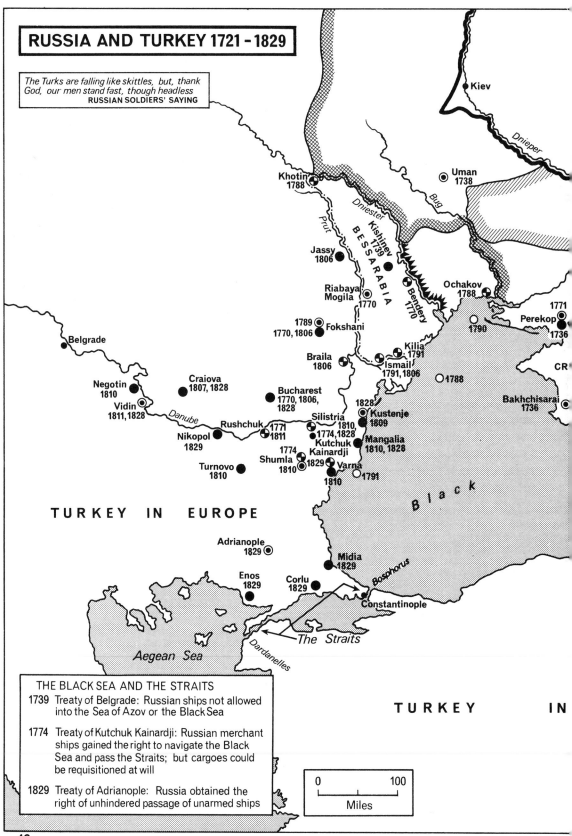

RUSSIA AND TURKEY 1721 - 1829

The Turks are falling like skittles, but, thank God, our men stand fast, though headless
RUSSIAN SOLDIERS' SAYING

Kiev

Dnieper

Khotin
1788

Uman
1738

Dniester

Bug

Kishinev
1739

BESSARABIA

Jassy
1806

Riabaya
Mogila
1770

Bendery
1770

Ochakov
1788

1771
1790

Perekop
1736

1789
1770, 1806

Fokshani

Kilia
1791

CR

Belgrade

Braila
1806

Ismail
1791, 1806

1788

Bakhchisarai
1736

Craiova
1807, 1828

Negotin
1810

Vidin
1811, 1828

Danube

Bucharest
1770, 1806,
1828

Silistria

1828
Kustenje
1809

Rushchuk
1771
1811

Nikopol
1829

1810
1774, 1828

Kutchuk
Kainardji

Mangalia
1810, 1828

1774
Shumla
1810

1829

Varna
1810

1791

Turnovo
1810

TURKEY   IN   EUROPE

B l a c k

Adrianople
1829

Midia
1829

Enos
1829

Corlu
1829

Bosphorus

Constantinople

The Straits

Dardanelles

Aegean Sea

TURKEY   IN

THE BLACK SEA AND THE STRAITS

1739 Treaty of Belgrade: Russian ships not allowed
into the Sea of Azov or the Black Sea

1774 Treaty of Kutchuk Kainardji: Russian merchant
ships gained the right to navigate the Black
Sea and pass the Straits; but cargoes could
be requisitioned at will

1829 Treaty of Adrianople: Russia obtained the
right of unhindered passage of unarmed ships

0   100

Miles

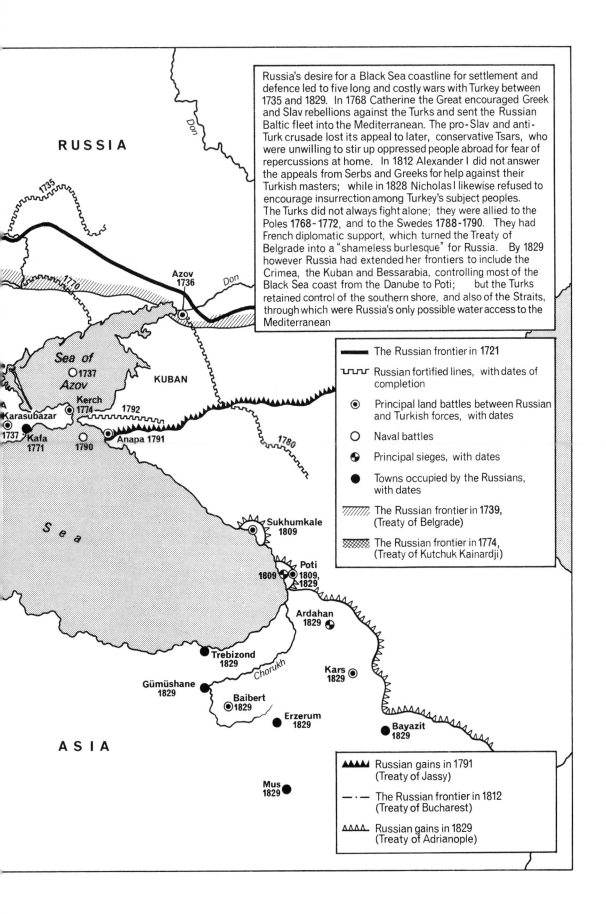

RUSSIA

Russia's desire for a Black Sea coastline for settlement and defence led to five long and costly wars with Turkey between 1735 and 1829. In 1768 Catherine the Great encouraged Greek and Slav rebellions against the Turks and sent the Russian Baltic fleet into the Mediterranean. The pro-Slav and anti-Turk crusade lost its appeal to later, conservative Tsars, who were unwilling to stir up oppressed people abroad for fear of repercussions at home. In 1812 Alexander I did not answer the appeals from Serbs and Greeks for help against their Turkish masters; while in 1828 Nicholas I likewise refused to encourage insurrection among Turkey's subject peoples. The Turks did not always fight alone; they were allied to the Poles 1768-1772, and to the Swedes 1788-1790. They had French diplomatic support, which turned the Treaty of Belgrade into a "shameless burlesque" for Russia. By 1829 however Russia had extended her frontiers to include the Crimea, the Kuban and Bessarabia, controlling most of the Black Sea coast from the Danube to Poti; but the Turks retained control of the southern shore, and also of the Straits, through which were Russia's only possible water access to the Mediterranean

Don

1735

Azov
1736

Don

Sea of
Azov   KUBAN
○1737

Kerch
1774   1792

Karasubazar
1737   Kafa
       1771   1790   Anapa 1791

1780

S e a

Sukhumkale
1809

Poti
1809   ⊕ 1809,
              1829

Ardahan
1829 ⊕

Trebizond
1829

Chorukh   Kars
                 1829 ◉

Gümüşhane
1829   Baibert
             ◉1829

             Erzerum
             1829   Bayazit
                               1829

ASIA

Mus
1829 ●

RUSSIA AND SWEDEN 1700-1809

0 — 300
Miles

From 1621 Sweden controlled the Baltic Sea and the Gulfs of Finland and Bothnia. In 1700 Peter the Great allied Russia with Poland and Denmark, in 1714 with Prussia and Hanover. His first conquest was Ingria, giving Russia a small but valued outlet on the Baltic. After several defeats, the Russians finally broke Sweden's dominance in 1721. Russia's annexation of Finland in 1809 further extended her control of the Baltic.

LAPLAND

Tornea

Uleaborg

Gulf of Bothnia

Vasa

FINLAND

KARELIA

Kexholm

Nystad
Abo

Helsingfors

Vyborg

Nöteborg

ALAND IS.

St Petersburg

Gulf of Finland

Narva

INGRIA

DAGO

Reval

Ivangorod

Novgorod

ESTLAND

ÖSEL

Dorpat

Pskov

SWEDEN

Stockholm

GOTLAND

LIVLAND

Riga

Baltic Sea

DENMARK

Copenhagen

Stralsund

BORNHOLM

POLAND

Stettin

SWEDISH POMERANIA

HANOVER

PRUSSIA

	Sweden in 1700
███	Swedish territory conquered by Peter the Great during the Great Northern War 1700-1721, and annexed to Russia at the Treaty of Nystad 1721
▨	Conquered by Russia, 1743
▨	Swedish territory conquered by Alexander I and annexed to Russia in 1809

47

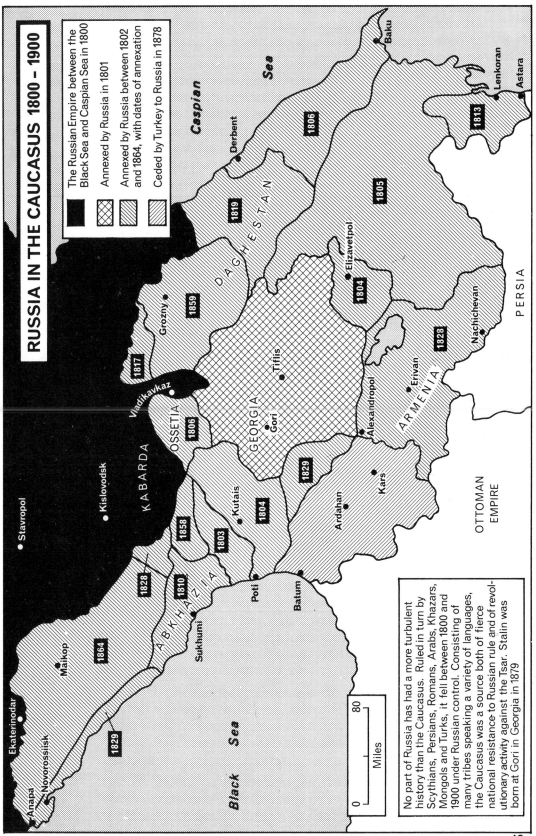

RUSSIA IN THE CAUCASUS 1800 – 1900

The Russian Empire between the
Black Sea and Caspian Sea in 1800

Annexed by Russia in 1801

Annexed by Russia between 1802
and 1864, with dates of annexation

Ceded by Turkey to Russia in 1878

Caspian Sea

Baku

Lenkoran

Astara

1813

Derbent

1806

1805

PERSIA

DAGHESTAN

1819

Elizavetpol

1804

Nachichevan

1859

Grozny

1817

Tiflis

1828

ARMENIA

Erivan

Vladikavkaz

OSSETIA

1806

GEORGIA

Gori

Alexandropol

KABARDA

1829

Kislovodsk

Kars

Stavropol

Kutais

1804

Ardahan

1858

1803

OTTOMAN
EMPIRE

1828

ABKHAZIA

1810

Poti

Batum

Ekaterinodar

Maikop

1864

Sukhumi

Novorossiisk

Anapa

1829

Black Sea

80

Miles

0

No part of Russia has had a more turbulent
history than the Caucasus. Ruled in turn by
Scythians, Persians, Romans, Arabs, Khazars,
Mongols and Turks, it fell between 1800 and
1900 under Russian control. Consisting of
many tribes speaking a variety of languages,
the Caucasus was a source both of fierce
national resistance to Russian rule and of revolutionary activity against the Tsar. Stalin was
born at Gori in Georgia in 1879

48

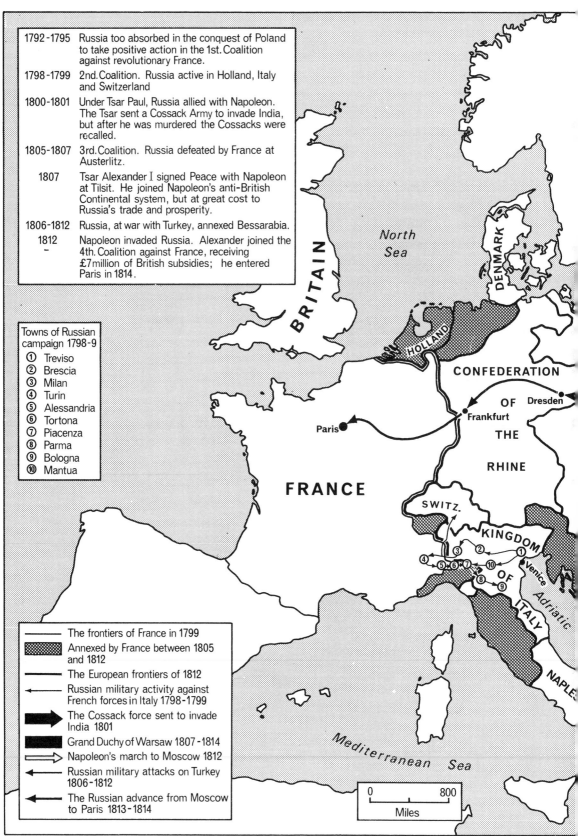

1792-1795   Russia too absorbed in the conquest of Poland to take positive action in the 1st. Coalition against revolutionary France.

1798-1799   2nd. Coalition. Russia active in Holland, Italy and Switzerland

1800-1801   Under Tsar Paul, Russia allied with Napoleon. The Tsar sent a Cossack Army to invade India, but after he was murdered the Cossacks were recalled.

1805-1807   3rd. Coalition. Russia defeated by France at Austerlitz.

1807   Tsar Alexander I signed Peace with Napoleon at Tilsit. He joined Napoleon's anti-British Continental system, but at great cost to Russia's trade and prosperity.

1806-1812   Russia, at war with Turkey, annexed Bessarabia.

1812 –   Napoleon invaded Russia. Alexander joined the 4th. Coalition against France, receiving £7 million of British subsidies; he entered Paris in 1814.

Towns of Russian campaign 1798-9

① Treviso
② Brescia
③ Milan
④ Turin
⑤ Alessandria
⑥ Tortona
⑦ Piacenza
⑧ Parma
⑨ Bologna
⑩ Mantua

BRITAIN

North Sea

DENMARK

CONFEDERATION

OF

Dresden

Frankfurt

THE

Paris

RHINE

FRANCE

HOLLAND

SWITZ.

KINGDOM

OF

ITALY

Venice

Adriatic

NAPLES

Mediterranean Sea

——— The frontiers of France in 1799

▨ Annexed by France between 1805 and 1812

——— The European frontiers of 1812

◄— Russian military activity against French forces in Italy 1798-1799

◄■ The Cossack force sent to invade India 1801

■ Grand Duchy of Warsaw 1807-1814

⇨ Napoleon's march to Moscow 1812

◄— Russian military attacks on Turkey 1806-1812

◄— The Russian advance from Moscow to Paris 1813-1814

0   800
Miles

RUSSIA AND EUROPE 1789-1815

R U S S I A

Tver

Moscow

Borodino

Viazma

Riazan

Smolensk

Tula

Riga

Baltic Sea

Borisov

Tilsit

RUSSIA

Kalisz

GRAND
DUCHY
OF WARSAW

Napoleon championed Polish independence, and many Polish
emigres joined him after 1795. In 1807 he established a
Grand Duchy of Warsaw, entirely out of Prussian and Austrian
Poland. The Russians planned to crush this new state, but to
forestall them Napoleon marched to Moscow in 1812. 85,000
Poles served in his army. After his defeat most of the Grand
Duchy was transferred to Russia, giving Russia a further
3 million Polish and 300,000 Jewish citizens.

Austerlitz

Vienna

AUSTRIA

Jassy

BESS-
ARABIA

Ismail

RUMANIANS

Bucharest

CROATS

Iasika

SERBS

Tirnovo

Shumla

Varna

Black Sea

BULGARS

TURKEY IN EUROPE

GREEKS

TURKEY   IN   ASIA

Balkan peoples under Turkish rule,
whom Alexander planned to enlist
in an anti-French crusade in return
for helping them obtain independence from Turkey. The plan failed.

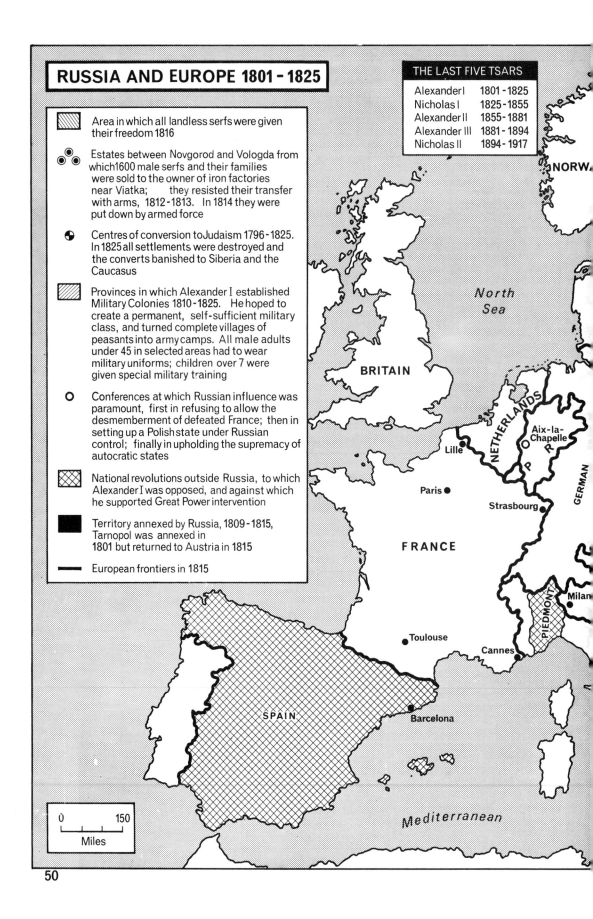

RUSSIA AND EUROPE 1801 - 1825

Area in which all landless serfs were given their freedom 1816

Estates between Novgorod and Vologda from which 1600 male serfs and their families were sold to the owner of iron factories near Viatka; they resisted their transfer with arms, 1812-1813. In 1814 they were put down by armed force

Centres of conversion to Judaism 1796-1825. In 1825 all settlements were destroyed and the converts banished to Siberia and the Caucasus

Provinces in which Alexander I established Military Colonies 1810-1825. He hoped to create a permanent, self-sufficient military class, and turned complete villages of peasants into army camps. All male adults under 45 in selected areas had to wear military uniforms; children over 7 were given special military training

Conferences at which Russian influence was paramount, first in refusing to allow the desmemberment of defeated France; then in setting up a Polish state under Russian control; finally in upholding the supremacy of autocratic states

National revolutions outside Russia, to which Alexander I was opposed, and against which he supported Great Power intervention

Territory annexed by Russia, 1809-1815, Tarnopol was annexed in 1801 but returned to Austria in 1815

European frontiers in 1815

NORW.

North Sea

BRITAIN

NETHERLANDS

Aix-la-Chapelle

O P E R

Lille

GERMAN

Paris ●

Strasbourg ●

FRANCE

Milan

PIEDMONT

Toulouse ●

Cannes

SPAIN

Barcelona ●

0   150
Miles

Mediterranean

50

FINLAND

Viatka●

Vologda

ALAND
ISLANDS

SWEDEN

St.
Petersburg●

Novgorod●

Moscow●

Tula◑

Saratov⊕

R U S S I A

Baltic Sea

Mogilev●

Bobrov◑

Pavlovsk◑

POLAND

Carlsbad○

Lemberg●
Tarnopol

Ekaterinoslav●

Prague●   ○Troppau

BESSARABIA

Nikolaev●

Vienna○

AUSTRIA–
HUNGARY

Laibach
○

Bucharest●

Black Sea

Belgrade●

T   U   R

Cattaro

Rome

Constantinople●   K   E   Y

NAPLES

Naples●

GREECE

Athens

Sea

Like Catherine the Great on her accession,
Alexander I was looked to on his accession
(in 1801) as a potential source of liberal-
ization. In the war against Napoleon he acted
as the enemy of tyrants and friend of the
oppressed. But by 1820 he had become a
pillar of autocracy both in Russia and
abroad. Under Alexander, Russia's western
frontier reached its furthest western extent,
and from 1820 to 1917 it was unchanged

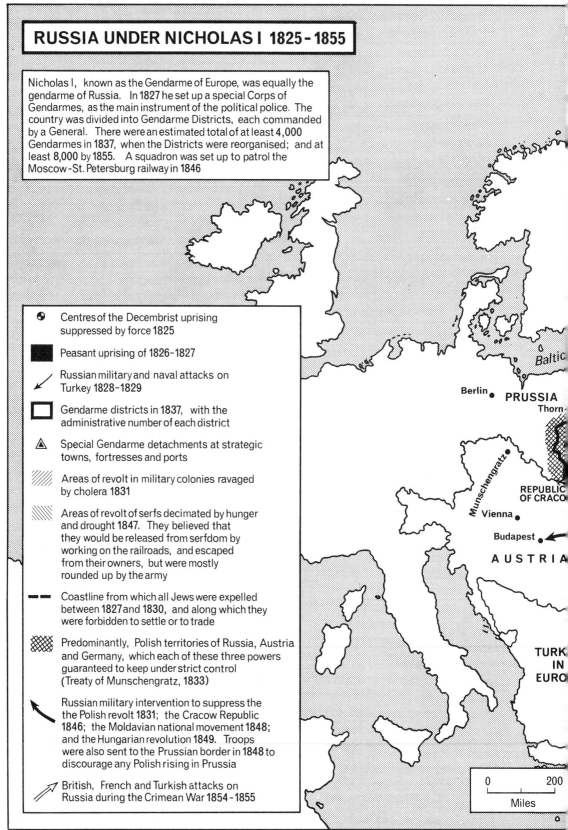

RUSSIA UNDER NICHOLAS I 1825-1855

Nicholas I, known as the Gendarme of Europe, was equally the gendarme of Russia. In 1827 he set up a special Corps of Gendarmes, as the main instrument of the political police. The country was divided into Gendarme Districts, each commanded by a General. There were an estimated total of at least 4,000 Gendarmes in 1837, when the Districts were reorganised; and at least 8,000 by 1855. A squadron was set up to patrol the Moscow-St. Petersburg railway in 1846

⊕   Centres of the Decembrist uprising suppressed by force 1825

■   Peasant uprising of 1826-1827

↙   Russian military and naval attacks on Turkey 1828-1829

▭   Gendarme districts in 1837, with the administrative number of each district

△   Special Gendarme detachments at strategic towns, fortresses and ports

▨   Areas of revolt in military colonies ravaged by cholera 1831

▨   Areas of revolt of serfs decimated by hunger and drought 1847. They believed that they would be released from serfdom by working on the railroads, and escaped from their owners, but were mostly rounded up by the army

▬ ▬   Coastline from which all Jews were expelled between 1827 and 1830, and along which they were forbidden to settle or to trade

▩   Predominantly, Polish territories of Russia, Austria and Germany, which each of these three powers guaranteed to keep under strict control (Treaty of Munschengratz, 1833)

◤   Russian military intervention to suppress the the Polish revolt 1831; the Cracow Republic 1846; the Moldavian national movement 1848; and the Hungarian revolution 1849. Troops were also sent to the Prussian border in 1848 to discourage any Polish rising in Prussia

↗   British, French and Turkish attacks on Russia during the Crimean War 1854-1855

Baltic

Berlin ● PRUSSIA

Thorn

Munschengratz ●

REPUBLIC OF CRACOW

Vienna ●

Budapest ●

AUSTRIA

TURKEY IN EUROPE

0   200

Miles

51

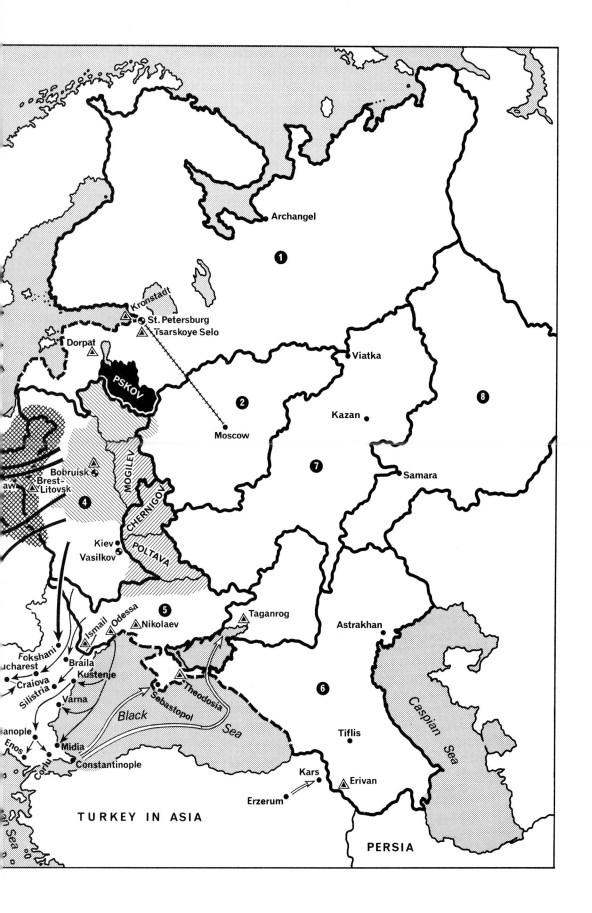

Archangel

①

Kronstadt
St. Petersburg
Tsarskoye Selo

Dorpat

Viatka

PSKOV

②

Kazan

⑧

Moscow

MOGILEV

Bobruisk
Brest-
Litovsk

CHERNIGOV

④

Samara

⑦

POLTAVA

Kiev
Vasilkov

Astrakhan

⑤

Odessa

Ismail

Nikolaev

Taganrog

⑥

Fokshani
ucharest

Braila
Kustenje

Theodosia

Tiflis

Craiova
Silistria

Varna

Sebastopol

Caspian Sea

anople
Enos

Midia
Constantinople

Black

Sea

Kars

Erivan

Erzerum

TURKEY IN ASIA

PERSIA

THE POLISH REVOLT IN 1831

After Napoleon's defeat in 1814, Russia set up its new Polish territory as a separate kingdom, CONGRESS POLAND, ruled directly by the Tsar. After 1814, Alexander I adopted a liberal, pro-Polish policy. But in 1825 his successor, Nicholas I, began to restrict Polish liberties. In 1830 the Poles rose in open war against Russian rule. They hoped for help from France, but it never came. The revolt was crushed by superior Russian force.

Palanga

Memel

Königsberg

Danzig

P R U S S I A

Masurian Lakes

Vilna

Suvalki

Grodno

Posen

Warsaw

Bialystok

R U S S I A

Pripet Marshes

Brest-Litovsk

Pinsk

Kalisz

Lodz

Piotrkow

Breslau

Kovel

SILESIA

Czenstochowa

Krasnik

REPUBLIC OF CRACOW

Cracow

Tarnow

GALICIA

Przemysl

Lvov

AUSTRIA

Tarnopol

Scale: 0 — 50 Miles

	Congress Poland, ruled by the Russian Tsar 1815-1914
	Principal areas of Polish partisan activity in 1831 against the local Russian authorities
⊙	Battles between Russian and Polish troops in 1831
↗	Polish troop movements. All these ended in exile across the Prussian, Austrian and Cracovian borders

THE POLISH REVOLT IN 1861

The Polish rising of 1831 was largely the work of the Polish aristocracy and land-owners. But by 1860 discontent against Russian rule had spread to the middle classes and intelligentsia. The revolt of 1861 took place throughout Congress Poland. It was crushed after three years of bitter fighting, during which time the Russians had to call in Austrian and Prussian military help

0   50
Miles

Memel

Danzig

Königsberg

PRUSSIA

Masurian
Lakes

Mlava

Kovno

Troki

Vilna

Bialystok

RUSSIA

Pripet

Marshes

Warsaw

Kalisz

Radomsk

Czenstochowa

Lublin

Krasnik

Zamosc

Kovel

Cracow

Tarnow

Przemysl

Lvov

Brody

AUSTRIA

Congress Poland, ruled by the Russian Tsar 1815-1914

○   Centres of the Polish revolt 1861-1863

Prussian and Austrian troops helping Russia to suppress the uprising

◉   Principal battles

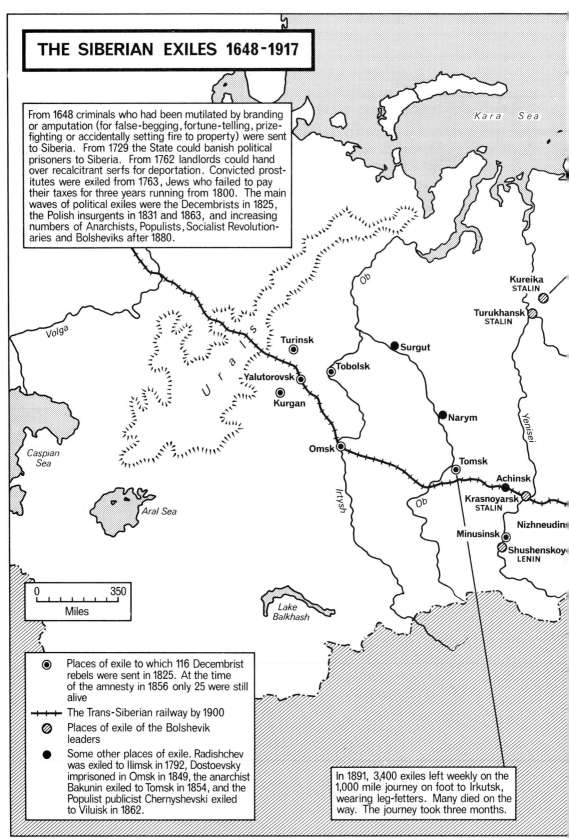

THE SIBERIAN EXILES 1648-1917

From 1648 criminals who had been mutilated by branding or amputation (for false-begging, fortune-telling, prize-fighting or accidentally setting fire to property) were sent to Siberia. From 1729 the State could banish political prisoners to Siberia. From 1762 landlords could hand over recalcitrant serfs for deportation. Convicted prostitutes were exiled from 1763, Jews who failed to pay their taxes for three years running from 1800. The main waves of political exiles were the Decembrists in 1825, the Polish insurgents in 1831 and 1863, and increasing numbers of Anarchists, Populists, Socialist Revolutionaries and Bolsheviks after 1880.

Kara Sea

Volga

Urals

Turinsk

Surgut

Yalutorovsk

Tobolsk

Kurgan

Narym

Caspian Sea

Omsk

Tomsk

Irtysh

Ob

Achinsk

Krasnoyarsk
STALIN

Aral Sea

Yenisei

Kureika
STALIN

Turukhansk
STALIN

Nizhneudins

Minusinsk

Shushenskoy
LENIN

0   350
Miles

Lake Balkhash

⊙   Places of exile to which 116 Decembrist rebels were sent in 1825. At the time of the amnesty in 1856 only 25 were still alive

+++   The Trans-Siberian railway by 1900

⊘   Places of exile of the Bolshevik leaders

●   Some other places of exile. Radishchev was exiled to Ilimsk in 1792, Dostoevsky imprisoned in Omsk in 1849, the anarchist Bakunin exiled to Tomsk in 1854, and the Populist publicist Chernyshevski exiled to Viluisk in 1862.

In 1891, 3,400 exiles left weekly on the 1,000 mile journey on foot to Irkutsk, wearing leg-fetters. Many died on the way. The journey took three months.

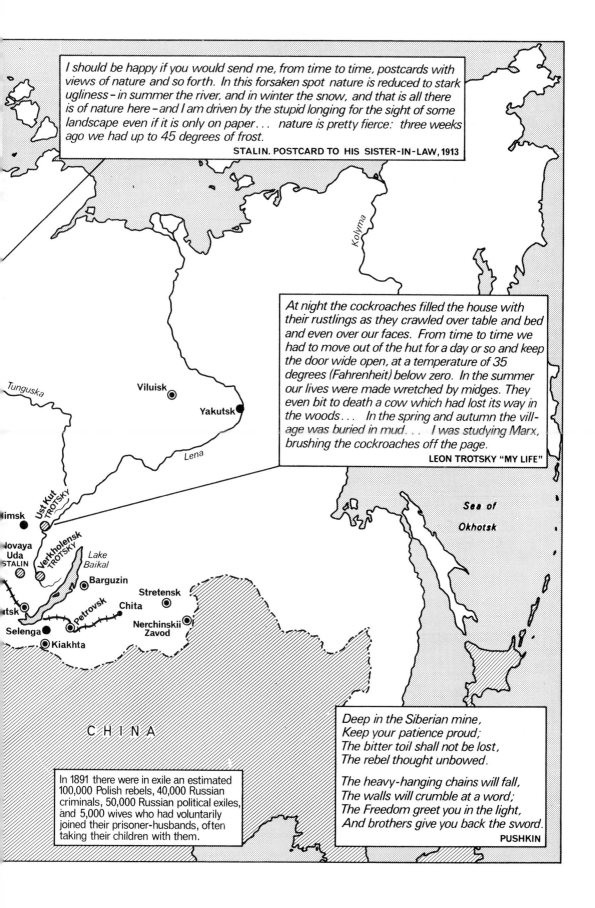

I should be happy if you would send me, from time to time, postcards with views of nature and so forth. In this forsaken spot nature is reduced to stark ugliness – in summer the river, and in winter the snow, and that is all there is of nature here – and I am driven by the stupid longing for the sight of some landscape even if it is only on paper... nature is pretty fierce: three weeks ago we had up to 45 degrees of frost.

STALIN. POSTCARD TO HIS SISTER-IN-LAW, 1913

At night the cockroaches filled the house with their rustlings as they crawled over table and bed and even over our faces. From time to time we had to move out of the hut for a day or so and keep the door wide open, at a temperature of 35 degrees (Fahrenheit) below zero. In the summer our lives were made wretched by midges. They even bit to death a cow which had lost its way in the woods... In the spring and autumn the village was buried in mud... I was studying Marx, brushing the cockroaches off the page.

LEON TROTSKY "MY LIFE"

Deep in the Siberian mine,
Keep your patience proud;
The bitter toil shall not be lost,
The rebel thought unbowed.

The heavy-hanging chains will fall,
The walls will crumble at a word;
The Freedom greet you in the light,
And brothers give you back the sword.

PUSHKIN

In 1891 there were in exile an estimated 100,000 Polish rebels, 40,000 Russian criminals, 50,000 Russian political exiles, and 5,000 wives who had voluntarily joined their prisoner-husbands, often taking their children with them.

Tunguska

Viluisk

Yakutsk

Lena

Kolyma

Sea of Okhotsk

Ust Kut TROTSKY

Nimsk

Novaya Uda STALIN

Verkholensk TROTSKY

Lake Baikal

Barguzin

Stretensk

Chita

Petrovsk

Nerchinskii Zavod

itsk

Selenga

Kiakhta

C H I N A

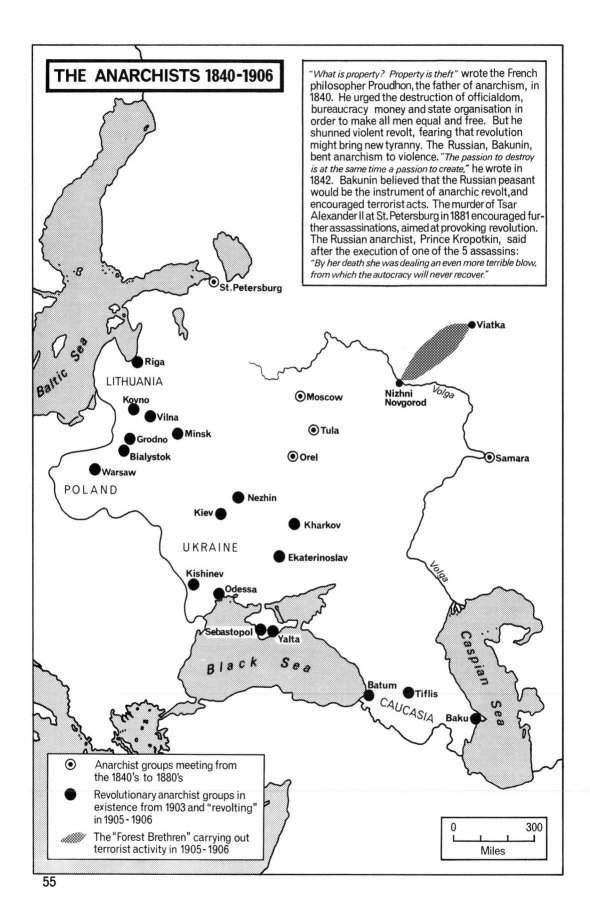

THE ANARCHISTS 1840-1906

"What is property? Property is theft" wrote the French philosopher Proudhon, the father of anarchism, in 1840. He urged the destruction of officialdom, bureaucracy money and state organisation in order to make all men equal and free. But he shunned violent revolt, fearing that revolution might bring new tyranny. The Russian, Bakunin, bent anarchism to violence. *"The passion to destroy is at the same time a passion to create,"* he wrote in 1842. Bakunin believed that the Russian peasant would be the instrument of anarchic revolt, and encouraged terrorist acts. The murder of Tsar Alexander II at St. Petersburg in 1881 encouraged further assassinations, aimed at provoking revolution. The Russian anarchist, Prince Kropotkin, said after the execution of one of the 5 assassins: *"By her death she was dealing an even more terrible blow, from which the autocracy will never recover."*

St.Petersburg

Viatka

Baltic Sea

Riga

LITHUANIA

Kovno

Vilna

Grodno

Minsk

Bialystok

Warsaw

POLAND

Moscow

Nizhni Novgorod

Volga

Tula

Orel

Samara

Nezhin

Kiev

Kharkov

UKRAINE

Ekaterinoslav

Kishinev

Odessa

Volga

Sebastopol

Yalta

Black Sea

Caspian Sea

Batum

Tiflis

CAUCASIA

Baku

Legend:
- ◉ Anarchist groups meeting from the 1840's to 1880's
- ● Revolutionary anarchist groups in existence from 1903 and "revolting" in 1905 - 1906
- ▨ The "Forest Brethren" carrying out terrorist activity in 1905 - 1906

0   300

Miles

RUSSIAN INDUSTRY BY 1860

0   200
Miles

Archangel

Urals

Vyborg

Schlüsselburg

Reval

St.Petersburg — 540,000

Narva

LEATHER

Kama

Viatka

GOLD

Perm

COAL

WOOL

Dorpat

Pskov

Yaroslavl

Volga

COAL

COPPER

LEATHER

Mitau

Riga — 77,000

Tver

Vladimir

LINEN

Kazan — 63,000

Ufa

Libau

Yegorevsk

LEATHER

Moscow — 460,000

Nizhni Novgorod

COPPER

Baltic Sea

WOOL

Dvinsk

Kovno

Kaluga

Tula

LEATHER

Riazan

LINEN

Ural

Vilna — 69,000

Grodno

LEATHER

Orel

Bialystok

Warsaw

LINEN

LINEN

WOOL

Saratov — 84,000

Lodz

Chernigov

Voronezh

LINEN

Dnieper

Kiev — 68,000

LINEN

Kharkov

Poltava

Donets

COAL

Don

Volga

Kishinev — 94,000

64,000

Nikolaev

Odessa — 120,000

Caspian Sea

TOBACCO

POPULATION
1811: 41,000,000
1863: 74,000,000

Black Sea

Caucasus

Baku

OIL

— The Russian frontier 1815-1914

● Principal cities, with their estimated population in 1860

╫╫╫ Railways built by 1860

┼┼┼ Railways under construction in 1860

⊙ Factory development before 1860

⊕ Towns with large factory growth from 1860

▬ Industries expanding rapidly from 1860

▓ Centres of the iron and steel production

▨ Sugar factories

PRINCIPAL IMPORTS: Cotton, machine tools, alcohol, dyes, fruit and nuts, wool, tea, olive and vegetable oil, silk, sugar, zinc, steel, iron, copper, horses. cattle, poultry, salt. Over 80% of all imports and exports went through the ports of St. Petersburg and Odessa

PRINCIPAL EXPORTS: Wheat, rye, cereals, flour, flax, hemp, wool, animal fat, lard, seeds, wood, wood products, paper

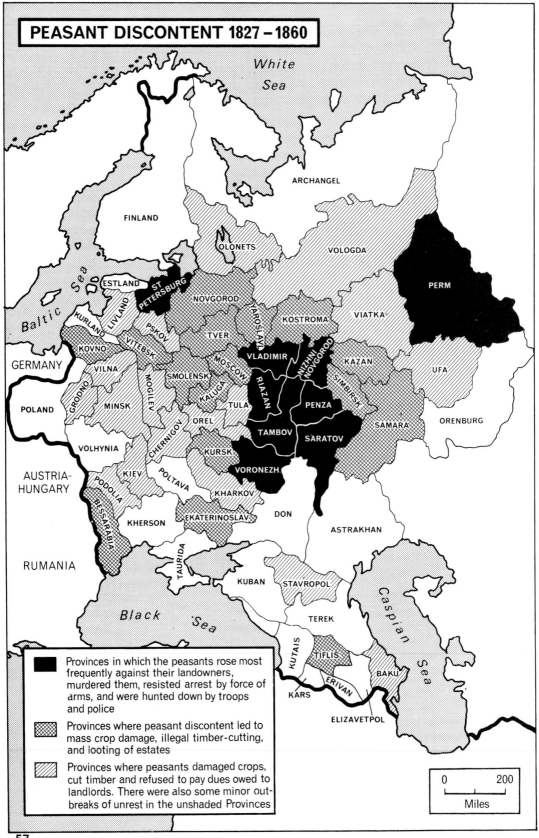

PEASANT DISCONTENT 1827–1860

White Sea

ARCHANGEL

FINLAND

OLONETS

VOLOGDA

PERM

ESTLAND

Baltic Sea

ST PETERSBURG

NOVGOROD

KOSTROMA

VIATKA

KURLAND

LIVLAND

PSKOV

YAROSLAVL

KOVNO

VITEBSK

TVER

MOSCOW

VLADIMIR

NIZHNI NOVGOROD

KAZAN

UFA

GERMANY

VILNA

MOGILEV

SMOLENSK

KALUGA

RIAZAN

SIMBIRSK

GRODNO

MINSK

TULA

PENZA

ORENBURG

POLAND

OREL

SAMARA

VOLHYNIA

CHERNIGOV

TAMBOV

SARATOV

AUSTRIA-HUNGARY

KIEV

POLTAVA

KURSK

PODOLIA

VORONEZH

KHARKOV

DON

ASTRAKHAN

BESSARABIA

KHERSON

EKATERINOSLAV

RUMANIA

TAURIDA

KUBAN

STAVROPOL

Caspian Sea

Black Sea

TEREK

KUTAIS

TIFLIS

BAKU

ERIVAN

KARS

ELIZAVETPOL

Miles

Provinces in which the peasants rose most frequently against their landowners, murdered them, resisted arrest by force of arms, and were hunted down by troops and police

Provinces where peasant discontent led to mass crop damage, illegal timber-cutting, and looting of estates

Provinces where peasants damaged crops, cut timber and refused to pay dues owed to landlords. There were also some minor outbreaks of unrest in the unshaded Provinces

0   200

SERFS IN 1860

White Sea

Baltic Sea

VOLOGDA

PERM

GERMANY

NOVGOROD

PSKOV

KOVNO

VITEBSK

TVER

YAROSLAVL

KOSTROMA

VILNA

GRODNO

MOGILEV

SMOLENSK

MOSCOW

VLADIMIR

NIZHNI NOVGOROD

SIMBIRSK

MINSK

KALUGA

RIAZAN

PENZA

TULA

AUSTRIA-HUNGARY

VOLHYNIA

KIEV

CHERNIGOV

OREL

TAMBOV

SARATOV

KURSK

PODOLIA

POLTAVA

VORONEZH

KHARKOV

RUMANIA

KHERSON

EKATERINOSLAV

DON

KUBAN

Black Sea

Caspian Sea

KUTAIS

TIFLIS

TURKEY

PERSIA

Provinces where over half of the peasants were serfs

Provinces where 36% to 55% of the peasants were serfs

Provinces where 16% to 35% of the peasants were serfs

0   200
Miles

58

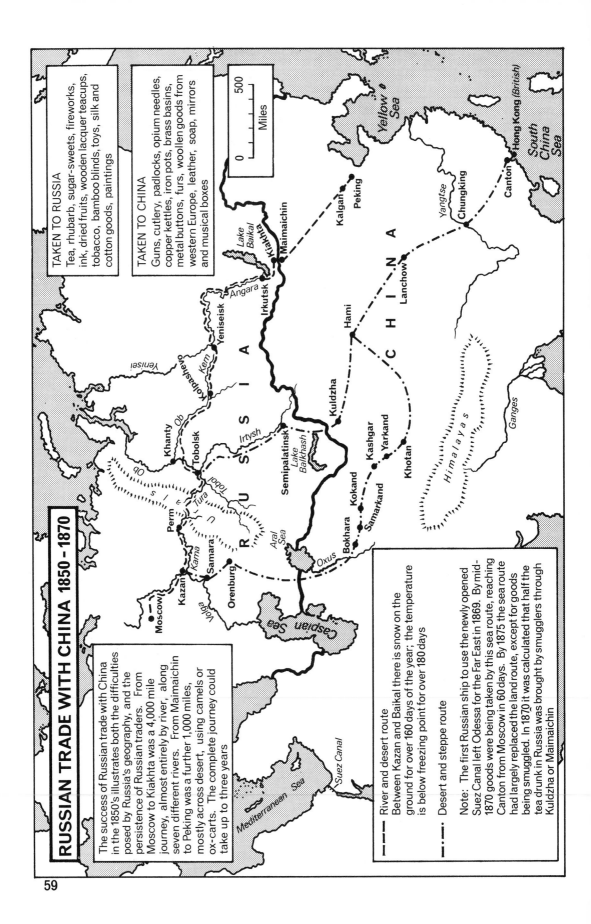

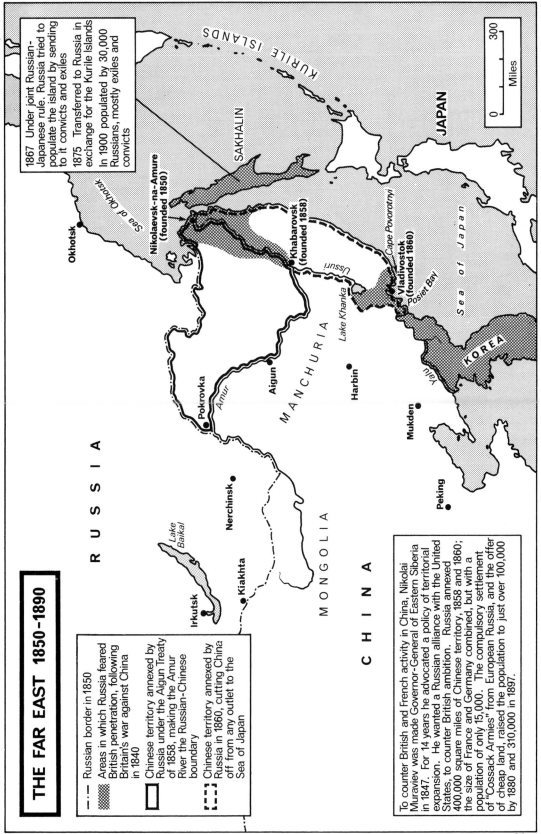

THE FAR EAST 1850–1890

- –·– Russian border in 1850

- Areas in which Russia feared British penetration, following Britain's war against China in 1840

- Chinese territory annexed by Russia under the Aigun Treaty of 1858, making the Amur River the Russian-Chinese boundary

- Chinese territory annexed by Russia in 1860, cutting China off from any outlet to the Sea of Japan

1867 Under joint Russian-Japanese rule. Russia tried to populate the island by sending to it convicts and exiles

1875 Transferred to Russia in exchange for the Kurile Islands In 1900 populated by 30,000 Russians, mostly exiles and convicts

KURILE ISLANDS

SAKHALIN

Sea of Okhotsk

Okhotsk

Nikolaevsk-na-Amure (founded 1850)

JAPAN

Sea of Japan

Khabarovsk (founded 1858)

Cape Povorotnyi

Vladivostok (founded 1860)

Posiet Bay

Ussuri

Ussuri

Lake Khanka

KOREA

Yalu

R U S S I A

Amur

Pokrovka

Aigun

MANCHURIA

Harbin

Mukden

Lake Baikal

Nerchinsk

Irkutsk

Kiakhta

M O N G O L I A

C H I N A

Peking

0   300
Miles

To counter British and French activity in China, Nikolai Muraviev was made Governor-General of Eastern Siberia in 1847. For 14 years he advocated a policy of territorial expansion. He wanted a Russian alliance with the United States, to counter British ambition. Russia annexed 400,000 square miles of Chinese territory, 1858 and 1860; the size of France and Germany combined, but with a population of only 15,000. The compulsory settlement of "Cossack Armies" from European Russia, and the offer of cheap land, raised the population to just over 100,000 by 1880 and 310,000 in 1897.

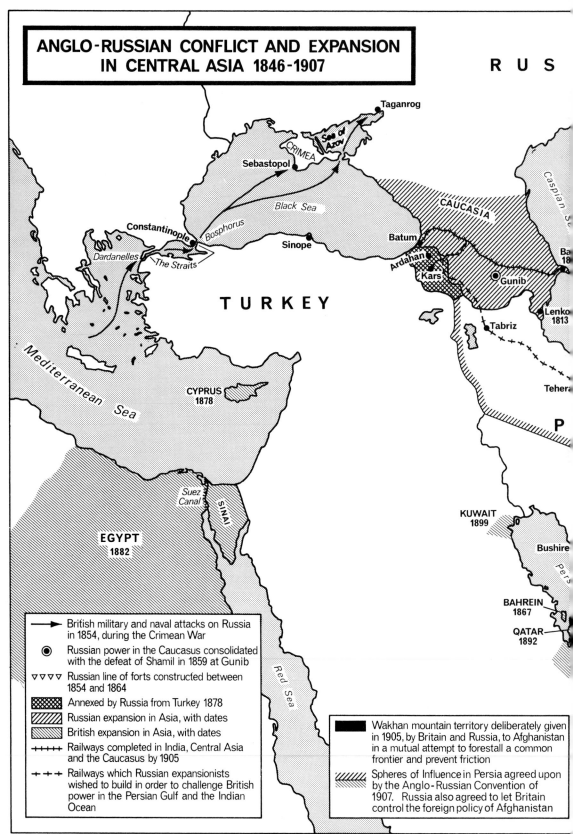

ANGLO-RUSSIAN CONFLICT AND EXPANSION IN CENTRAL ASIA 1846-1907

R U S

Taganrog

Sea of Azov

CRIMEA

Sebastopol

Black Sea

Constantinople

Bosphorus

Dardanelles

The Straits

Sinope

CAUCASIA

Caspian Se

Batum

Ardahan

Kars

Gunib

Ba
18

Lenko
1813

Tabriz

Tehera

T U R K E Y

Mediterranean Sea

CYPRUS
1878

P

Suez
Canal

SINAI

KUWAIT
1899

Bushire

EGYPT
1882

Pers

Red Sea

BAHREIN
1867

QATAR
1892

British military and naval attacks on Russia in 1854, during the Crimean War

Russian power in the Caucasus consolidated with the defeat of Shamil in 1859 at Gunib

Russian line of forts constructed between 1854 and 1864

Annexed by Russia from Turkey 1878

Russian expansion in Asia, with dates

British expansion in Asia, with dates

Railways completed in India, Central Asia and the Caucasus by 1905

Railways which Russian expansionists wished to build in order to challenge British power in the Persian Gulf and the Indian Ocean

Wakhan mountain territory deliberately given in 1905, by Britain and Russia, to Afghanistan in a mutual attempt to forestall a common frontier and prevent friction

Spheres of Influence in Persia agreed upon by the Anglo-Russian Convention of 1907. Russia also agreed to let Britain control the foreign policy of Afghanistan

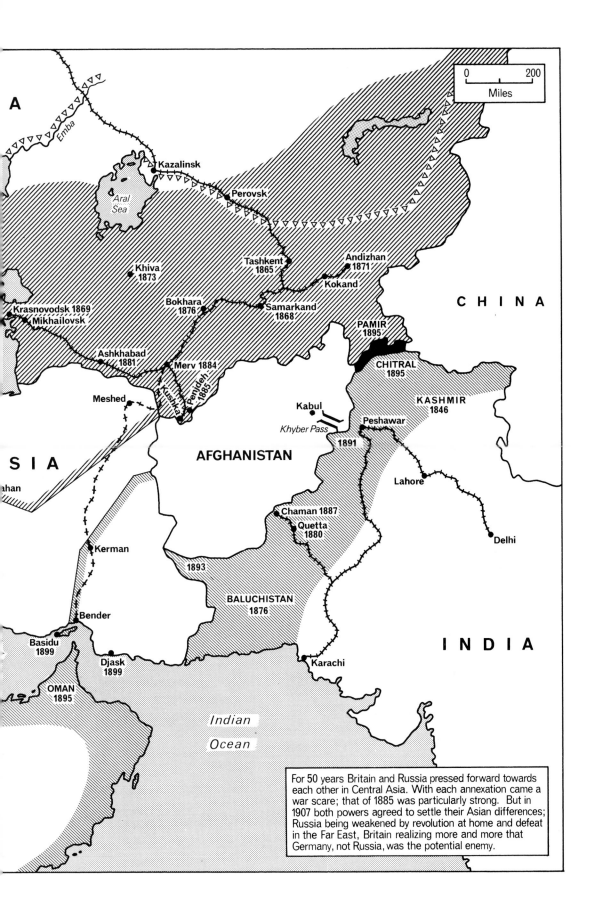

A

Emba

Kazalinsk

Aral
Sea

Perovsk

Khiva
1873

Tashkent
1865

Andizhan
1871

Kokand

Krasnovodsk 1869
Mikhailovsk

Bokhara
1876

Samarkand
1868

CHINA

PAMIR
1895

Ashkhabad
1881

Merv 1884

Kushka

Penideh
1885

CHITRAL
1875

Meshed

KASHMIR
1846

Kabul

Khyber Pass

Peshawar

1891

SIA

AFGHANISTAN

ahan

Lahore

Chaman 1887

Quetta
1880

Delhi

Kerman

1893

BALUCHISTAN
1876

INDIA

Bender

Basidu
1899

Djask
1899

Karachi

OMAN
1895

Indian
Ocean

0   200
Miles

For 50 years Britain and Russia pressed forward towards
each other in Central Asia. With each annexation came a
war scare; that of 1885 was particularly strong. But in
1907 both powers agreed to settle their Asian differences;
Russia being weakened by revolution at home and defeat
in the Far East, Britain realizing more and more that
Germany, not Russia, was the potential enemy.

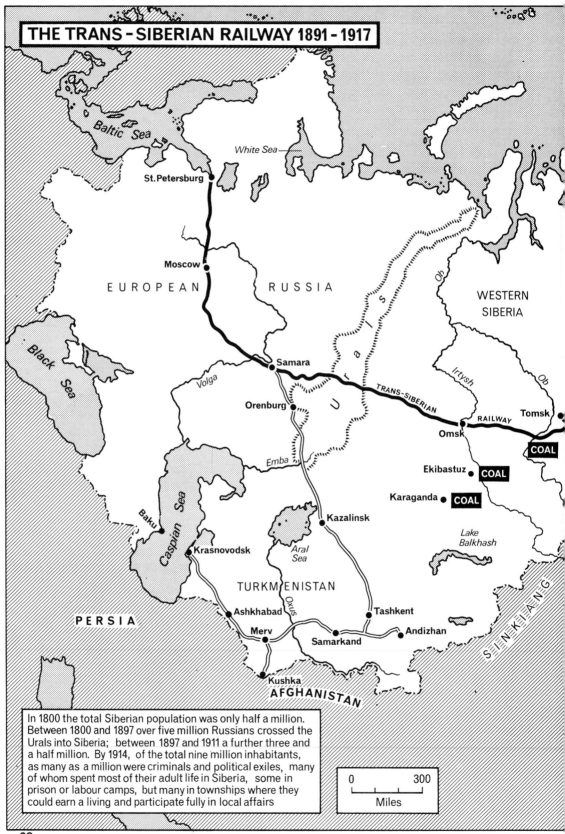

THE TRANS-SIBERIAN RAILWAY 1891-1917

Baltic Sea

White Sea

St.Petersburg

Moscow

EUROPEAN   RUSSIA

WESTERN
SIBERIA

Black Sea

Volga

Samara

U r a l s

Irtysh

Ob

TRANS-SIBERIAN

Orenburg

RAILWAY

Tomsk

Emba

Omsk

COAL

Ekibastuz   **COAL**

Karaganda   **COAL**

Kazalinsk

*Lake
Balkhash*

Baku

Caspian Sea

Krasnovodsk

*Aral
Sea*

TURKMENISTAN

Oxus

PERSIA

Ashkhabad

Tashkent

Merv

Andizhan

Samarkand

S I N K I A N G

Kushka

AFGHANISTAN

In 1800 the total Siberian population was only half a million.
Between 1800 and 1897 over five million Russians crossed the
Urals into Siberia; between 1897 and 1911 a further three and
a half million. By 1914, of the total nine million inhabitants,
as many as a million were criminals and political exiles, many
of whom spent most of their adult life in Siberia, some in
prison or labour camps, but many in townships where they
could earn a living and participate fully in local affairs

0   300
Miles

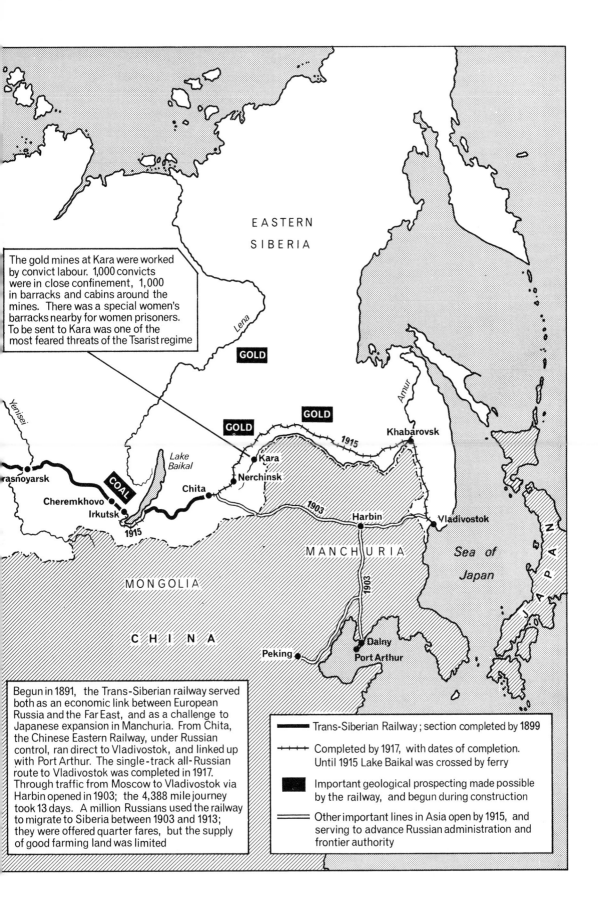

The gold mines at Kara were worked by convict labour. 1,000 convicts were in close confinement, 1,000 in barracks and cabins around the mines. There was a special women's barracks nearby for women prisoners. To be sent to Kara was one of the most feared threats of the Tsarist regime

EASTERN SIBERIA

GOLD

GOLD

GOLD

Khabarovsk

1915

Amur

Lena

Kara

Nerchinsk

Yenisei

rasnoyarsk

COAL

Lake Baikal

Chita

1903

Harbin

Vladivostok

Cheremkhovo

Irkutsk

1915

MANCHURIA

Sea of Japan

MONGOLIA

1903

CHINA

Dalny

Peking

Port Arthur

JAPAN

Begun in 1891, the Trans-Siberian railway served both as an economic link between European Russia and the Far East, and as a challenge to Japanese expansion in Manchuria. From Chita, the Chinese Eastern Railway, under Russian control, ran direct to Vladivostok, and linked up with Port Arthur. The single-track all-Russian route to Vladivostok was completed in 1917. Through traffic from Moscow to Vladivostok via Harbin opened in 1903; the 4,388 mile journey took 13 days. A million Russians used the railway to migrate to Siberia between 1903 and 1913; they were offered quarter fares, but the supply of good farming land was limited

Trans-Siberian Railway; section completed by 1899

++++ Completed by 1917, with dates of completion. Until 1915 Lake Baikal was crossed by ferry

Important geological prospecting made possible by the railway, and begun during construction

Other important lines in Asia open by 1915, and serving to advance Russian administration and frontier authority

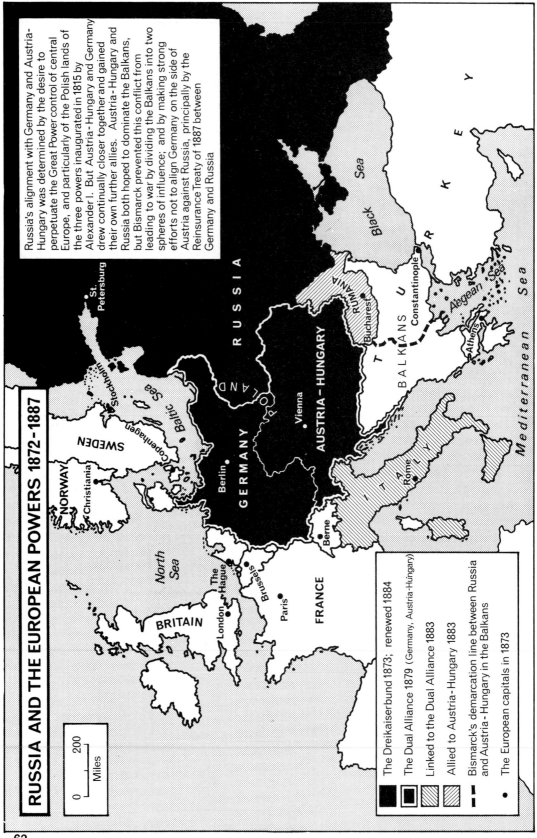

RUSSIA AND THE EUROPEAN POWERS 1872-1887

Russia's alignment with Germany and Austria-Hungary was determined by the desire to perpetuate the Great Power control of central Europe, and particularly of the Polish lands of the three powers inaugurated in 1815 by Alexander I. But Austria-Hungary and Germany drew continually closer together and gained their own further allies. Austria-Hungary and Russia both hoped to dominate the Balkans, but Bismarck prevented this conflict from leading to war by dividing the Balkans into two spheres of influence; and by making strong efforts not to align Germany on the side of Austria against Russia, principally by the Reinsurance Treaty of 1887 between Germany and Russia

St. Petersburg

Stockholm

SWEDEN

NORWAY
Christiania

Baltic Sea

Copenhagen

Berlin

GERMANY

POLAND

RUSSIA

Vienna

AUSTRIA-HUNGARY

RUMA-NIA

Bucharest

Black Sea

Constantinople

T
U
R
K
E
Y

BALKANS

Aegean Sea

Athens

Mediterranean Sea

Rome

ITALY

Berne

North Sea

The Hague

London

Brussels

Paris

FRANCE

BRITAIN

0   200
Miles

The Dreikaiserbund 1873; renewed 1884

The Dual Alliance 1879 (Germany, Austria-Hungary)

Linked to the Dual Alliance 1883

Allied to Austria-Hungary 1883

Bismarck's demarcation line between Russia
and Austria-Hungary in the Balkans

The European capitals in 1873

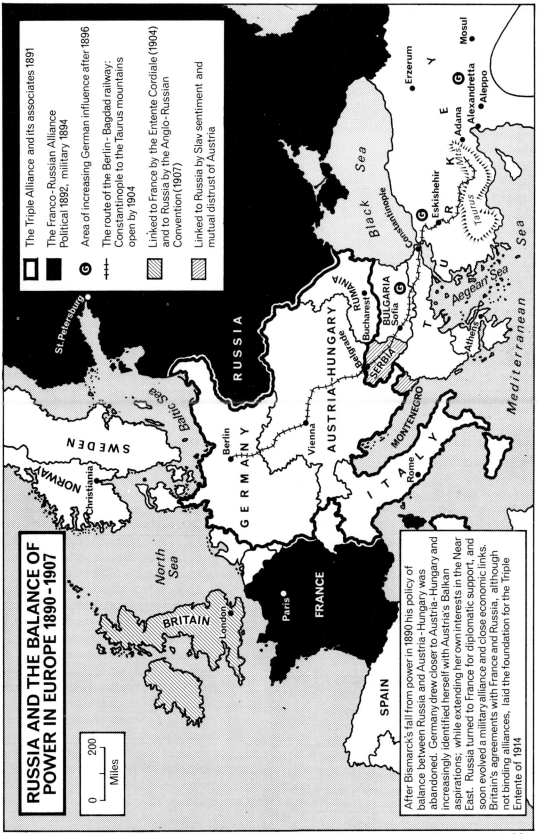

RUSSIA AND THE BALANCE OF POWER IN EUROPE 1890–1907

Miles
0   200

The Triple Alliance and its associates 1891

The Franco-Russian Alliance Political 1892, military 1894

Ⓖ Area of increasing German influence after 1896

┼┼┼ The route of the Berlin- Bagdad railway: Constantinople to the Taurus mountains open by 1904

Linked to France by the Entente Cordiale (1904) and to Russia by the Anglo-Russian Convention (1907)

Linked to Russia by Slav sentiment and mutual distrust of Austria

After Bismarck's fall from power in 1890 his policy of balance between Russia and Austria–Hungary was abandoned. Germany drew closer to Austria–Hungary and increasingly identified herself with Austria's Balkan aspirations; while extending her own interests in the Near East. Russia turned to France for diplomatic support, and soon evolved a military alliance and close economic links. Britain's agreements with France and Russia, although not binding alliances, laid the foundation for the Triple Entente of 1914

NORWAY
SWEDEN
Christiania

St.Petersburg

Baltic Sea

RUSSIA

North Sea

GERMANY
Berlin

BRITAIN
London

FRANCE
Paris

SPAIN

Vienna

AUSTRIA-HUNGARY

ITALY
Rome

MONTENEGRO

SERBIA
Belgrade

RUMANIA
Bucharest

BULGARIA Ⓖ
Sofia

Athens

Aegean Sea

Black Sea

Constantinople
Ⓖ Eskishehir

TURKEY
Taurus Mts.
Adana Ⓖ
Alexandretta
Aleppo

Erzerum

Mosul

Mediterranean Sea

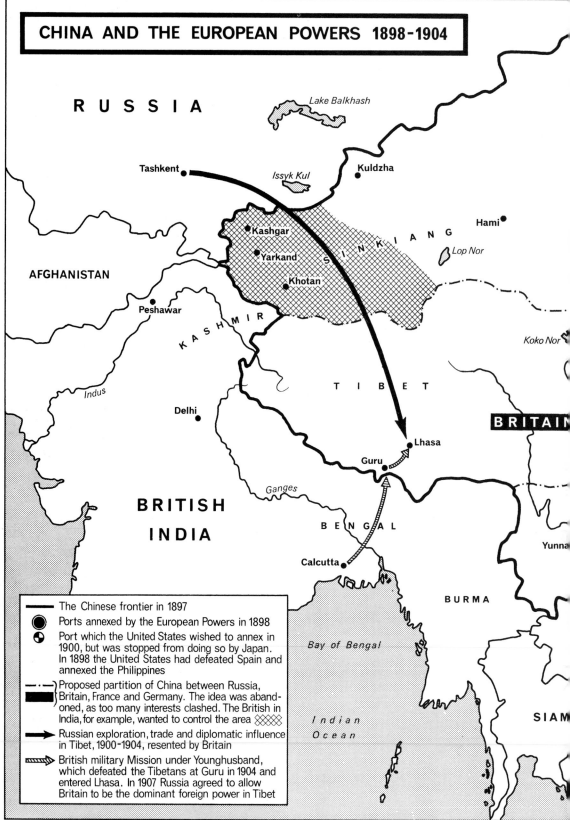

CHINA AND THE EUROPEAN POWERS 1898-1904

RUSSIA

Lake Balkhash

Tashkent •

Issyk Kul

Kuldzha •

Hami •

S I N K I A N G

• Kashgar

Lop Nor

AFGHANISTAN

• Yarkand

• Khotan

• Peshawar

Koko Nor

K A S H M I R

Indus

T I B E T

• Delhi

BRITAIN

• Lhasa

Guru •

Ganges

BRITISH

INDIA

B E N G A L

Yunna

• Calcutta

BURMA

Bay of Bengal

SIAM

Indian
Ocean

——— The Chinese frontier in 1897

● Ports annexed by the European Powers in 1898

◑ Port which the United States wished to annex in 1900, but was stopped from doing so by Japan. In 1898 the United States had defeated Spain and annexed the Philippines

—·—·— Proposed partition of China between Russia, Britain, France and Germany. The idea was abandoned, as too many interests clashed. The British in India, for example, wanted to control the area ⊠⊠⊠⊠

——➤ Russian exploration, trade and diplomatic influence in Tibet, 1900-1904, resented by Britain

⇢⇢⇢▷ British military Mission under Younghusband, which defeated the Tibetans at Guru in 1904 and entered Lhasa. In 1907 Russia agreed to allow Britain to be the dominant foreign power in Tibet

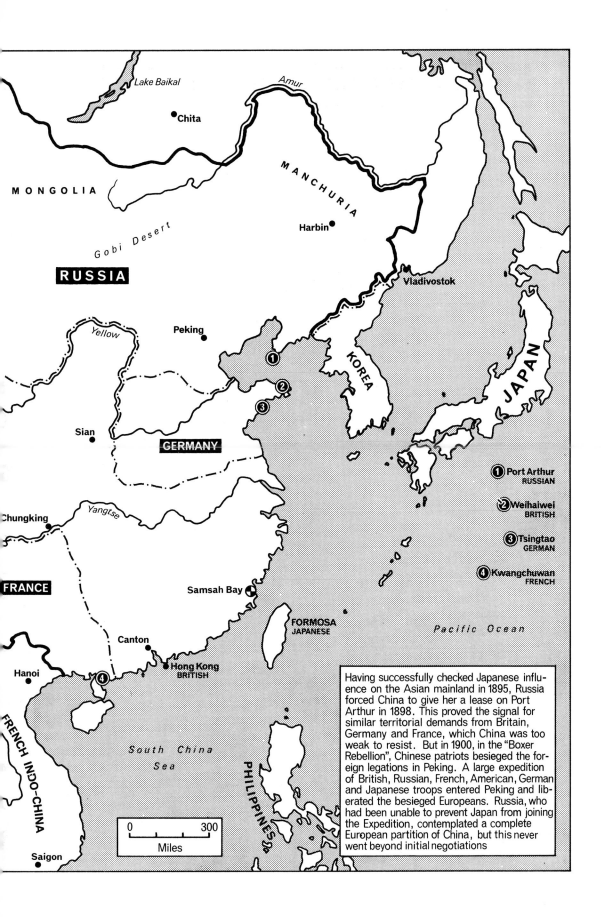

Lake Baikal

Amur

•Chita

MONGOLIA

MANCHURIA

Gobi Desert

Harbin•

RUSSIA

Vladivostok

Yellow

Peking•

KOREA

①

②

③

Sian•

GERMANY

JAPAN

Yangtse

Chungking•

①Port Arthur
RUSSIA

②Weihaiwei
BRITISH

③Tsingtao
GERMAN

FRANCE

④Kwangchuwan
FRENCH

Samsah Bay

FORMOSA
JAPANESE

Pacific Ocean

Canton•

Hanoi•

④

Hong Kong
BRITISH

FRENCH INDO-CHINA

South China
Sea

PHILIPPINES

0   300
Miles

Saigon•

Having successfully checked Japanese influence on the Asian mainland in 1895, Russia
forced China to give her a lease on Port
Arthur in 1898. This proved the signal for
similar territorial demands from Britain,
Germany and France, which China was too
weak to resist. But in 1900, in the "Boxer
Rebellion", Chinese patriots besieged the foreign legations in Peking. A large expedition
of British, Russian, French, American, German
and Japanese troops entered Peking and liberated the besieged Europeans. Russia, who
had been unable to prevent Japan from joining
the Expedition, contemplated a complete
European partition of China, but this never
went beyond initial negotiations

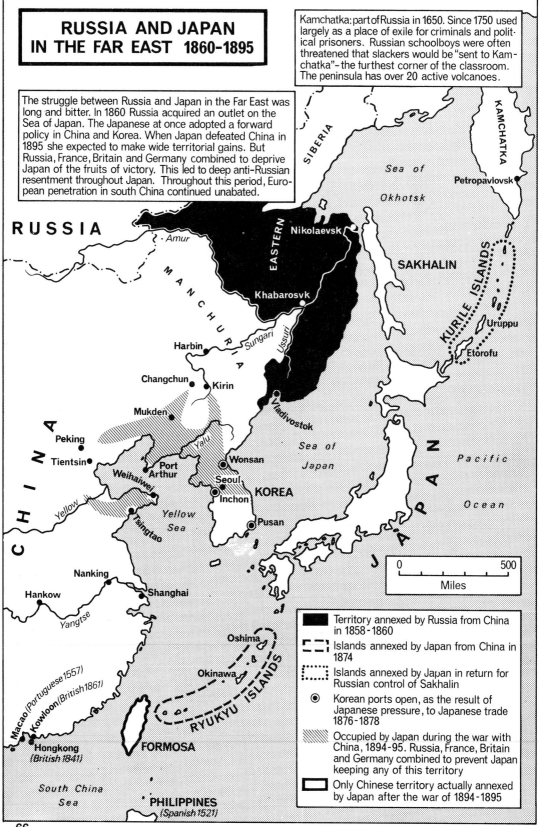

RUSSIA AND JAPAN IN THE FAR EAST 1860-1895

Kamchatka: part of Russia in 1650. Since 1750 used largely as a place of exile for criminals and political prisoners. Russian schoolboys were often threatened that slackers would be "sent to Kamchatka" – the furthest corner of the classroom. The peninsula has over 20 active volcanoes.

The struggle between Russia and Japan in the Far East was long and bitter. In 1860 Russia acquired an outlet on the Sea of Japan. The Japanese at once adopted a forward policy in China and Korea. When Japan defeated China in 1895 she expected to make wide territorial gains. But Russia, France, Britain and Germany combined to deprive Japan of the fruits of victory. This led to deep anti-Russian resentment throughout Japan. Throughout this period, European penetration in south China continued unabated.

RUSSIA

KAMCHATKA

SIBERIA

Sea of Okhotsk

Petropavlovsk

EASTERN

Amur

Nikolaevsk

SAKHALIN

KURILE ISLANDS

MANCHURIA

Khabarosvk

Sungari

Harbin

Ussuri

Uruppu

Etorofu

Changchun   Kirin

Mukden

Vladivostok

Peking

Yalu

Tientsin

Sea of Japan

JAPAN

Pacific

Port Arthur

Weihaiwei

Wonsan

Seoul

KOREA

Inchon

Ocean

Tsingtao

Yellow Sea

Pusan

Nanking

Hankow

Shanghai

Yangtse

Oshima

Okinawa

RYUKYU ISLANDS

Macao (Portuguese 1557)

Kowloon (British 1861)

Hongkong (British 1841)

FORMOSA

South China Sea

PHILIPPINES (Spanish 1521)

0	500

Miles

■ Territory annexed by Russia from China in 1858-1860

▢ Islands annexed by Japan from China in 1874

⋯ Islands annexed by Japan in return for Russian control of Sakhalin

◉ Korean ports open, as the result of Japanese pressure, to Japanese trade 1876-1878

▨ Occupied by Japan during the war with China, 1894-95. Russia, France, Britain and Germany combined to prevent Japan keeping any of this territory

▢ Only Chinese territory actually annexed by Japan after the war of 1894-1895

66

0   300
Miles

WAR DEAD 1904-05	
Russian	120,000
Japanese	75,000

R U S S I A

Chita
Nerchinsk
Amur
Nikolaevsk
Argun
SAKHALIN
M A N C H U R I A
Hailar
Amur
Khabarovsk
Tsitsihar
Harbin
Sungari
C H I N A
Mukden
Vladivostok
Yalu
Peking
Sea of Japan
Port Arthur
KOREA
Seoul
J A P A N
Yellow Sea
Tsushima Strait
Tokyo

The Trans-Siberian Railway by 1895

Under increasing Russian control after 1895

Leased by Russia from China in 1898, together with the right to build a railway to Harbin; (completed by 1904)

The Chinese Eastern Railway, controlled by Russia after its completion in 1903

Russian economic penetration. Russia refused to allow Japan a sphere of influence in Korea

Japanese naval and military attacks 1904-1905

Annexed by Japan in 1905

After successfully halting Japanese expansion in 1895, the Russians adopted an active expansionist policy. For 10 years they pressed forward in Manchuria, and discussed the partition of China with the British Government in 1900. But Japan sought revenge for the humiliation of 1895, and in 1902 neutralized Britain by the Anglo-Japanese Alliance. In February 1904, under Russian provocation, Japan attacked Port Arthur. Russia was defeated on land and sea, and a peace treaty was signed in the United States in Sept. 1905. The grave demoralization created by Russia's defeat led to a mass of revolutionary outbreaks in Russia, and to a serious weakening of the Tsarist mystique.

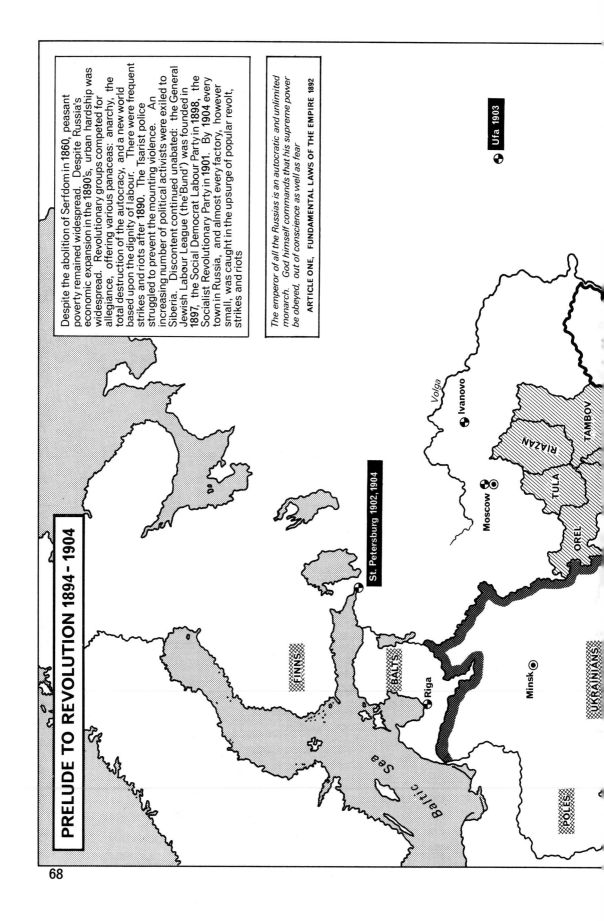

PRELUDE TO REVOLUTION 1894 - 1904

Despite the abolition of Serfdom in 1860, peasant poverty remained widespread. Despite Russia's economic expansion in the 1890's, urban hardship was widespread. Revolutionary groups competed for allegiance, offering various panaceas: anarchy, the total destruction of the autocracy, and a new world based upon the dignity of labour. There were frequent strikes and riots after 1890. The Tsarist police struggled to prevent the mounting violence. An increasing number of political activists were exiled to Siberia. Discontent continued unabated: the General Jewish Labour League (the 'Bund') was founded in 1897, the Social Democrat Labour Party in 1898, the Socialist Revolutionary Party in 1901. By 1904 every town in Russia, and almost every factory, however small, was caught in the upsurge of popular revolt, strikes and riots

The emperor of all the Russias is an autocratic and unlimited monarch. God himself commands that his supreme power be obeyed, out of conscience as well as fear

ARTICLE ONE, FUNDAMENTAL LAWS OF THE EMPIRE 1892

Ufa 1903

Volga

Ivanovo

St. Petersburg 1902, 1904

Moscow

FINNS

BALTS

Riga

Minsk

RIAZAN

TULA

TAMBOV

OREL

Baltic Sea

POLES

UKRAINIANS

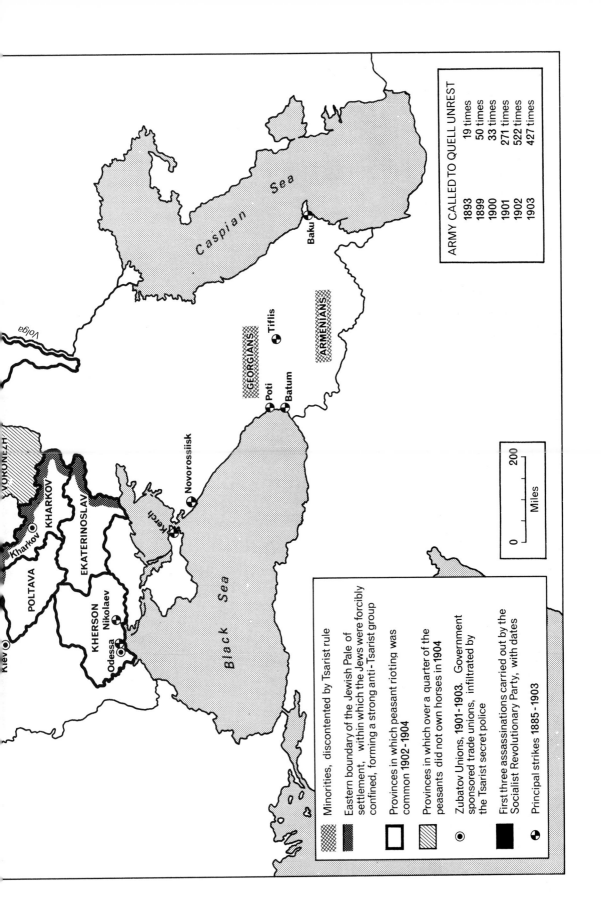

ARMY CALLED TO QUELL UNREST

1893	19 times
1899	50 times
1900	33 times
1901	271 times
1902	522 times
1903	427 times

Caspian Sea

Volga

Baku

GEORGIANS

Tiflis

ARMENIANS

Poti
Batum

Novorossiisk

VORONEZH

KHARKOV
Kharkov

EKATERINOSLAV

POLTAVA

KHERSON
Nikolaev

Odessa

Kerch

Kiev

Black Sea

0   200
Miles

Minorities, discontented by Tsarist rule

Eastern boundary of the Jewish Pale of
settlement, within which the Jews were forcibly
confined, forming a strong anti-Tsarist group

Provinces in which peasant rioting was
common 1902-1904

Provinces in which over a quarter of the
peasants did not own horses in 1904

Zubatov Unions, 1901-1903. Government
sponsored trade unions, infiltrated by
the Tsarist secret police

First three assassinations carried out by the
Socialist Revolutionary Party, with dates

Principal strikes 1885-1903

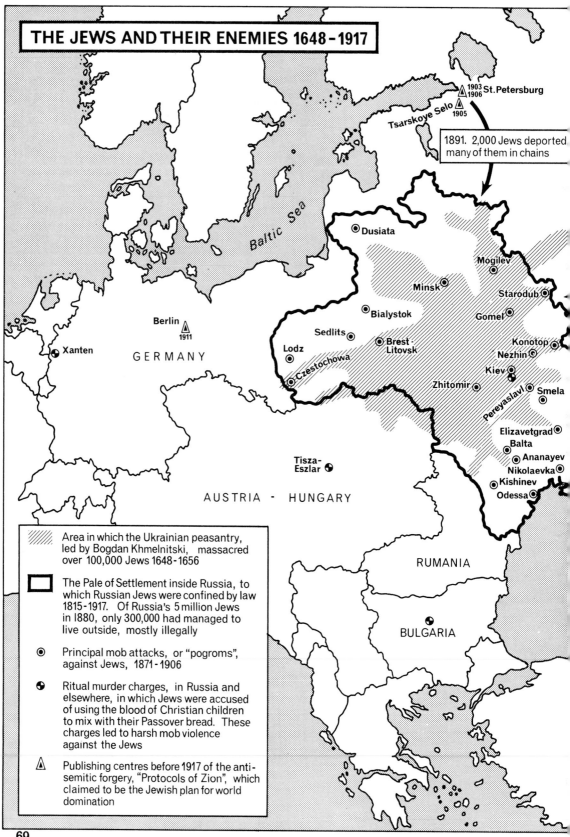

THE JEWS AND THEIR ENEMIES 1648-1917

St.Petersburg △ 1903 1906

Tsarskoye Selo △ 1905

1891. 2,000 Jews deported many of them in chains

Dusiata ⊙

Mogilev ⊙

Minsk ⊙

Starodub ⊙

Bialystok ⊙

Gomel ⊙

Sedlits ⊙

Lodz ⊙

Brest-Litovsk ⊙

Konotop ⊙

Nezhin ⊙

BERLIN △ 1911

GERMANY

Xanten ⊙

Czestochowa ⊙

Kiev ⊙

Zhitomir ⊙

Pereyaslavl ⊙

Smela ⊙

Elizavetgrad ⊙
Balta ⊙

Tisza-Eszlar ◓

Ananayev ⊙

Nikolaevka ⊙

AUSTRIA - HUNGARY

Kishinev ⊙

Odessa ⊙

Baltic Sea

RUMANIA

BULGARIA ◓

Area in which the Ukrainian peasantry, led by Bogdan Khmelnitski, massacred over 100,000 Jews 1648-1656

The Pale of Settlement inside Russia, to which Russian Jews were confined by law 1815-1917. Of Russia's 5 million Jews in 1880, only 300,000 had managed to live outside, mostly illegally

⊙ Principal mob attacks, or "pogroms", against Jews, 1871-1906

◓ Ritual murder charges, in Russia and elsewhere, in which Jews were accused of using the blood of Christian children to mix with their Passover bread. These charges led to harsh mob violence against the Jews

△ Publishing centres before 1917 of the anti-semitic forgery, "Protocols of Zion", which claimed to be the Jewish plan for world domination

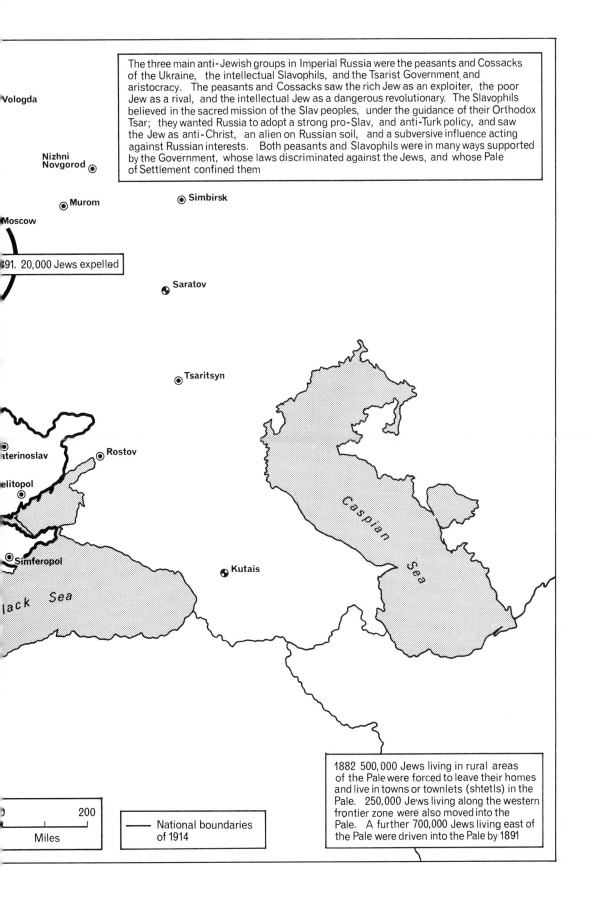

Vologda

Nizhni
Novgorod ⊙

⊙ Murom   ⊙ Simbirsk

Moscow

891. 20,000 Jews expelled

⊕ Saratov

⊙ Tsaritsyn

The three main anti-Jewish groups in Imperial Russia were the peasants and Cossacks
of the Ukraine, the intellectual Slavophils, and the Tsarist Government, and
aristocracy. The peasants and Cossacks saw the rich Jew as an exploiter, the poor
Jew as a rival, and the intellectual Jew as a dangerous revolutionary. The Slavophils
believed in the sacred mission of the Slav peoples, under the guidance of their Orthodox
Tsar; they wanted Russia to adopt a strong pro-Slav, and anti-Turk policy, and saw
the Jew as anti-Christ, an alien on Russian soil, and a subversive influence acting
against Russian interests. Both peasants and Slavophils were in many ways supported
by the Government, whose laws discriminated against the Jews, and whose Pale
of Settlement confined them

aterinoslav
⊙ Rostov

elitopol

⊙Simferopol

⊕ Kutais

Caspian Sea

lack Sea

200

Miles

—— National boundaries
of 1914

1882 500,000 Jews living in rural areas
of the Pale were forced to leave their homes
and live in towns or townlets (shtetls) in the
Pale. 250,000 Jews living along the western
frontier zone were also moved into the
Pale. A further 700,000 Jews living east of
the Pale were driven into the Pale by 1891

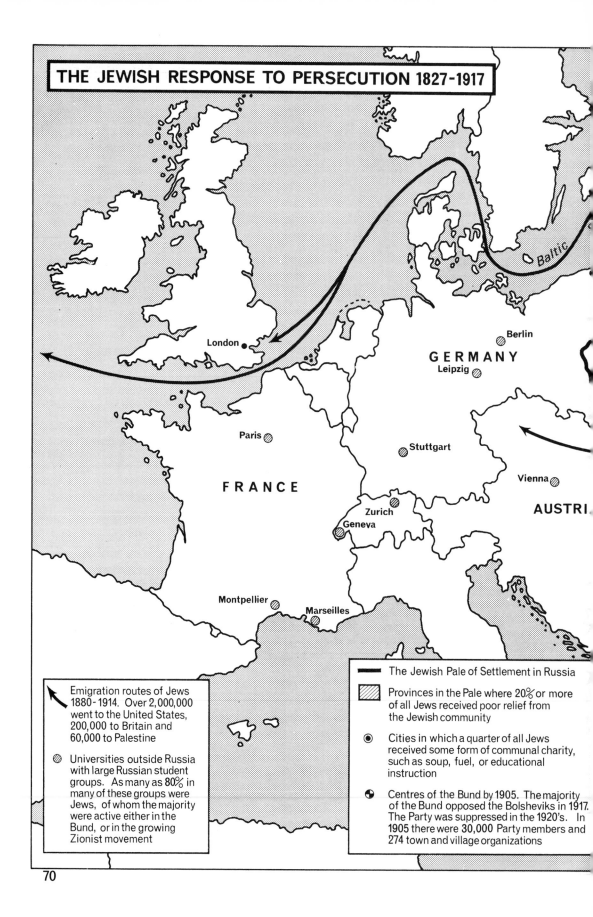

THE JEWISH RESPONSE TO PERSECUTION 1827-1917

Baltic

London

GERMANY

Berlin

Leipzig

Paris

Stuttgart

Vienna

FRANCE

Zurich

Geneva

AUSTRI

Montpellier

Marseilles

Emigration routes of Jews 1880-1914. Over 2,000,000 went to the United States, 200,000 to Britain and 60,000 to Palestine

Universities outside Russia with large Russian student groups. As many as 80% in many of these groups were Jews, of whom the majority were active either in the Bund, or in the growing Zionist movement

The Jewish Pale of Settlement in Russia

Provinces in the Pale where 20% or more of all Jews received poor relief from the Jewish community

Cities in which a quarter of all Jews received some form of communal charity, such as soup, fuel, or educational instruction

Centres of the Bund by 1905. The majority of the Bund opposed the Bolsheviks in 1917. The Party was suppressed in the 1920's. In 1905 there were 30,000 Party members and 274 town and village organizations

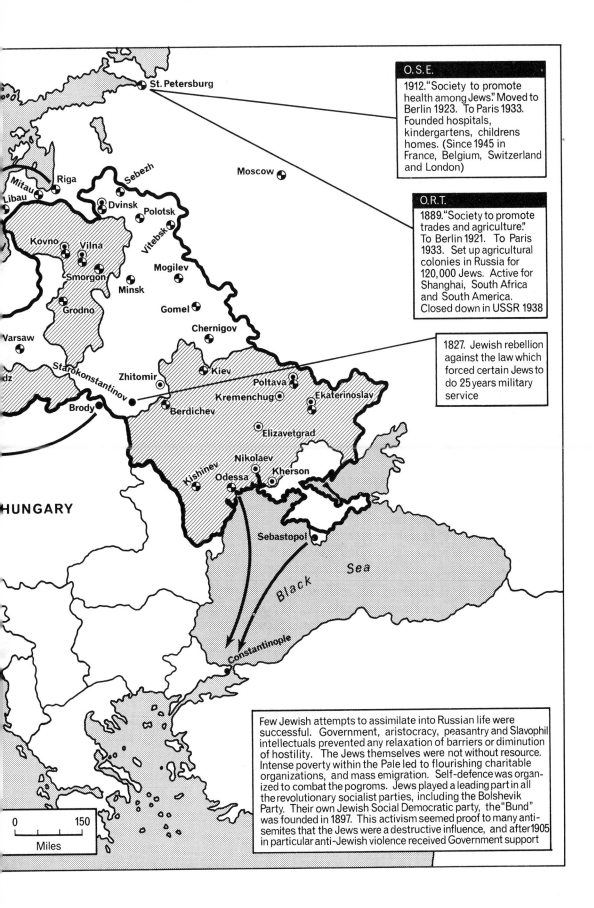

O.S.E.

1912. "Society to promote health among Jews." Moved to Berlin 1923. To Paris 1933. Founded hospitals, kindergartens, childrens homes. (Since 1945 in France, Belgium, Switzerland and London)

O.R.T.

1889. "Society to promote trades and agriculture." To Berlin 1921. To Paris 1933. Set up agricultural colonies in Russia for 120,000 Jews. Active for Shanghai, South Africa and South America. Closed down in USSR 1938

1827. Jewish rebellion against the law which forced certain Jews to do 25 years military service

St. Petersburg

Moscow

Riga
Mitau
Libau
Sebezh
Dvinsk
Polotsk
Kovno
Vilna
Smorgon
Vitebsk
Grodno
Minsk
Mogilev
Gomel
Varsaw
Starokonstantinov
Zhitomir
Chernigov
Kiev
dz
Brody
Berdichev
Poltava
Kremenchug
Ekaterinoslav
Elizavetgrad
Kishinev
Nikolaev
Odessa
Kherson

HUNGARY

Sebastopol

Black Sea

Constantinople

Few Jewish attempts to assimilate into Russian life were successful. Government, aristocracy, peasantry and Slavophil intellectuals prevented any relaxation of barriers or diminution of hostility. The Jews themselves were not without resource. Intense poverty within the Pale led to flourishing charitable organizations, and mass emigration. Self-defence was organized to combat the pogroms. Jews played a leading part in all the revolutionary socialist parties, including the Bolshevik Party. Their own Jewish Social Democratic party, the "Bund" was founded in 1897. This activism seemed proof to many anti-semites that the Jews were a destructive influence, and after 1905 in particular anti-Jewish violence received Government support

```
0        150
   Miles
```

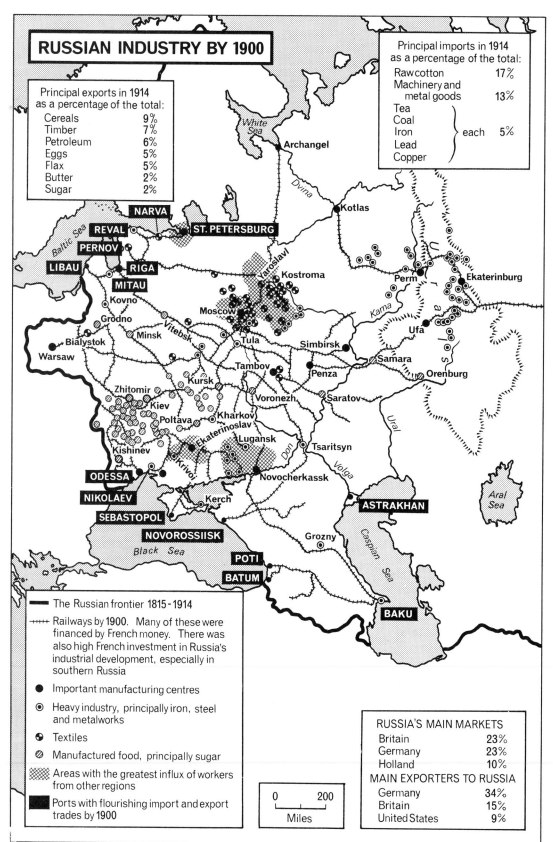

RUSSIAN INDUSTRY BY 1900

Principal exports in 1914
as a percentage of the total:

Cereals	9%
Timber	7%
Petroleum	6%
Eggs	5%
Flax	5%
Butter	2%
Sugar	2%

Principal imports in 1914
as a percentage of the total:

Raw cotton	17%
Machinery and metal goods	13%
Tea	
Coal	
Iron } each	5%
Lead	
Copper	

White Sea

Archangel

Dvina

Kotlas

NARVA

REVAL   ST. PETERSBURG

PERNOV

Baltic Sea

LIBAU   RIGA

MITAU

Kovno

Grodno

Yaroslavl   Kostroma

Moscow

Perm   Ekaterinburg

Kama

Minsk   Vitebsk

Tula

Ufa

Bialystok

Warsaw

Simbirsk

Samara

Kursk

Tambov

Penza

Orenburg

Zhitomir

Kiev

Voronezh

Saratov

Poltava   Kharkov

Ural

Kishinev   Ekaterinoslav   Lugansk

Krivoi   Don   Tsaritsyn

ODESSA

Novocherkassk

Volga

NIKOLAEV

Kerch

Aral Sea

SEBASTOPOL

ASTRAKHAN

NOVOROSSIISK

Grozny

Black Sea

POTI

Caspian Sea

BATUM

BAKU

── The Russian frontier 1815-1914

┼┼┼┼ Railways by 1900. Many of these were
   financed by French money. There was
   also high French investment in Russia's
   industrial development, especially in
   southern Russia

● Important manufacturing centres

◉ Heavy industry, principally iron, steel
   and metalworks

✪ Textiles

⊘ Manufactured food, principally sugar

▧ Areas with the greatest influx of workers
   from other regions

■ Ports with flourishing import and export
   trades by 1900

0   200
├────────┤
   Miles

RUSSIA'S MAIN MARKETS

Britain	23%
Germany	23%
Holland	10%

MAIN EXPORTERS TO RUSSIA

Germany	34%
Britain	15%
United States	9%

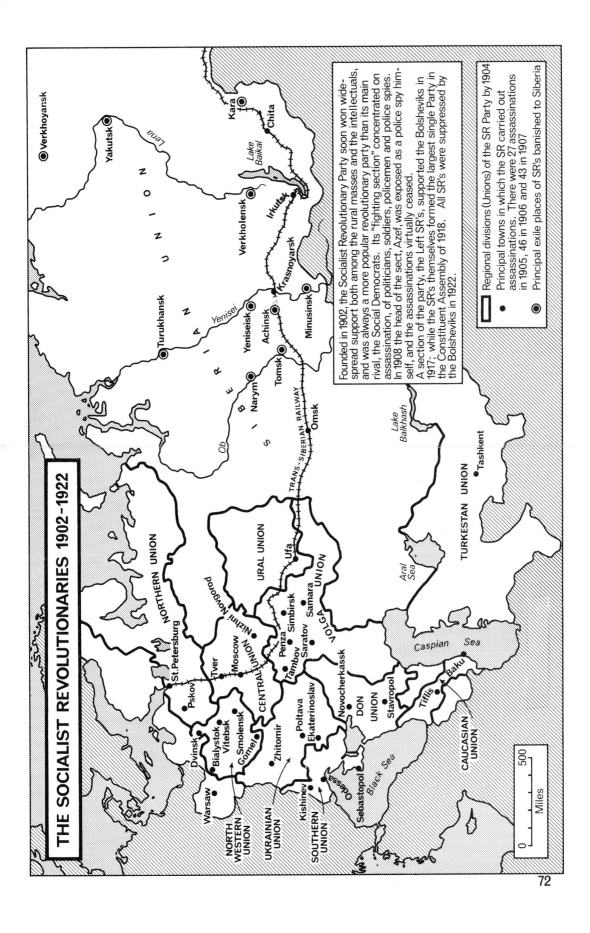

THE SOCIALIST REVOLUTIONARIES 1902-1922

Founded in 1902, the Socialist Revolutionary Party soon won widespread support both among the rural masses and the intellectuals, and was always a more popular revolutionary party than its main rival, the Social Democrats. Its "fighting section" concentrated on assassination, of politicians, soldiers, policemen and police spies. In 1908 the head of the sect, Azef, was exposed as a police spy himself, and the assassinations virtually ceased.

A section of the party, the Left SR's, supported the Bolsheviks in 1917; while the SR's themselves formed the largest single Party in the Constituent Assembly of 1918. All SR's were suppressed by the Bolsheviks in 1922.

☐ Regional divisions (Unions) of the SR Party by 1904

• Principal towns in which the SR carried out
   assassinations. There were 27 assassinations
   in 1905, 46 in 1906 and 43 in 1907

◉ Principal exile places of SR's banished to Siberia

72

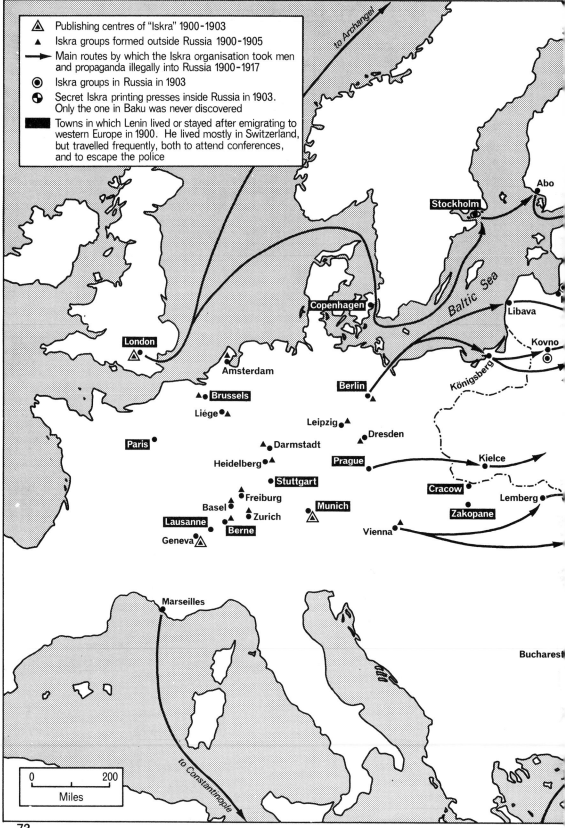

Legend:

⚠ Publishing centres of "Iskra" 1900-1903

▲ Iskra groups formed outside Russia 1900-1905

→ Main routes by which the Iskra organisation took men and propaganda illegally into Russia 1900-1917

◉ Iskra groups in Russia in 1903

◓ Secret Iskra printing presses inside Russia in 1903. Only the one in Baku was never discovered

■ Towns in which Lenin lived or stayed after emigrating to western Europe in 1900. He lived mostly in Switzerland, but travelled frequently, both to attend conferences, and to escape the police

to Archangel

Abo

Stockholm

Baltic Sea

Copenhagen

Libava

Kovno

Berlin

Königsberg

London

Amsterdam

Brussels

Liége

Leipzig

Dresden

Paris

Darmstadt

Heidelberg

Prague

Kielce

Stuttgart

Cracow

Lemberg

Freiburg

Munich

Zakopane

Basel

Lausanne

Zurich

Berne

Vienna

Geneva

Marseilles

Bucharest

to Constantinople

0   200
Miles

73

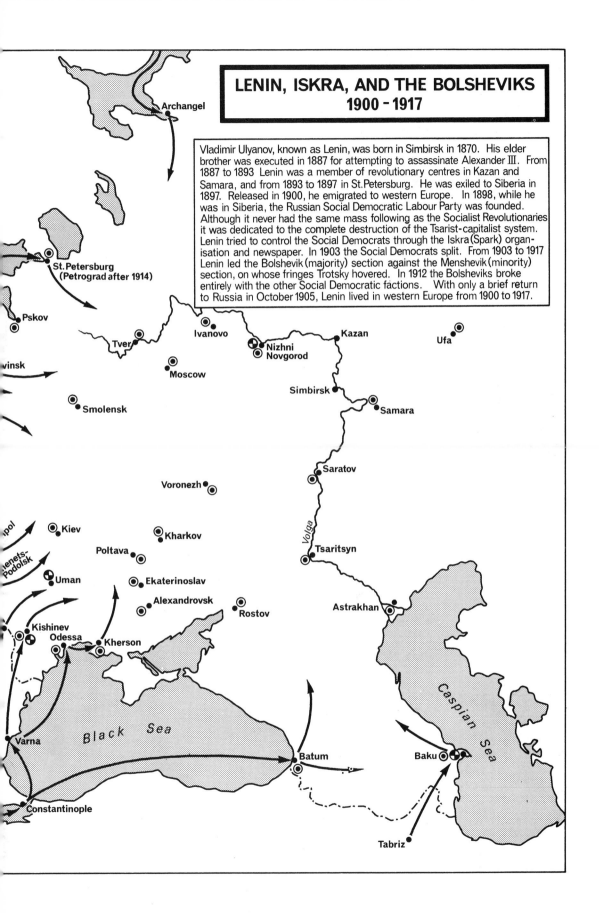

LENIN, ISKRA, AND THE BOLSHEVIKS
1900 - 1917

Vladimir Ulyanov, known as Lenin, was born in Simbirsk in 1870. His elder brother was executed in 1887 for attempting to assassinate Alexander III. From 1887 to 1893 Lenin was a member of revolutionary centres in Kazan and Samara, and from 1893 to 1897 in St.Petersburg. He was exiled to Siberia in 1897. Released in 1900, he emigrated to western Europe. In 1898, while he was in Siberia, the Russian Social Democratic Labour Party was founded. Although it never had the same mass following as the Socialist Revolutionaries it was dedicated to the complete destruction of the Tsarist-capitalist system. Lenin tried to control the Social Democrats through the Iskra (Spark) organisation and newspaper. In 1903 the Social Democrats split. From 1903 to 1917 Lenin led the Bolshevik (majority) section against the Menshevik (minority) section, on whose fringes Trotsky hovered. In 1912 the Bolsheviks broke entirely with the other Social Democratic factions. With only a brief return to Russia in October 1905, Lenin lived in western Europe from 1900 to 1917.

Archangel

St.Petersburg
(Petrograd after 1914)

Pskov

vinsk

Tver

Ivanovo

Nizhni
Novgorod

Kazan

Ufa

Moscow

Smolensk

Simbirsk

Samara

Saratov

Voronezh

Volga

Kiev

Kharkov

enets-
Podolsk

Poltava

pol

Uman

Ekaterinoslav

Tsaritsyn

Alexandrovsk

Rostov

Astrakhan

Kishinev
Odessa

Kherson

Caspian Sea

Black Sea

Varna

Batum

Baku

Constantinople

Tabriz

THE PROVINCES AND POPULATION OF EUROPEAN RUSSIA IN 1900

White Sea

NORWAY

ARCHANGEL

SWEDEN

FINLAND

VOLOGDA

OLONETS

Baltic Sea

ESTLAND

ST PETERSBURG

NOVGOROD

PERM

KURLAND

LIVLAND

PSKOV

KOSTROMA

VIATKA

KOVNO

VITEBSK

TVER

YAROSLAVL

GERMANY

VILNA

MOSCOW

VLADIMIR

NIZHNI NOVGOROD

KAZAN

UFA

GRODNO

SMOLENSK

KALUGA

RIAZAN

SIMBIRSK

POLISH PROVINCES

MINSK

MOGILEV

TULA

PENZA

OREL

ORENBURG

VOLHYNIA

CHERNIGOV

TAMBOV

SARATOV

SAMARA

AUSTRIA-HUNGARY

KIEV

POLTAVA

KURSK

PODOLIA

VORONEZH

KHARKOV

BESSARABIA

KHERSON

EKATERINOSLAV

DON

ASTRAKHAN

RUMANIA

TAURIDA

KUBAN

STAVROPOL

Caspian Sea

Black Sea

TEREK

TURKEY

TRANS-CAUCASIAN PROVINCES

PERSIA

The first official Russian census was held in 1897. The total population was just over 129 million - nearly as large as the combined populations of Britain, France, and Germany. Over 80% of all Russians were peasants. Finland was an autonomous Duchy, and, like Poland, was subdivided into Provinces

MAIN NATIONAL & ETHNIC GROUPS IN EUROPEAN RUSSIA IN 1900	
Russians	55 million
Ukrainians	22 million
Poles	8 million
White Russians	6 million
Jews	5 million
Balts	4 million
Caucasians	3 million
Germans	2 million

THE 1905 REVOLUTION IN THE COUNTRYSIDE

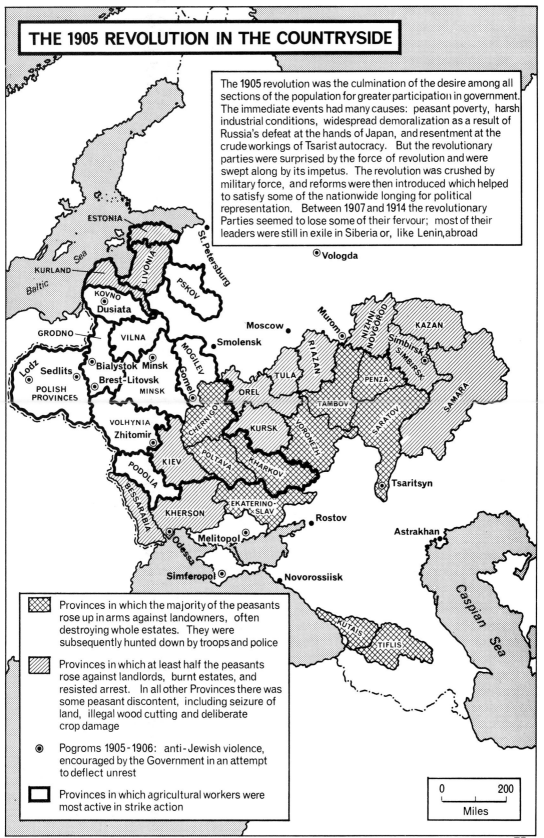

The 1905 revolution was the culmination of the desire among all sections of the population for greater participation in government. The immediate events had many causes: peasant poverty, harsh industrial conditions, widespread demoralization as a result of Russia's defeat at the hands of Japan, and resentment at the crude workings of Tsarist autocracy. But the revolutionary parties were surprised by the force of revolution and were swept along by its impetus. The revolution was crushed by military force, and reforms were then introduced which helped to satisfy some of the nationwide longing for political representation. Between 1907 and 1914 the revolutionary Parties seemed to lose some of their fervour; most of their leaders were still in exile in Siberia or, like Lenin, abroad

Provinces in which the majority of the peasants rose up in arms against landowners, often destroying whole estates. They were subsequently hunted down by troops and police

Provinces in which at least half the peasants rose against landlords, burnt estates, and resisted arrest. In all other Provinces there was some peasant discontent, including seizure of land, illegal wood cutting and deliberate crop damage

◉ Pogroms 1905-1906: anti-Jewish violence, encouraged by the Government in an attempt to deflect unrest

Provinces in which agricultural workers were most active in strike action

0   200
Miles

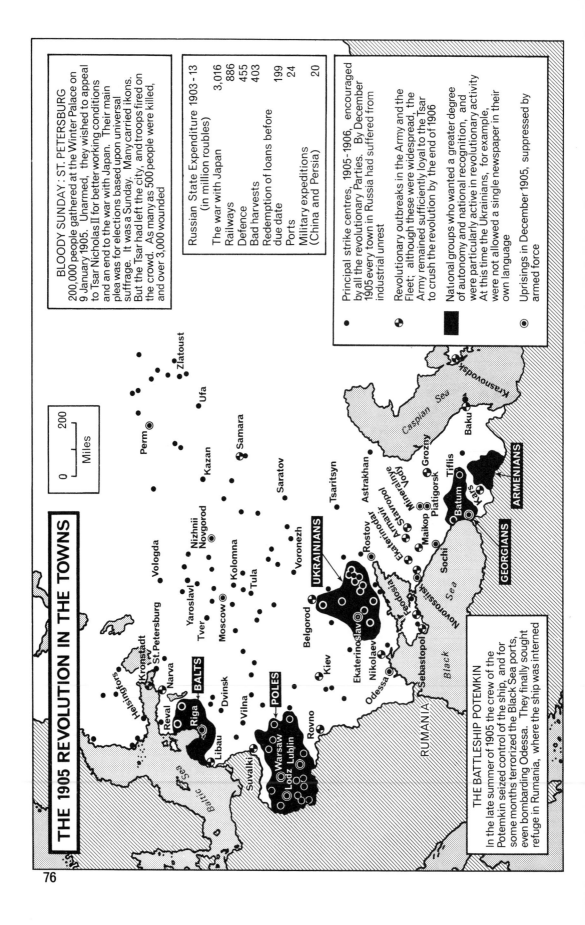

THE 1905 REVOLUTION IN THE TOWNS

BLOODY SUNDAY: ST. PETERSBURG

200,000 people gathered at the Winter Palace on 9 January 1905. Unarmed, they wished to appeal to Tsar Nicholas II for better working conditions and an end to the war with Japan. Their main plea was for elections based upon universal suffrage. It was a Sunday. Many carried ikons. But the Tsar had left the city, and troops fired on the crowd. As many as 500 people were killed, and over 3,000 wounded

Russian State Expenditure 1903 - 13
(in million roubles)

The war with Japan	3,016
Railways	886
Defence	455
Bad harvests	403
Redemption of loans before due date	199
Ports	24
Military expeditions (China and Persia)	20

- Principal strike centres, 1905-1906, encouraged by all the revolutionary Parties. By December 1905 every town in Russia had suffered from industrial unrest

- Revolutionary outbreaks in the Army and the Fleet; although these were widespread, the Army remained sufficiently loyal to the Tsar to crush the revolution by the end of 1906

- National groups who wanted a greater degree of autonomy and national recognition, and were particularly active in revolutionary activity At this time the Ukrainians, for example, were not allowed a single newspaper in their own language

- Uprisings in December 1905, suppressed by armed force

THE BATTLESHIP POTEMKIN

In the late summer of 1905 the crew of the Potemkin seized control of the ship, and for some months terrorized the Black Sea ports, even bombarding Odessa. They finally sought refuge in Rumania, where the ship was interned

0   200
Miles

Zlatoust
Ufa
Samara
Perm
Kazan
Saratov
Vologda
Nizhnii Novgorod
Kolomna
Tula
Voronezh
Yaroslavl
Tver
Moscow
Tsaritsyn
Astrakhan
Krasnovodsk
Caspian Sea
Baku
Grozny
Mineralnye Vody
Piatigorsk
Tiflis
Batum
Kars
ARMENIANS
GEORGIANS
Sochi
Novorossisk
Black Sea
Armavir
Stavropol
Maikop
Ekaterinodar
Rostov
UKRAINIANS
Belgorod
Ekaterinoslav
Nikolaev
Odessa
Feodosia
Sebastopol
RUMANIA
Kiev
Rovno
Lublin
Warsaw
Lodz
POLES
Suvalki
Vilna
Dvinsk
Libau
Riga
Reval
BALTS
Narva
Helsingfors
Kronstadt
St.Petersburg
Baltic Sea

76

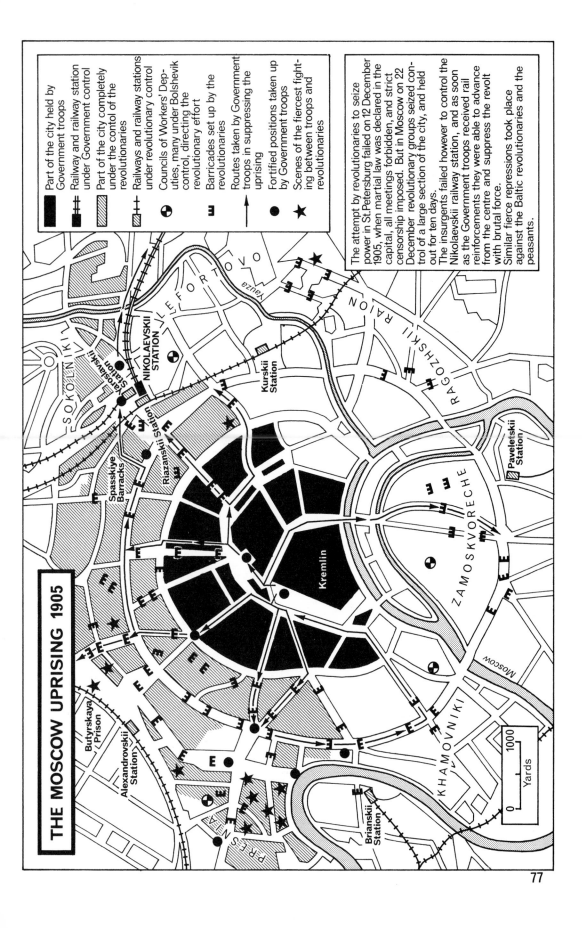

THE MOSCOW UPRISING 1905

Legend:

- Part of the city held by Government troops
- Railway and railway station under Government control
- Part of the city completely under the control of the revolutionaries
- Railways and railway stations under revolutionary control
- Councils of Workers' Deputies, many under Bolshevik control, directing the revolutionary effort
- Barricades set up by the revolutionaries
- Routes taken by Government troops in suppressing the uprising
- Fortified positions taken up by Government troops
- Scenes of the fiercest fighting between troops and revolutionaries

The attempt by revolutionaries to seize power in St.Petersburg failed on 12 December 1905, when martial law was declared in the capital, all meetings forbidden, and strict censorship imposed. But in Moscow on 22 December revolutionary groups seized control of a large section of the city, and held out for ten days.

The insurgents failed however to control the Nikolaevskii railway station, and as soon as the Government troops received rail reinforcements they were able to advance from the centre and suppress the revolt with brutal force.

Similar fierce repressions took place against the Baltic revolutionaries and the peasants.

Map labels: SOKOLNIKI, LEFORTOVO, Yauza, Starosievskii Station, NIKOLAEVSKII STATION, Kurskii Station, Riazanskii Station, Spasskiye Barracks, Kremlin, ZAMOSKVORECHE, Paveletskii Station, RAGOZHSKII RAION, Moscow, Moscow, KHAMOVNIKI, Butyrskaya Prison, Alexandrovskii Station, PRESNIA, Brianskii Station

Yards 0 1000

RUSSIA AND THE BALKANS 1876-1885

0   100
Miles

Russia wanted to drive the Turk from Europe and dominate the
Balkans.   Britain supported Russian protests against Turkish
atrocities against the Bulgarians in 1875, which led Russia to
attack Turkey. After defeating the Turks at Plevna in 1876 Russia
tried to set up a large independent Bulgaria, but Britain and
Austria-Hungary challenged Russia's aspirations, and under
German mediation Russia agreed to the creation of a much
smaller Bulgaria. Austria advanced her own Balkan interests
by occupying the former Turkish province of Bosnia, which she
formally annexed in 1908, and entering Novi Pazar.

RUSSIA

AUSTRIA-HUNGARY

R U M A N I A

BOSNIA
Sarajevo●
Belgrade ●

Bucharest ●
Constanza ●

SERBIA

Danube

NOVI PAZAR
Nish ●

Plevna
Silistria
B U L G A R I A
Varna
Tirnovo ●
Burgas ●

Cattaro ●
Sofia ●
EAST RUMELIA

MONTENEGRO

Skopje ●

Adrianople ●
Midia ●

MACEDONIA
Kavalla ●
Rodosto ●
San
Stephano ●

Constantinople

Dedeagatch
Chanak ●

Adriatic Sea

Aegean Sea

TURKEY –

IN – ASIA

G R E E C E
Athens ●

Black Sea

— · — · The boundary of Turkey-in-Europe 1876

☐ Russian proposal for an independent "Big
Bulgaria", agreed to by the Turks at the
Treaty of San Stephano 1878

■ Bulgaria, autonomous, not independent,
as allowed by Britain and Germany by
the Treaty of Berlin 1878

▨ Turkish territory added to Serbia, Rumania
and Montenegro (who each gained their
independence from Turkey) by the Treaty of
Berlin 1878; and to Greece in 1881

▩ Occupied by Austria-Hungary in 1878

▧ Added to Bulgaria in 1885, when Bulgaria
became fully independent of Turkey

RUSSIA, THE BALKANS, AND THE COMING OF WAR 1912–1914

0   500

Miles

North Sea

BRITAIN

Ice Sea

Baltic

St. Petersburg

Reval

Riga

BALTIC PROVINCES

Moscow

RUSSIA

Danzig

FRANCE

Paris

Berlin

GERMANY

Breslau

Warsaw

POLISH PROVINCES

Pripet Marshes

Kiev

VOLHYNIA

Lemberg

Vienna

Budapest

AUSTRIA - HUNGARY

Adriatic Sea

BOSNIA

Sarajevo

Belgrade

SERBIA

RUMANIA

Black Sea

MONTENEGRO

ALBANIA

Skopje

BULGARIA

Constantinople

Bosphorus

Dardanelles

TURKEY

GREECE

Aegean Sea

Russia's mid-century alignment with
Germany was changed during the 1880's
to a new alignment with France,
while at the same time Austria and
Germany drew closer together. In the
two Balkan Wars of 1912 and 1913
Turkey was driven almost entirely
from Europe, but Russia's position
did not improve; for as a result of
Turkey's defeat Austrian influence
increased even further. In June 1914
a Bosnian Serb murdered the Austrian
heir to the throne, Archduke Franz-
Ferdinand, at Sarajevo. Austria
invaded Serbia on 28 July 1914.
Russia then declared war on Austria.
Germany supported her ally Austria
and declared war on Russia. France
and Britain joined Russia against
Germany and Austria. Turkey
attacked Russia in October 1914

Countries in which Austrian and German influence
worked against Russia. Greece had a pro-German
King; Turkey a pro-German Minister of War and
virtual dictator; Bulgaria and Rumania had both
accepted alliance with the Central Powers

Area of Russia in which Germany hoped to expand
as a result of war

Russia's only two Balkan Allies, both threatened by
Austria. Austria had created the state of Albania
in 1912 in order to cut Serbia off from the sea.

Countries in western Europe sympathetic to Russia.
France had a military alliance with Russia dating from
1894. Britain a convention dating from 1907

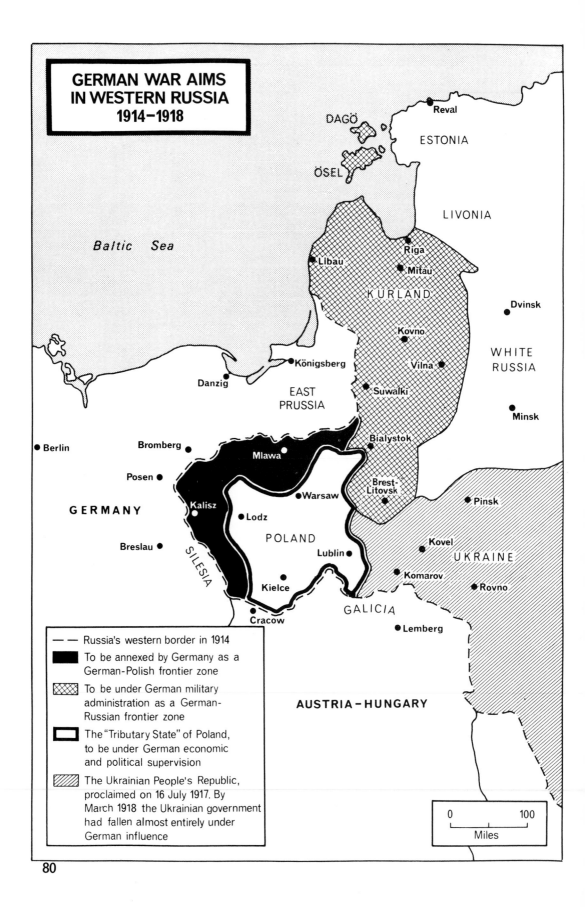

GERMAN WAR AIMS
IN WESTERN RUSSIA
1914–1918

DAGÖ

Reval

ESTONIA

ÖSEL

LIVONIA

Baltic Sea

Libau
Riga
Mitau

KURLAND

Dvinsk

Kovno

WHITE
RUSSIA

Königsberg

Vilna

Danzig

EAST
PRUSSIA

Suwalki

Minsk

Berlin

Bromberg

Mlawa

Bialystok

Posen

Warsaw

Brest-
Litovsk

Pinsk

GERMANY

Kalisz

Lodz

POLAND

Kovel

UKRAINE

Breslau

SILESIA

Lublin

Komarov

Rovno

Kielce

Cracow

GALICIA

Lemberg

Russia's western border in 1914

To be annexed by Germany as a
German-Polish frontier zone

To be under German military
administration as a German-
Russian frontier zone

The "Tributary State" of Poland,
to be under German economic
and political supervision

The Ukrainian People's Republic,
proclaimed on 16 July 1917. By
March 1918 the Ukrainian government
had fallen almost entirely under
German influence

AUSTRIA–HUNGARY

0   100

Miles

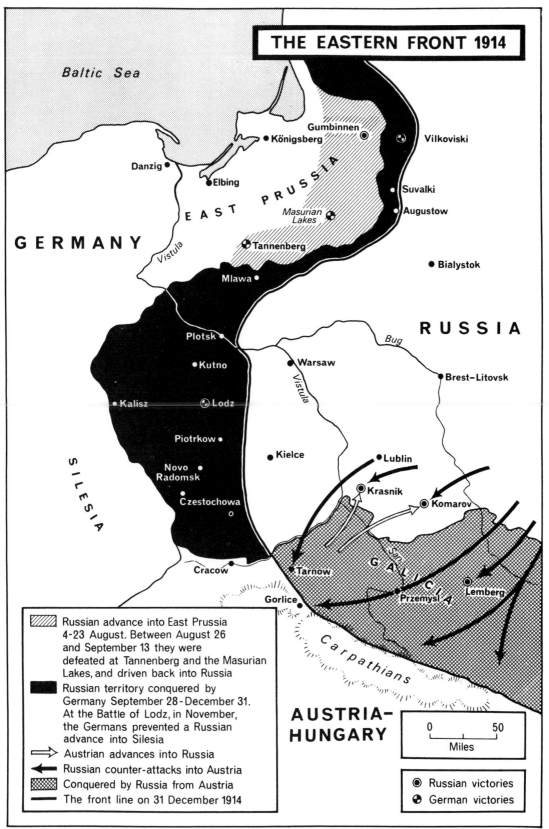

THE EASTERN FRONT 1914

Baltic Sea

GERMANY

Danzig ●

● Königsberg

Gumbinnen ◎

Vilkoviski

● Elbing

E A S T   P R U S S I A

Suvalki ○

Augustow ●

Masurian Lakes ◎

● Bialystok

◉ Tannenberg

Vistula

Mlawa ●

Plotsk ●

R U S S I A

Bug

● Kutno

● Warsaw

Vistula

● Brest–Litovsk

● Kalisz

⊕ Lodz

Piotrkow ●

● Kielce

S I L E S I A

Novo Radomsk ●

● Lublin

Czestochowa ●

⊙ Krasnik

◉ Komarov

G A L I C I A

Cracow ●

Tarnow ●

● Lemberg

Gorlice ●

Przemysl ◉

Carpathians

AUSTRIA-HUNGARY

Scale: 0 — 50 Miles

Legend

▨ Russian advance into East Prussia 4-23 August. Between August 26 and September 13 they were defeated at Tannenberg and the Masurian Lakes, and driven back into Russia

■ Russian territory conquered by Germany September 28-December 31. At the Battle of Lodz, in November, the Germans prevented a Russian advance into Silesia

⇨ Austrian advances into Russia

← Russian counter-attacks into Austria

▨ Conquered by Russia from Austria

— The front line on 31 December 1914

◉ Russian victories
⊕ German victories

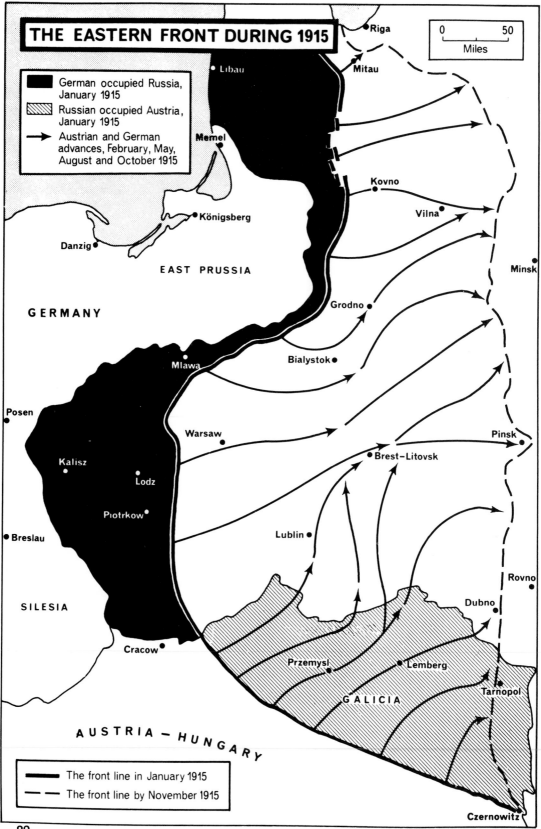

THE EASTERN FRONT DURING 1915

German occupied Russia, January 1915

Russian occupied Austria, January 1915

Austrian and German advances, February, May, August and October 1915

0   50
Miles

Riga

Libau

Mitau

Memel

Kovno

Königsberg

Vilna

Danzig

EAST PRUSSIA

Minsk

GERMANY

Grodno

Mlawa

Bialystok

Posen

Warsaw

Pinsk

Kalisz

Lodz

Brest–Litovsk

Piotrkow

Breslau

Lublin

SILESIA

Rovno

Dubno

Cracow

Przemysl

Lemberg

Tarnopol

GALICIA

AUSTRIA – HUNGARY

Czernowitz

The front line in January 1915

The front line by November 1915

82

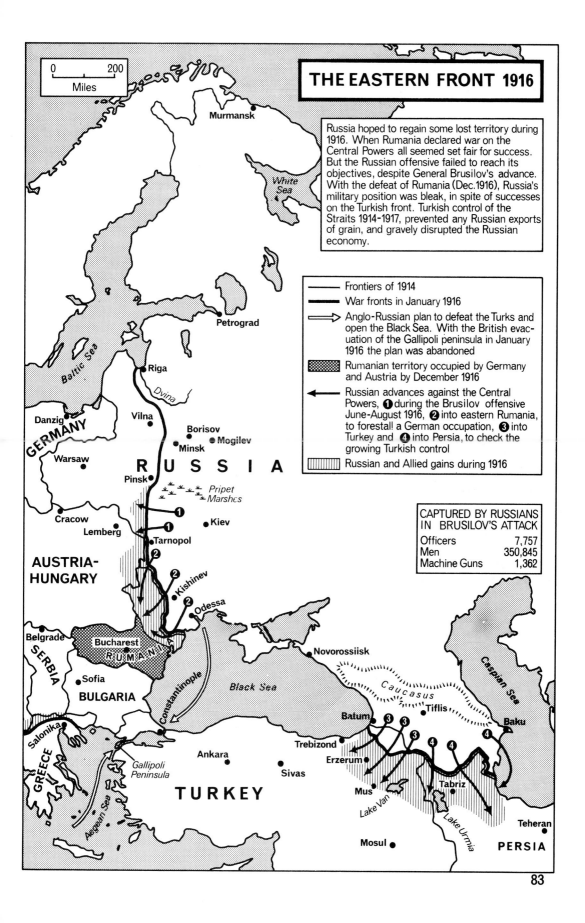

THE EASTERN FRONT 1916

Russia hoped to regain some lost territory during 1916. When Rumania declared war on the Central Powers all seemed set fair for success. But the Russian offensive failed to reach its objectives, despite General Brusilov's advance. With the defeat of Rumania (Dec.1916), Russia's military position was bleak, in spite of successes on the Turkish front. Turkish control of the Straits 1914-1917, prevented any Russian exports of grain, and gravely disrupted the Russian economy.

———	Frontiers of 1914
▬▬▬	War fronts in January 1916
⇒	Anglo-Russian plan to defeat the Turks and open the Black Sea. With the British evacuation of the Gallipoli peninsula in January 1916 the plan was abandoned
▨	Rumanian territory occupied by Germany and Austria by December 1916
←	Russian advances against the Central Powers, ❶ during the Brusilov offensive June-August 1916, ❷ into eastern Rumania, to forestall a German occupation, ❸ into Turkey and ❹ into Persia, to check the growing Turkish control
▥	Russian and Allied gains during 1916

CAPTURED BY RUSSIANS IN BRUSILOV'S ATTACK

Officers	7,757
Men	350,845
Machine Guns	1,362

Murmansk

White Sea

Baltic Sea

Petrograd

Riga

Dvina

Danzig

Vilna

GERMANY

Borisov

Mogilev

Minsk

Warsaw

R U S S I A

Pinsk

Pripet Marshes

Cracow

Lemberg

Tarnopol

Kiev

AUSTRIA-HUNGARY

Kishinev

Odessa

Belgrade

Bucharest

RUMANIA

Novorossiisk

Caucasus

Caspian Sea

SERBIA

Sofia

BULGARIA

Constantinople

Black Sea

Tiflis

Baku

Batum

Salonika

GREECE

Aegean Sea

Gallipoli Peninsula

Ankara

Sivas

T U R K E Y

Trebizond

Erzerum

Mus

Lake Van

Tabriz

Lake Urmia

Teheran

Mosul

PERSIA

0   200
Miles

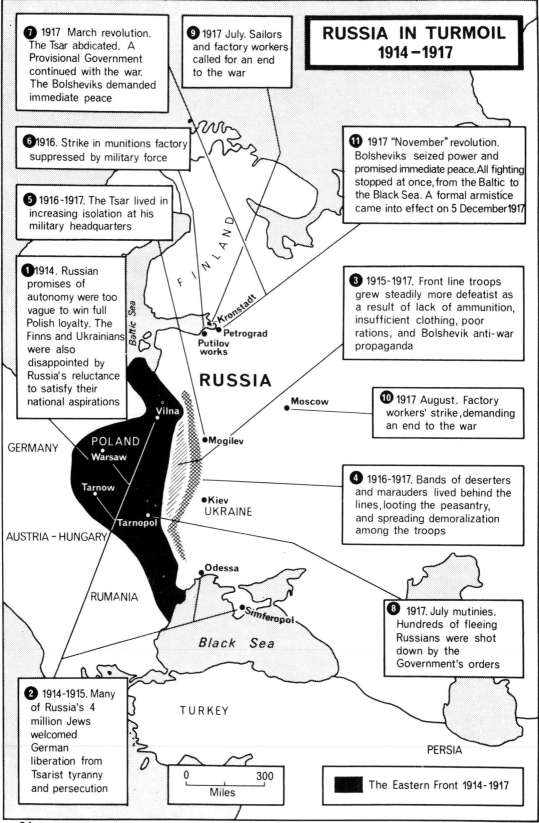

RUSSIA IN TURMOIL
1914–1917

7 1917 March revolution. The Tsar abdicated. A Provisional Government continued with the war. The Bolsheviks demanded immediate peace

9 1917 July. Sailors and factory workers called for an end to the war

6 1916. Strike in munitions factory suppressed by military force

5 1916-1917. The Tsar lived in increasing isolation at his military headquarters

1 1914. Russian promises of autonomy were too vague to win full Polish loyalty. The Finns and Ukrainians were also disappointed by Russia's reluctance to satisfy their national aspirations

11 1917 "November" revolution. Bolsheviks seized power and promised immediate peace. All fighting stopped at once, from the Baltic to the Black Sea. A formal armistice came into effect on 5 December 1917

3 1915-1917. Front line troops grew steadily more defeatist as a result of lack of ammunition, insufficient clothing, poor rations, and Bolshevik anti-war propaganda

10 1917 August. Factory workers' strike, demanding an end to the war

4 1916-1917. Bands of deserters and marauders lived behind the lines, looting the peasantry, and spreading demoralization among the troops

8 1917. July mutinies. Hundreds of fleeing Russians were shot down by the Government's orders

2 1914-1915. Many of Russia's 4 million Jews welcomed German liberation from Tsarist tyranny and persecution

FINLAND

Baltic Sea

Kronstadt

Petrograd

Putilov works

RUSSIA

Moscow

GERMANY

POLAND

Warsaw

Mogilev

Vilna

Tarnow

Tarnopol

Kiev

UKRAINE

AUSTRIA – HUNGARY

RUMANIA

Odessa

Simferopol

Black Sea

TURKEY

PERSIA

0   300
Miles

⬛ The Eastern Front 1914-1917

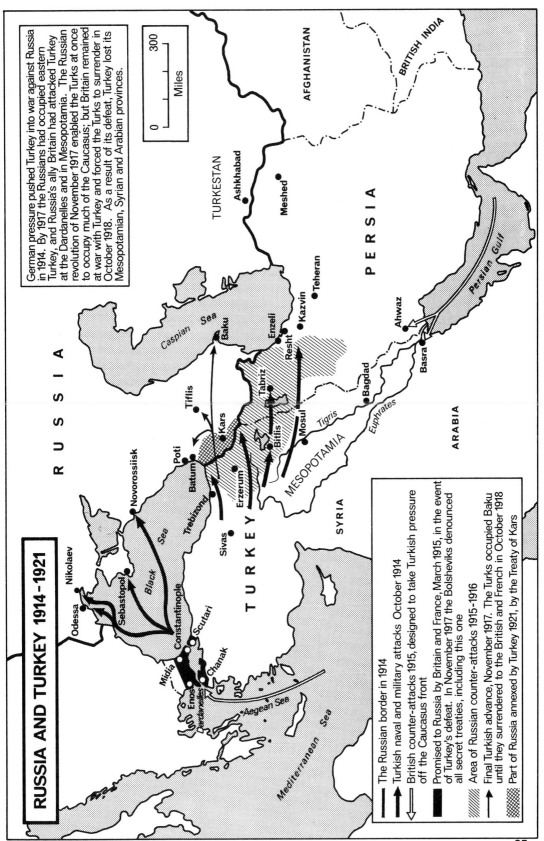

RUSSIA AND TURKEY 1914-1921

German pressure pushed Turkey into war against Russia in 1914. By 1917 the Russians had occupied eastern Turkey, and Russia's ally Britain had attacked Turkey at the Dardanelles and in Mesopotamia. The Russian revolution of November 1917 enabled the Turks at once to occupy much of the Caucasus; but Britain remained at war with Turkey and forced the Turks to surrender in October 1918. As a result of its defeat, Turkey lost its Mesopotamian, Syrian and Arabian provinces.

300

0   Miles

AFGHANISTAN

BRITISH INDIA

TURKESTAN

Ashkhabad

Meshed

P E R S I A

Teheran

Persian Gulf

R U S S I A

Caspian Sea

Baku

Enzeli

Kazvin

Resht

Ahwaz

Tiflis

Tabriz

Basra

Kars

Bagdad

Bitlis

Mosul

Tigris

Euphrates

Poti

Battum

MESOPOTAMIA

Novorossiisk

Erzerum

ARABIA

Trebizond

SYRIA

Nikolaev

Sivas

Odessa

Sebastopol

Black Sea

T U R K E Y

Constantinople

Scutari

Midia

Chanak

Enos

Dardanelles

Aegean Sea

Mediterranean Sea

The Russian border in 1914

Turkish naval and military attacks October 1914

British counter-attacks 1915, designed to take Turkish pressure off the Caucasus front

Promised to Russia by Britain and France, March 1915, in the event of Turkey's defeat. In November 1917 the Bolsheviks denounced all secret treaties, including this one

Area of Russian counter-attacks 1915-1916

Final Turkish advance, November 1917. The Turks occupied Baku until they surrendered to the British and French in October 1918

Part of Russia annexed by Turkey 1921, by the Treaty of Kars

85

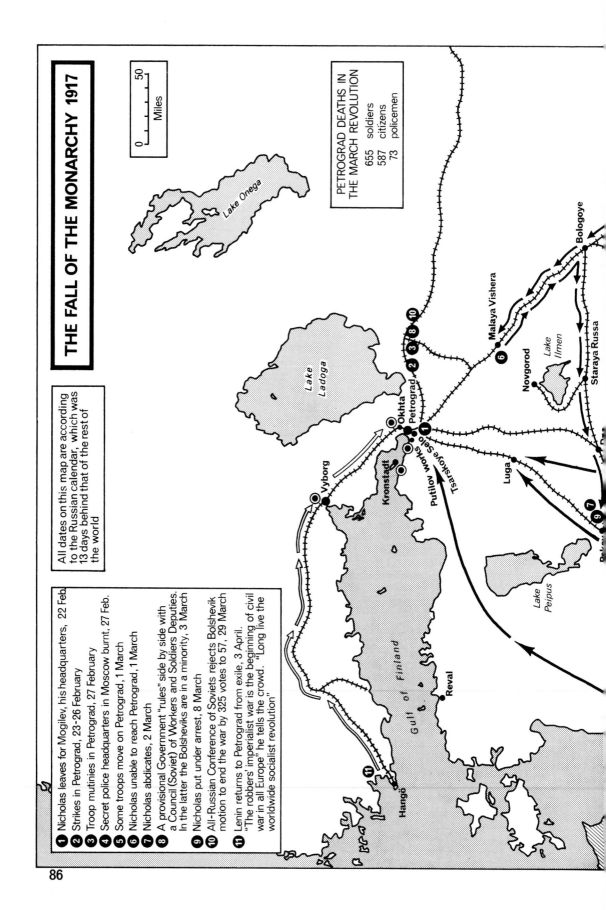

THE FALL OF THE MONARCHY 1917

0   50
Miles

PETROGRAD DEATHS IN
THE MARCH REVOLUTION

655   soldiers
587   citizens
73   policemen

All dates on this map are according
to the Russian calendar, which was
13 days behind that of the rest of
the world

Lake Onega

Lake Ladoga

Lake Ilmen

Lake Peipus

Gulf of Finland

Bologoye

Malaya Vishera

Staraya Russa

Novgorod

Luga

Okhta
Petrograd
Tsarskoye Selo
Putilov works
Kronstadt

Vyborg

Reval

Hangö

1 Nicholas leaves for Mogilev, his headquarters, 22 Feb.

2 Strikes in Petrograd, 23-26 February

3 Troop mutinies in Petrograd, 27 February

4 Secret police headquarters in Moscow burnt, 27 Feb.

5 Some troops move on Petrograd, 1 March

6 Nicholas unable to reach Petrograd, 1 March

7 Nicholas abdicates, 2 March

8 A provisional Government "rules" side by side with
a Council (Soviet) of Workers and Soldiers Deputies.
In the latter the Bolsheviks are in a minority, 3 March

9 Nicholas put under arrest, 8 March

10 All-Russian Conference of Soviets rejects Bolshevik
motion to end the war by 325 votes to 57, 29 March

11 Lenin returns to Petrograd from exile, 3 April.
"The robbers' imperialist war is the beginning of civil
war in all Europe" he tells the crowd. "Long live the
worldwide socialist revolution"

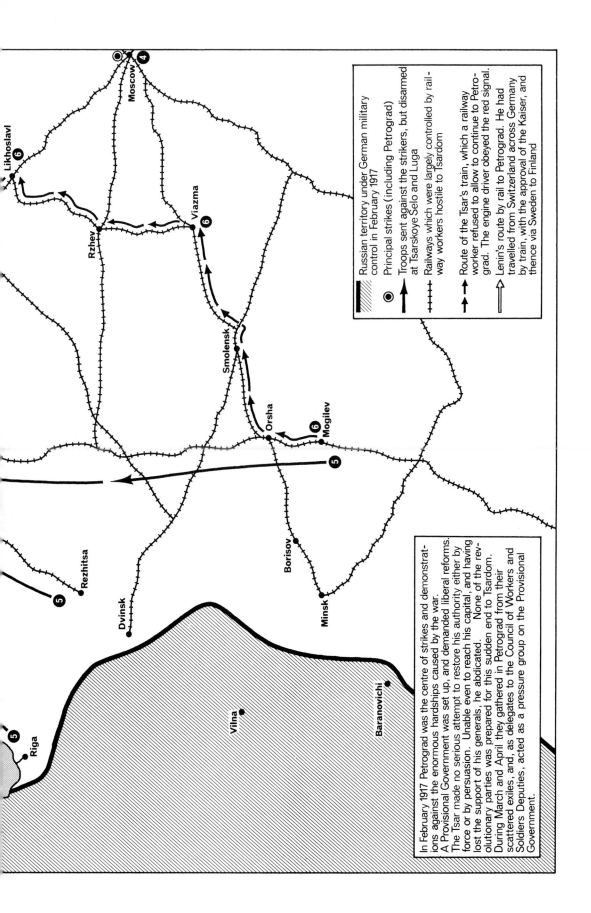

LENIN'S RETURN TO RUSSIA 1917

Our tactics: absolute distrust; no support of new Government; Kerensky particularly suspect; to arm proletariat only guarantee; no rapprochement with other parties. This last is conditio sine qua non

LENIN TO BOLSHEVIKS IN SWEDEN TELEGRAM FROM BERN 26 MARCH 1917

0   250

Miles

North Cape

Murmansk

SWEDEN

Vyborg

Hangö

Petrograd

Stockholm

Baltic Sea

Scapa Flow

North Sea

BRITAIN

Liverpool

Trelleborg

London

English Channel

Berlin

GERMANY

Paris

Cracow

FRANCE

Berne

SWITZ

Innsbruck

Vienna

AUSTRIA-HUNGARY

RUSSIA

Odessa

ITALY

Black Sea

BULGARIA

Aegean Sea

TURKEY

On 7 August 1914 Lenin was arrested in Cracow by the Austrians as an enemy alien and spy. He was released on 23 Aug., the Austrian Government having been persuaded that he was even more an enemy of Tsardom, and could "render great services" to Austria by fomenting anti-Tsarist troubles

◼ The Central Powers and their conquests in February 1917

◀–·– Lenin's route from Austria to Switzerland, 1914

····▶ Lenin's first proposed route back to Russia, which proved impossible for fear of arrest by the British

▶ Lenin's actual route 9-16 April 1917

▨ Sea routes to Russia closed by Central Power minefields

When revolution broke out in Petrograd in February 1917, Lenin, the Bolshevik leader, was in Switzerland. Wartime was not conducive to travel, nor did his plan to go through Britain prove possible. Instead, the German Government, eager to see dissension and chaos in Russia, agreed with alacrity to his request to travel across "enemy" territory, and provided him with facilities. Thus Imperial Germany served as a hand-maiden to the Russian revolution of October 1917

THE LOCATION OF THE BOLSHEVIK LEADERS DURING THE FIRST REVOLUTION OF 1917

The only Bolshevik leaders, none of them very senior, who happened to be in. Petrograd at the time of the February Revolution:
MOLOTOV, STEKLOV, SHLYAPNIKOV, LATSIS, and ZALUTSKI

Pacific Ocean

ALASKA

Bering Strait

Arctic Ocean

North Pole

CANADA

U.S.A.

New York

Halifax

GREENLAND

SIBERIA

ORDZHONIKIDZE
Pokrovsk

Lena

Chita

STALIN
Kureika

Turukhansk
SVERDLOV

Irkutsk

Yenisei

Achinsk
KAMENEV

Ob

Narym
RYKOV

CHINA

New York
BUKHARIN
TROTSKY Ⓜ
VOLODARSKY Ⓜ

Stockholm
KOLLONTAI
URITSKY Ⓜ

Atlantic Ocean

SWEDEN

TRANS-SIBERIAN RAILWAY

Urals

Stockholm

Petrograd

London
LITVINOV
CHICHERIN Ⓜ

Moscow
DZERZHINSKY

London

Paris
ANTONOV-OVSEENKO

Paris
FRANCE

TER-PETROSIAN
• Kharkov

Jassy
RAKOVSKY

Vladikavkaz
KIROV

SWITZERLAND
LENIN
LUNACHARSKY Ⓜ
RADEK
ZINOVIEV

SWITZERLAND

Black Sea

PERSIA

Mediterranean Sea

░░░ Territory controlled by Germany and her allies in March 1917

◉ Centre of the First Russian Revolution, and scene of all subsequent struggles for power during 1917

▬ The location of the Bolshevik leaders at the time of the March Revolution. The majority were in exile or out of Russia. They all made haste to return to Petrograd.
Ⓜ = Mensheviks and others who became Bolsheviks on their return to Petrograd

Most of the Social Democratic leaders of both the Bolshevik and Menshevik factions were abroad or in exile when revolution broke out in Russia in 1917. Those who were in Siberia reached Petrograd early in March, following the spontaneous amnesty of all political prisoners. Also returning in March were those living in Sweden. Next to return, in April, were the "specials" from Switzerland, led by Lenin. Finally, in May, came the "regulars" who had been in Switzerland, or elsewhere abroad.

THE WAR AND REVOLUTION JULY AND AUGUST 1917

In March 1917 the Provisional Government assured Britain and France that it would continue the war against the Central Powers. But the offensive launched on 1 July ended two weeks later in mutiny and failure. Mass demonstrations in Petrograd on 16 and 17 July, though leaderless, showed how hated the war had become, and the Bolsheviks soon dominated the Soviets by their cry of "Bread and Peace". The Provisional Government then published evidence of financial dealings between the Bolsheviks and German agents, forced Lenin to go into hiding in Finland, and arrested Trotsky. In August General Kornilov led an army against Petrograd, intending to crush the Soviets and stiffen the Provisional Government against concessions. The Bolsheviks took a leading part in the defence of the city, and greatly increased their military power, having been armed by the Provisional Government. They also gained support among the masses, who feared the return of autocracy

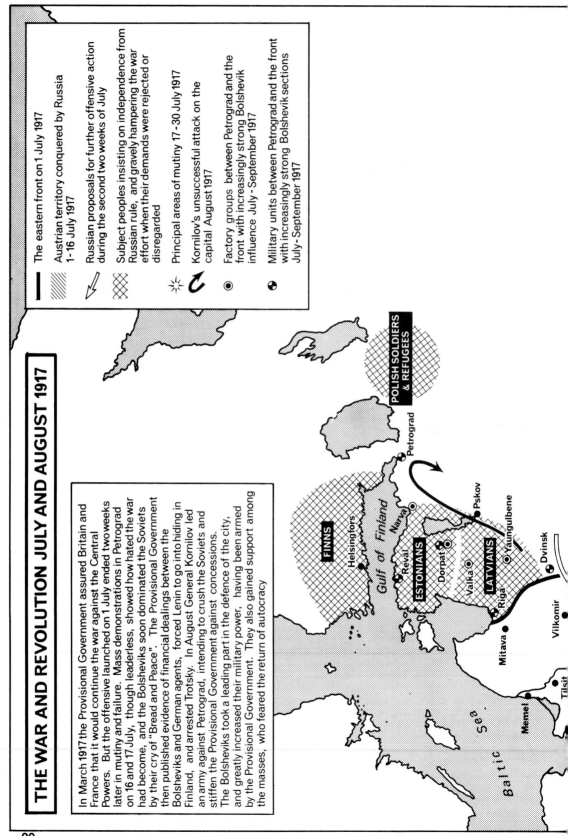

The eastern front on 1 July 1917

Austrian territory conquered by Russia 1- 16 July 1917

Russian proposals for further offensive action during the second two weeks of July

Subject peoples insisting on independence from Russian rule, and gravely hampering the war effort when their demands were rejected or disregarded

Principal areas of mutiny 17 - 30 July 1917

Kornilov's unsuccessful attack on the capital August 1917

Factory groups between Petrograd and the front with increasingly strong Bolshevik influence July - September 1917

Military units between Petrograd and the front with increasingly strong Bolshevik sections July - September 1917

POLISH SOLDIERS & REFUGEES

FINNS

Helsingfors

Gulf of Finland

Petrograd

Narva

Reval

ESTONIANS

Dorpat

Pskov

Valka

Vaungulbene

LATVIANS

Riga

Dvinsk

Mitava

Vilkomir

Baltic Sea

Memel

Tilsit

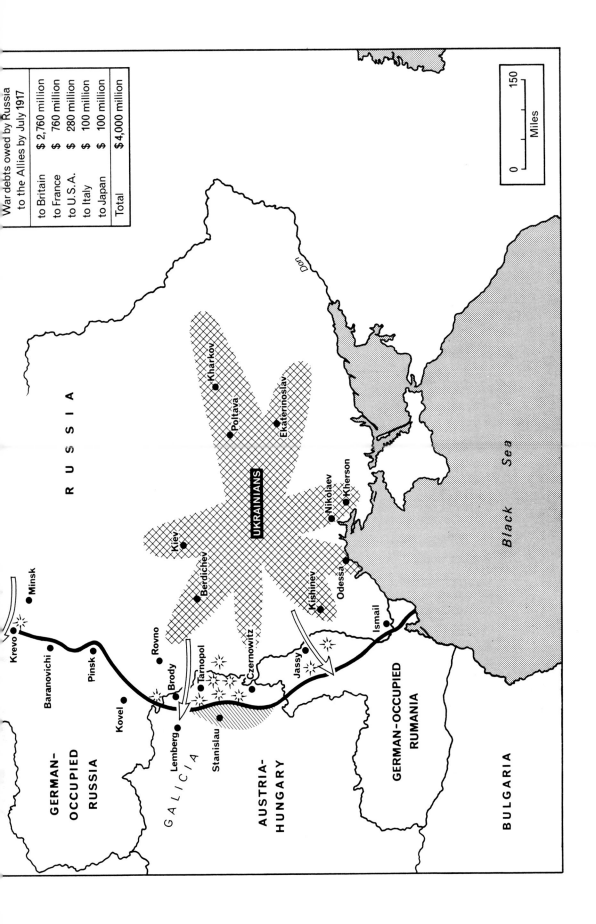

War debts owed by Russia
to the Allies by July 1917

to Britain	$	2,760 million
to France	$	760 million
to U.S.A.	$	280 million
to Italy	$	100 million
to Japan	$	100 million
Total	$	4,000 million

0   150
Miles

RUSSIA

GERMAN-
OCCUPIED
RUSSIA

Minsk

Krevo

Baranovichi

Pinsk

Kovel

Rovno

Brody

Lemberg

Stanislau

Tarnopol

Czernowitz

GALICIA

AUSTRIA-
HUNGARY

Jassy

Kishinev

Ismail

GERMAN-OCCUPIED
RUMANIA

BULGARIA

Kiev

Berdichev

UKRAINIANS

Poltava

Kharkov

Ekaterinoslav

Nikolaev

Kherson

Odessa

Don

Black Sea

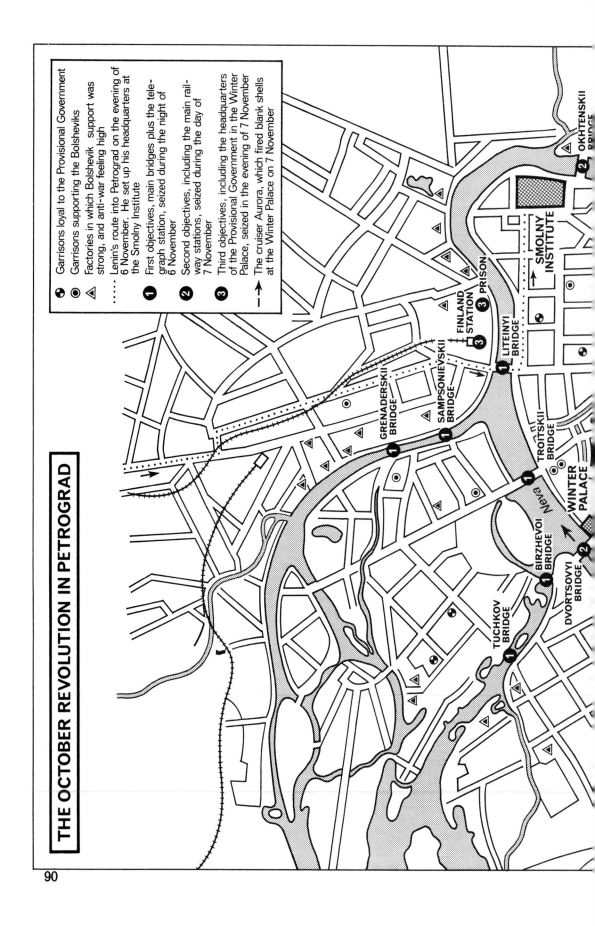

THE OCTOBER REVOLUTION IN PETROGRAD

⊕ Garrisons loyal to the Provisional Government

⊙ Garrisons supporting the Bolsheviks

◁ Factories in which Bolshevik support was strong, and anti-war feeling high

⋯ Lenin's route into Petrograd on the evening of 6 November. He set up his headquarters at the Smolny Institute

➊ First objectives, main bridges plus the telegraph station, seized during the night of 6 November

➋ Second objectives, including the main railway stations, seized during the day of 7 November

➌ Third objectives, including the headquarters of the Provisional Government in the Winter Palace, seized in the evening of 7 November

→ The cruiser Aurora, which fired blank shells at the Winter Palace on 7 November

SMOLNY INSTITUTE

OKHTENSKII BRIDGE ➋

PRISON

FINLAND STATION ➌

LITEINYI BRIDGE ➊

GRENADERSKII BRIDGE

SAMPSONIEVSKII BRIDGE ➊

➊

TROITSKII BRIDGE

WINTER PALACE ➌

Neva

BIRZHEVOI BRIDGE ➊

DVORTSOVYI BRIDGE ➋

TUCHKOV BRIDGE ➊

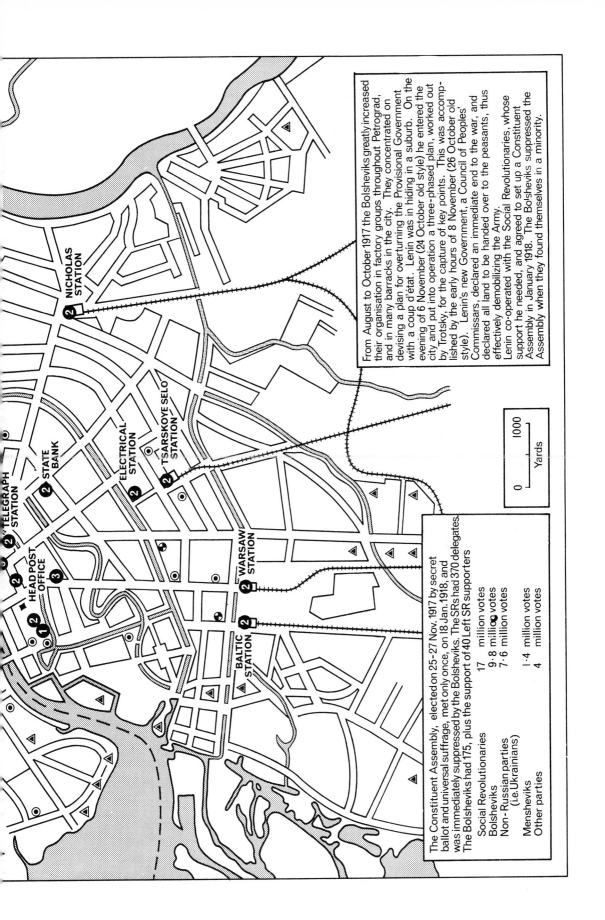

NICHOLAS STATION

TELEGRAPH STATION

STATE BANK

HEAD POST OFFICE

ELECTRICAL STATION

TSARSKOYE SELO STATION

WARSAW STATION

BALTIC STATION

0   1000
Yards

From August to October 1917 the Bolsheviks greatly increased their organisation in factory groups throughout Petrograd, and in many barracks in the city. They concentrated on devising a plan for overturning the Provisional Government with a coup d'état. Lenin was in hiding in a suburb. On the evening of 6 November (24 October old style) he entered the city and put into operation a three-phased plan, worked out by Trotsky, for the capture of key points. This was accomplished by the early hours of 8 November (26 October old style). Lenin's new Government, a Council of Peoples' Commissars, declared an immediate end to the war, and declared all land to be handed over to the peasants, thus effectively demobilizing the Army.
Lenin co-operated with the Social Revolutionaries, whose support he needed, and agreed to set up a Constituent Assembly in January 1918. The Bolsheviks suppressed the Assembly when they found themselves in a minority.

The Constituent Assembly, elected on 25-27 Nov. 1917 by secret ballot and universal suffrage, met only once, on 18 Jan. 1918, and was immediately suppressed by the Bolsheviks. The SRs had 370 delegates. The Bolsheviks had 175, plus the support of 40 Left SR supporters

Social Revolutionaries	17	million votes
Bolsheviks	9·8	million votes
Non-Russian parties (i.e. Ukrainians)	7·6	million votes
Mensheviks	1·4	million votes
Other parties	4	million votes

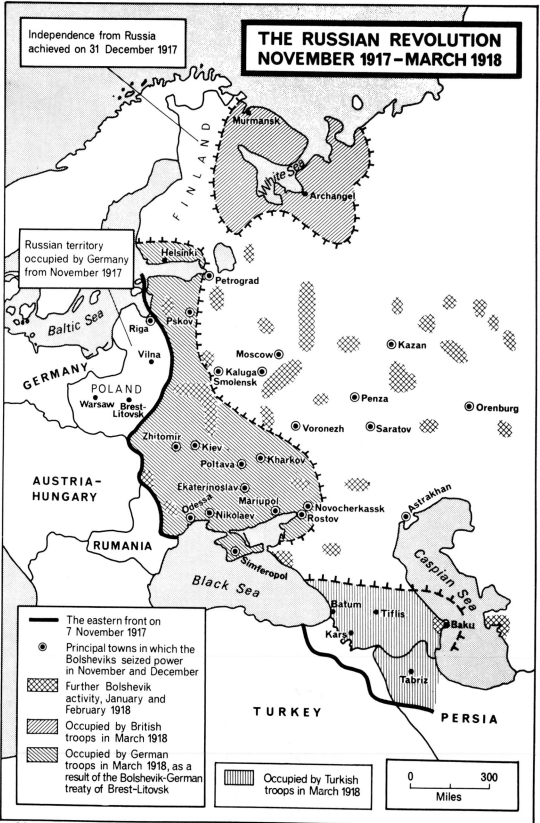

THE RUSSIAN REVOLUTION NOVEMBER 1917–MARCH 1918

Independence from Russia achieved on 31 December 1917

Russian territory occupied by Germany from November 1917

FINLAND

Murmansk

White Sea

Archangel

Helsinki

Petrograd

Baltic Sea

Riga

Pskov

GERMANY

Vilna

Moscow

Kazan

Kaluga

Smolensk

POLAND

Penza

Orenburg

Warsaw   Brest-Litovsk

Voronezh   Saratov

Zhitomir

Kiev

Poltava   Kharkov

AUSTRIA-HUNGARY

Ekaterinoslav

Astrakhan

Odessa   Mariupol

Novocherkassk

Nikolaev   Rostov

RUMANIA

Simferopol

Caspian Sea

Black Sea

Batum   Tiflis

Baku

Kars

The eastern front on 7 November 1917

Principal towns in which the Bolsheviks seized power in November and December

Further Bolshevik activity, January and February 1918

Occupied by British troops in March 1918

Occupied by German troops in March 1918, as a result of the Bolshevik-German treaty of Brest-Litovsk

Tabriz

TURKEY   PERSIA

Occupied by Turkish troops in March 1918

0   300
Miles

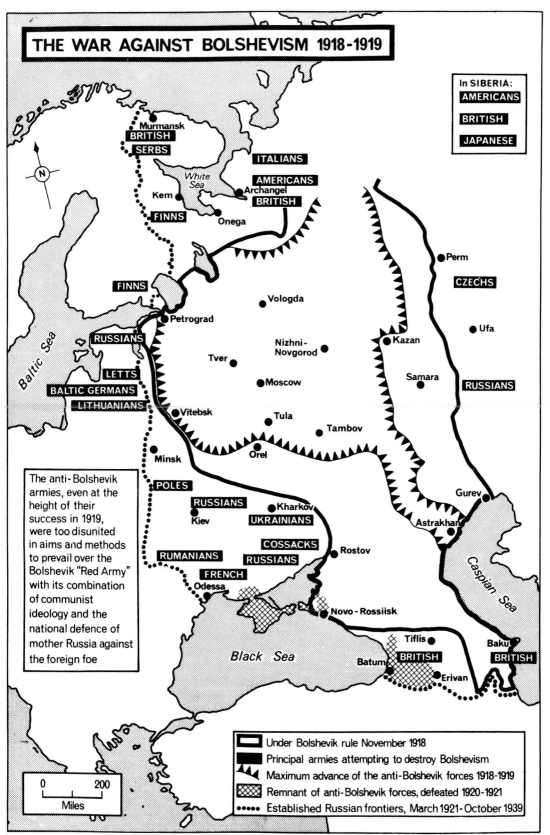

THE WAR AGAINST BOLSHEVISM 1918-1919

In SIBERIA:
AMERICANS
BRITISH
JAPANESE

Murmansk
BRITISH
SERBS

ITALIANS
AMERICANS

White Sea

Kem
Archangel
BRITISH

Onega

FINNS

Perm

CZECHS

FINNS

Vologda

Ufa

Petrograd

Nizhni-Novgorod

Kazan

Baltic Sea

RUSSIANS

Tver

Samara

LETTS

Moscow

RUSSIANS

BALTIC GERMANS
LITHUANIANS

Vitebsk

Tula

Minsk

Orel

Tambov

POLES

Gurev

RUSSIANS

Kharkov

Astrakhan

Kiev

UKRAINIANS

COSSACKS

Rostov

RUMANIANS
RUSSIANS

FRENCH

Caspian Sea

Odessa

Novo-Rossiisk

The anti-Bolshevik
armies, even at the
height of their
success in 1919,
were too disunited
in aims and methods
to prevail over the
Bolshevik "Red Army"
with its combination
of communist
ideology and the
national defence of
mother Russia against
the foreign foe

Tiflis

Baku

Batum
BRITISH
BRITISH

Erivan

Black Sea

	Under Bolshevik rule November 1918
	Principal armies attempting to destroy Bolshevism
	Maximum advance of the anti-Bolshevik forces 1918-1919
	Remnant of anti-Bolshevik forces, defeated 1920-1921
	Established Russian frontiers, March 1921-October 1939

0   200
Miles

92

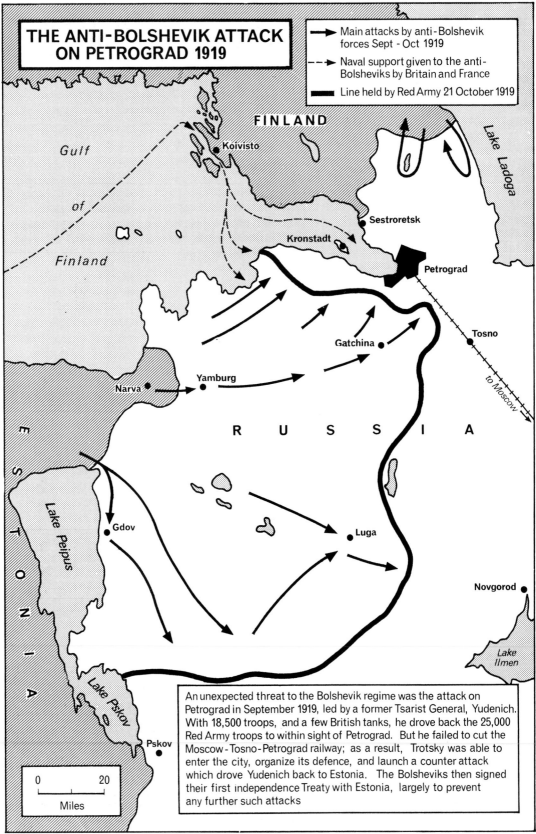

THE ANTI-BOLSHEVIK ATTACK ON PETROGRAD 1919

→ Main attacks by anti-Bolshevik forces Sept - Oct 1919

--→ Naval support given to the anti-Bolsheviks by Britain and France

▬ Line held by Red Army 21 October 1919

FINLAND

Gulf

of

Finland

Koivisto

Lake Ladoga

Sestroretsk

Kronstadt

Petrograd

Tosno

Gatchina

to Moscow

Yamburg

Narva

R U S S I A

E

S

T

Lake Peipus

O

Gdov

Luga

N

Novgorod

I

A

Lake Pskov

Lake Ilmen

Pskov

0   20

Miles

An unexpected threat to the Bolshevik regime was the attack on Petrograd in September 1919, led by a former Tsarist General, Yudenich. With 18,500 troops, and a few British tanks, he drove back the 25,000 Red Army troops to within sight of Petrograd. But he failed to cut the Moscow - Tosno - Petrograd railway; as a result, Trotsky was able to enter the city, organize its defence, and launch a counter attack which drove Yudenich back to Estonia. The Bolsheviks then signed their first independence Treaty with Estonia, largely to prevent any further such attacks

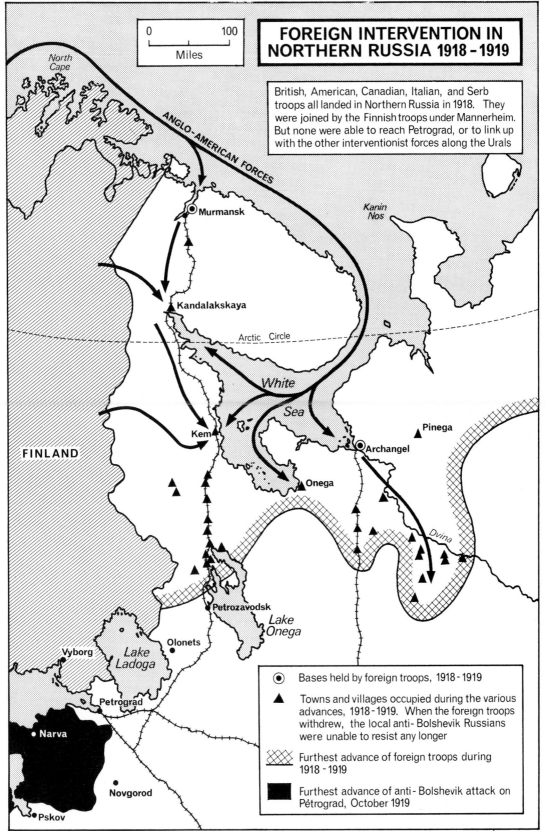

FOREIGN INTERVENTION IN NORTHERN RUSSIA 1918-1919

British, American, Canadian, Italian, and Serb troops all landed in Northern Russia in 1918. They were joined by the Finnish troops under Mannerheim. But none were able to reach Petrograd, or to link up with the other interventionist forces along the Urals

0   100
Miles

North Cape

ANGLO-AMERICAN FORCES

Murmansk

Kanin Nos

Kandalakskaya

Arctic Circle

White

Sea

Pinega

Kem

Archangel

FINLAND

Onega

Dvina

Petrozavodsk

Lake Onega

Olonets

Vyborg

Lake Ladoga

Petrograd

Narva

Novgorod

Pskov

⊙ Bases held by foreign troops, 1918-1919

▲ Towns and villages occupied during the various advances, 1918-1919. When the foreign troops withdrew, the local anti-Bolshevik Russians were unable to resist any longer

▨ Furthest advance of foreign troops during 1918-1919

■ Furthest advance of anti-Bolshevik attack on Pétrograd, October 1919

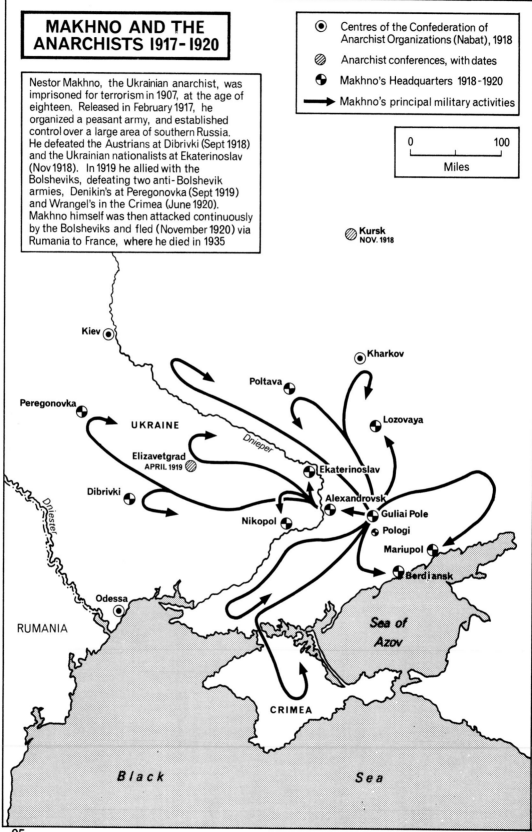

MAKHNO AND THE ANARCHISTS 1917-1920

Nestor Makhno, the Ukrainian anarchist, was imprisoned for terrorism in 1907, at the age of eighteen. Released in February 1917, he organized a peasant army, and established control over a large area of southern Russia. He defeated the Austrians at Dibrivki (Sept 1918) and the Ukrainian nationalists at Ekaterinoslav (Nov 1918). In 1919 he allied with the Bolsheviks, defeating two anti-Bolshevik armies, Denikin's at Peregonovka (Sept 1919) and Wrangel's in the Crimea (June 1920). Makhno himself was then attacked continuously by the Bolsheviks and fled (November 1920) via Rumania to France, where he died in 1935

Centres of the Confederation of Anarchist Organizations (Nabat), 1918

Anarchist conferences, with dates

Makhno's Headquarters 1918-1920

Makhno's principal military activities

0   100
Miles

Kursk
NOV. 1918

Kiev

Kharkov

Poltava

Peregonovka

UKRAINE

Lozovaya

Dnieper

Elizavetgrad
APRIL 1919

Dibrivki

Ekaterinoslav

Alexandrovsk

Nikopol

Guliai Pole

Pologi

Mariupol

Berdiansk

Dniester

Odessa

RUMANIA

Sea of
Azov

Black   Sea

CRIMEA

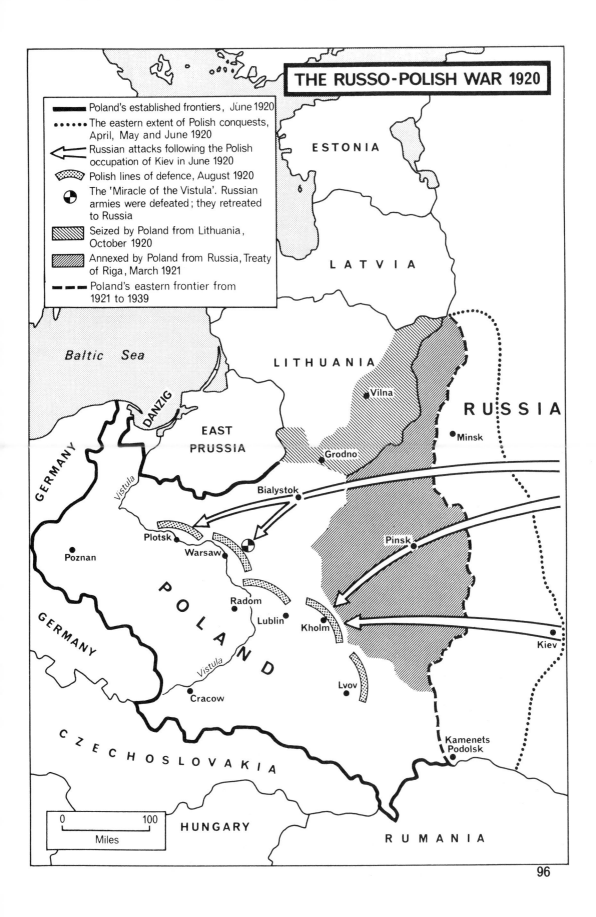

THE RUSSO-POLISH WAR 1920

Poland's established frontiers, June 1920

•••••• The eastern extent of Polish conquests, April, May and June 1920

⟵ Russian attacks following the Polish occupation of Kiev in June 1920

Polish lines of defence, August 1920

The 'Miracle of the Vistula'. Russian armies were defeated; they retreated to Russia

Seized by Poland from Lithuania, October 1920

Annexed by Poland from Russia, Treaty of Riga, March 1921

Poland's eastern frontier from 1921 to 1939

ESTONIA

LATVIA

Baltic Sea

LITHUANIA

Vilna

RUSSIA

Minsk

DANZIG

EAST PRUSSIA

Grodno

Vistula

Bialystok

Plotsk

Poznan

Warsaw

POLAND

Radom

Lublin

Pinsk

Kholm

Kiev

Vistula

Lvov

Cracow

GERMANY

GERMANY

C Z E C H O S L O V A K I A

Kamenets Podolsk

HUNGARY

RUMANIA

0   100
Miles

96

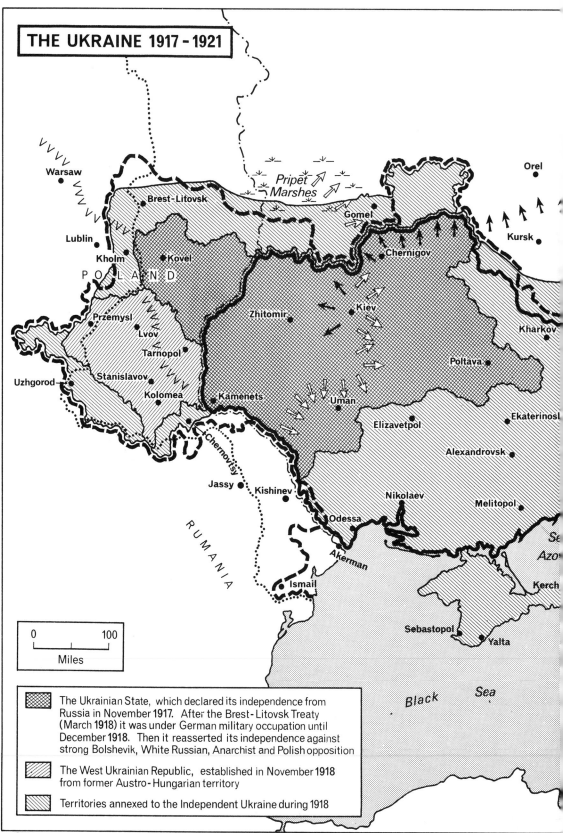

THE UKRAINE 1917 - 1921

Warsaw

Orel

Brest-Litovsk

Pripet Marshes

Gomel

Kursk

Lublin

Kholm

Kovel

Chernigov

P O L A N D

Przemysl

Zhitomir

Kiev

Kharkov

Lvov

Tarnopol

Poltava

Uzhgorod

Stanislavov

Kamenets

Kolomea

Uman

Ekaterinosl

Chernovtsi

Elizavetpol

Alexandrovsk

Jassy

Kishinev

Nikolaev

Melitopol

R U M A N I A

Odessa

Akerman

Ismail

Se Azo

Kerch

Sebastopol

Yalta

Black   Sea

0   100
Miles

The Ukrainian State, which declared its independence from
Russia in November 1917. After the Brest-Litovsk Treaty
(March 1918) it was under German military occupation until
December 1918. Then it reasserted its independence against
strong Bolshevik, White Russian, Anarchist and Polish opposition

The West Ukrainian Republic, established in November 1918
from former Austro-Hungarian territory

Territories annexed to the Independent Ukraine during 1918

Territory claimed by the Ukrainian nationalists as part of the "ethnographic" Ukraine

Boundary of the Ukrainian Soviet Socialist Republic **1921**

Western boundary of the Soviet Union **1921-1939**

Western boundary of the Soviet Union since **1945**

Furthest northern advance of Denikin's anti-Bolshevik armies, November **1919.** Denikin's Great Russian policies failed to gain him much Ukrainian support

Furthest eastern advance of the Polish Army in June **1920**

Furthest western advance of the Red Army by August **1920**

Voronezh

Buturlinovka

Lugansk

Taganrog

Rostov

Mariupol

Astrakhan

Caspian Sea

Ekaterinodar

Stavropol

Armavir

Mineralnye Vody

Mozdok

Novorossiisk

Tuapse

Sochi

Causasus

Batum

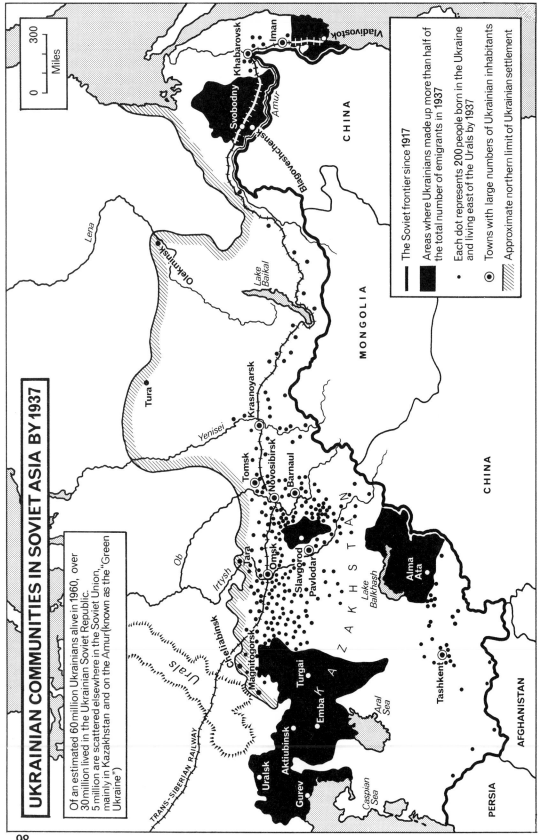

UKRAINIAN COMMUNITIES IN SOVIET ASIA BY 1937

Of an estimated 60 million Ukrainians alive in 1960, over 30 million lived in the Ukrainian Soviet Republic. 5 million are scattered elsewhere in the Soviet Union, mainly in Kazakhstan and on the Amur (known as the "Green Ukraine")

Legend:

— The Soviet frontier since 1917

▇ Areas where Ukrainians made up more than half of the total number of emigrants in 1937

• Each dot represents 200 people born in the Ukraine and living east of the Urals by 1937

◉ Towns with large numbers of Ukrainian inhabitants

▨ Approximate northern limit of Ukrainian settlement

Scale: 0 — 300 Miles

Place names: Vladivostok, Iman, Khabarovsk, Svobodny, Blagoveshchensk, Amur, Olekminsk, Lena, Lake Baikal, Tura, Yenisei, Krasnoyarsk, Tomsk, Novosibirsk, Barnaul, Ob, Irtysh, Tara, Omsk, Slavgorod, Pavlodar, Lake Balkhash, Alma Ata, KAZAKHSTAN, Cheliabinsk, Magnitogorsk, Urals, Turgai, Emba R., Aral Sea, Tashkent, Aktiubinsk, Uralsk, Gurev, Caspian Sea, TRANS-SIBERIAN RAILWAY, CHINA, MONGOLIA, PERSIA, AFGHANISTAN

98

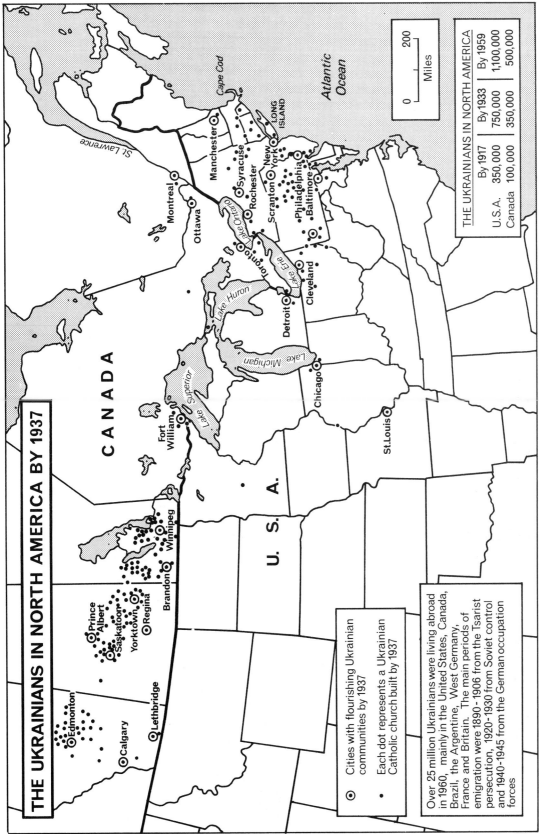

THE UKRAINIANS IN NORTH AMERICA BY 1937

CANADA

U. S. A.

Edmonton

Calgary

Lethbridge

Prince
Albert

Saskatoon

Yorkton

Regina

Brandon

Winnipeg

Fort
William

St. Louis

Chicago

Detroit

Cleveland

Toronto

Ottawa

Montreal

Manchester

Syracuse

Rochester

Scranton

New
York

LONG
ISLAND

Philadelphia

Baltimore

St. Lawrence

Lake Ontario

Lake Erie

Lake Huron

Lake Michigan

Lake Superior

Cape Cod

*Atlantic
Ocean*

THE UKRAINIANS IN NORTH AMERICA			
	By 1917	By 1933	By 1959
U.S.A.	350,000	750,000	1,100,000
Canada	100,000	350,000	500,000

0 ————— 200
Miles

◉ Cities with flourishing Ukrainian
communities by 1937

• Each dot represents a Ukrainian
Catholic church built by 1937

Over 25 million Ukrainians were living abroad
in 1960, mainly in the United States, Canada,
Brazil, the Argentine, West Germany,
France and Britain. The main periods of
emigration were 1890 - 1906 from the Tsarist
persecution, 1920-1930 from Soviet control
and 1940-1945 from the German occupation
forces

99

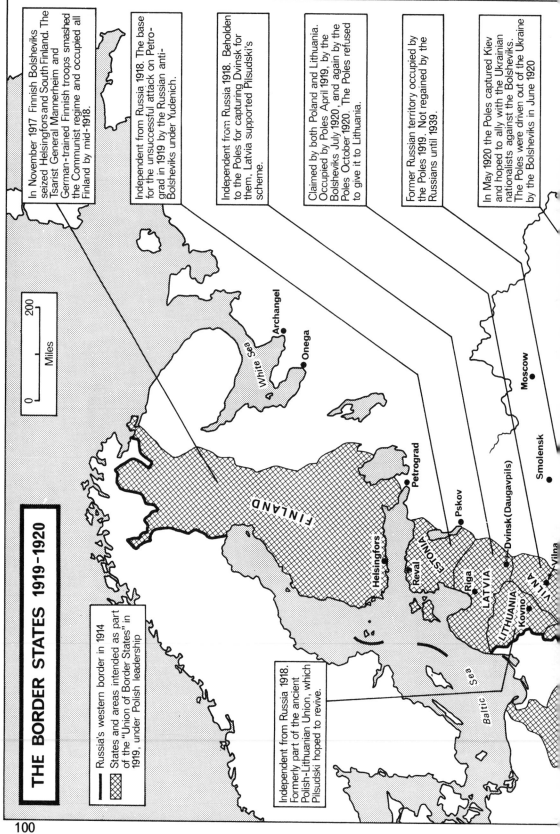

THE BORDER STATES 1919–1920

In November 1917 Finnish Bolsheviks seized Helsingfors and South Finland. The Tsarist General Mannerheim and German-trained Finnish troops smashed the Communist regime and occupied all Finland by mid-1918.

Independent from Russia 1918. The base for the unsuccessful attack on Petrograd in 1919 by the Russian anti-Bolsheviks under Yudenich.

Independent from Russia 1918. Beholden to the Poles for capturing Dvinsk for them, Latvia supported Pilsudski's scheme.

Claimed by both Poland and Lithuania. Occupied by Poles April 1919, by the Bolsheviks July 1920, and again by the Poles October 1920. The Poles refused to give it to Lithuania.

Former Russian territory occupied by the Poles 1919. Not regained by the Russians until 1939.

In May 1920 the Poles captured Kiev and hoped to ally with the Ukrainian nationalists against the Bolsheviks. The Poles were driven out of the Ukraine by the Bolsheviks in June 1920

——— Russia's western border in 1914

States and areas intended as part of the "Union of Border States" in 1919, under Polish leadership

Independent from Russia 1918. Formerly part of the ancient Polish-Lithuanian Union, which Pilsudski hoped to revive.

0   200
Miles

White Sea

Archangel

Onega

Petrograd

Pskov

Moscow

Smolensk

Helsingfors

Reval

ESTONIA

Riga

LATVIA

Dvinsk (Daugavpils)

Vilna

VILNA

LITHUANIA

Kovno

FINLAND

Baltic Sea

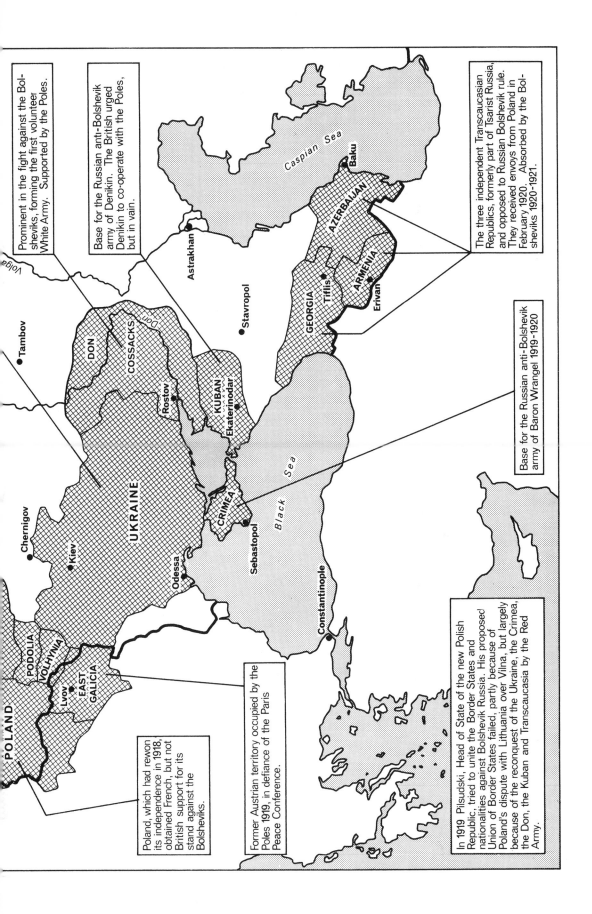

Prominent in the fight against the Bolsheviks, forming the first volunteer White Army. Supported by the Poles.

Base for the Russian anti-Bolshevik army of Denikin. The British urged Denikin to co-operate with the Poles, but in vain.

The three independent Transcaucasian Republics, formerly part of Tsarist Russia, and opposed to Russian Bolshevik rule. They received envoys from Poland in February 1920. Absorbed by the Bolsheviks 1920-1921.

Base for the Russian anti-Bolshevik army of Baron Wrangel 1919-1920

Poland, which had rewon its independence in 1918, obtained French, but not British support for its stand against the Bolsheviks.

Former Austrian territory occupied by the Poles 1919, in defiance of the Paris Peace Conference.

In 1919 Pilsudski, Head of State of the new Polish Republic, tried to unite the Border States and nationalities against Bolshevik Russia. His proposed Union of Border States failed, partly because of Poland's dispute with Lithuania over Vilna, but largely because of the reconquest of the Ukraine, the Crimea, the Don, the Kuban and Transcaucasia by the Red Army.

Volga

Caspian Sea

Baku

AZERBAIJAN

Astrakhan

ARMENIA

GEORGIA

Tiflis

Erivan

Stavropol

Tambov

DON

COSSACKS

Don

Rostov

KUBAN

Ekaterinodar

Black Sea

CRIMEA

Chernigov

Kiev

UKRAINE

Sebastopol

Odessa

Constantinople

POLAND

PODOLIA

VOLHYNIA

Lvov

EAST GALICIA

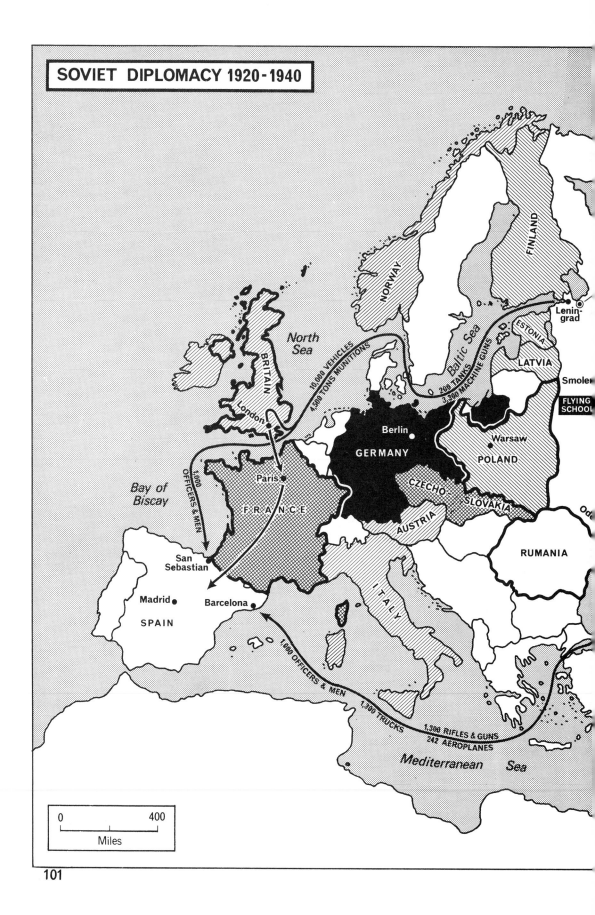

SOVIET DIPLOMACY 1920-1940

North Sea

NORWAY

FINLAND

Baltic Sea

Leningrad

ESTONIA

LATVIA

Smole

FLYING SCHOOL

BRITAIN

London

10,000 VEHICLES

4,500 TONS MUNITIONS

0. 200 TANKS

3,300 MACHINE GUNS

Berlin

GERMANY

Warsaw

POLAND

1,000 OFFICERS & MEN

Paris

FRANCE

CZECHO SLOVAKIA

Bay of Biscay

AUSTRIA

RUMANIA

San Sebastian

Od

Madrid

Barcelona

ITALY

SPAIN

1,000 OFFICERS & MEN

1,300 TRUCKS

1,300 RIFLES & GUNS
242 AEROPLANES

Mediterranean   Sea

0   400

Miles

101

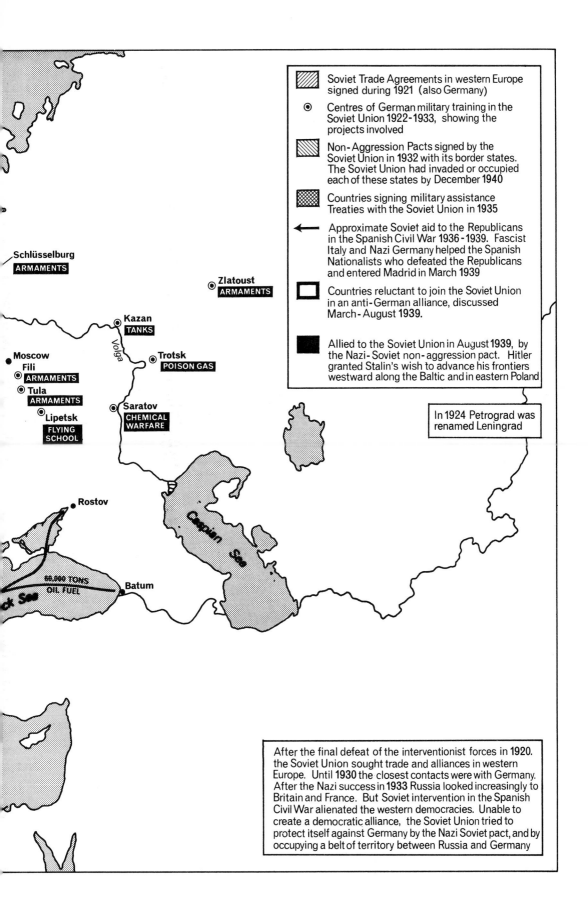

Schlüsselburg
ARMAMENTS

Zlatoust
ARMAMENTS

Kazan
TANKS

Moscow
Fili
ARMAMENTS
Tula
ARMAMENTS
Lipetsk
FLYING
SCHOOL

Volga

Trotsk
POISON GAS

Saratov
CHEMICAL
WARFARE

Rostov

60,000 TONS
OIL FUEL

Batum

Caspian Sea

Black Sea

▨ Soviet Trade Agreements in western Europe signed during 1921 (also Germany)

⊙ Centres of German military training in the Soviet Union 1922-1933, showing the projects involved

▨ Non-Aggression Pacts signed by the Soviet Union in 1932 with its border states. The Soviet Union had invaded or occupied each of these states by December 1940

▨ Countries signing military assistance Treaties with the Soviet Union in 1935

← Approximate Soviet aid to the Republicans in the Spanish Civil War 1936-1939. Fascist Italy and Nazi Germany helped the Spanish Nationalists who defeated the Republicans and entered Madrid in March 1939

☐ Countries reluctant to join the Soviet Union in an anti-German alliance, discussed March-August 1939.

■ Allied to the Soviet Union in August 1939, by the Nazi-Soviet non-aggression pact. Hitler granted Stalin's wish to advance his frontiers westward along the Baltic and in eastern Poland

In 1924 Petrograd was renamed Leningrad

After the final defeat of the interventionist forces in 1920. the Soviet Union sought trade and alliances in western Europe. Until 1930 the closest contacts were with Germany. After the Nazi success in 1933 Russia looked increasingly to Britain and France. But Soviet intervention in the Spanish Civil War alienated the western democracies. Unable to create a democratic alliance, the Soviet Union tried to protect itself against Germany by the Nazi Soviet pact, and by occupying a belt of territory between Russia and Germany

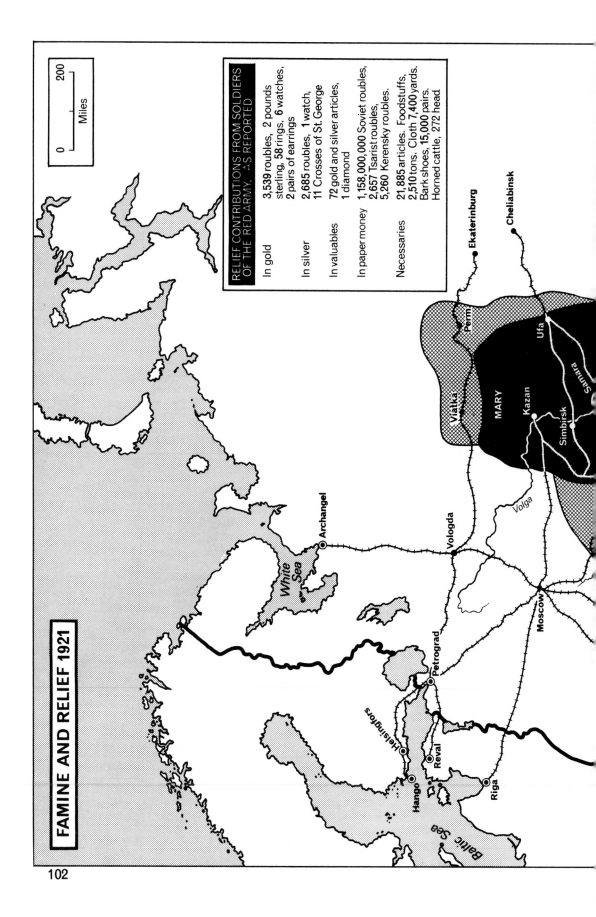

FAMINE AND RELIEF 1921

RELIEF CONTRIBUTIONS FROM SOLDIERS OF THE RED ARMY, AS REPORTED

In gold   3,539 roubles, 2 pounds sterling, 58 rings, 6 watches, 2 pairs of earrings

In silver   2,685 roubles, 1 watch, 11 Crosses of St. George

In valuables   72 gold and silver articles, 1 diamond

In paper money 1,158,000,000 Soviet roubles, 2,657 Tsarist roubles, 5,260 Kerensky roubles.

Necessaries   21,885 articles. Foodstuffs, 2,510 tons. Cloth 7,400 yards. Bark shoes, 15,000 pairs. Horned cattle, 272 head

Miles

0   200

Cheliabinsk

Ekaterinburg

Perm

Viatka

Ufa

MARY

Samara

Kazan

Simbirsk

Volga

Vologda

White Sea

Archangel

Moscow

Petrograd

Helsingfors

Reval

Hango

Riga

Baltic Sea

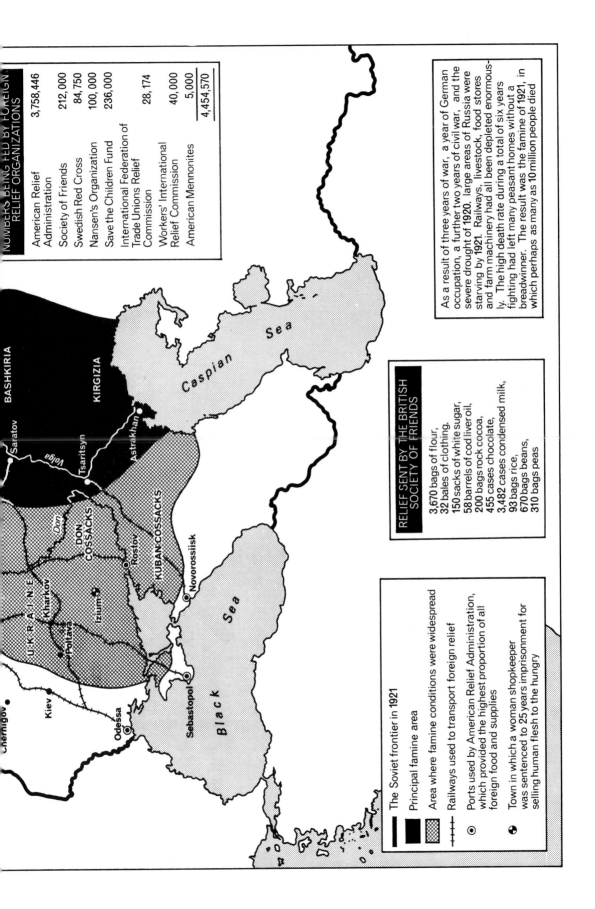

NUMBERS BEING FED BY FOREIGN
RELIEF ORGANIZATIONS

American Relief Administration	3,758,446
Society of Friends	212,000
Swedish Red Cross	84,750
Nansen's Organization	100,000
Save the Children Fund	236,000
International Federation of Trade Unions Relief Commission	28,174
Workers' International Relief Commission	40,000
American Mennonites	5,000
	4,454,570

As a result of three years of war, a year of German occupation, a further two years of civil war, and the severe drought of 1920, large areas of Russia were starving by 1921. Railways, livestock, food stores and farm machinery had all been depleted enormously. The high death rate during a total of six years fighting had left many peasant homes without a breadwinner. The result was the famine of 1921, in which perhaps as many as 10 million people died

BASHKIRIA

KIRGIZIA

Saratov

Caspian Sea

Tsaritsyn

Astrakhan

Volga

Kharkov

Poltava

Izium

Rostov

DON COSSACKS

Don

KUBAN COSSACKS

U·K·R·A·I·N·E

Novorossiisk

Black Sea

Sebastopol

Odessa

Kiev

Chernigov

RELIEF SENT BY THE BRITISH
SOCIETY OF FRIENDS

3,670 bags of flour,
32 bales of clothing,
150 sacks of white sugar,
58 barrels of cod liver oil,
200 bags rock cocoa,
455 cases chocolate,
3,482 cases condensed milk,
93 bags rice,
670 bags beans,
310 bags peas

The Soviet frontier in 1921

Principal famine area

Area where famine conditions were widespread

Railways used to transport foreign relief

Ports used by American Relief Administration, which provided the highest proportion of all foreign food and supplies

Town in which a woman shopkeeper was sentenced to 25 years imprisonment for selling human flesh to the hungry

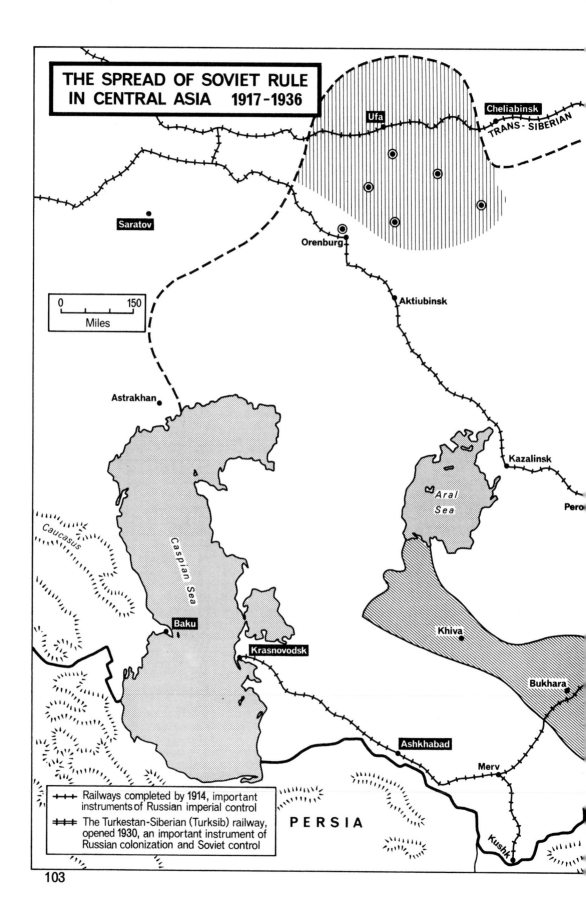

THE SPREAD OF SOVIET RULE
IN CENTRAL ASIA   1917-1936

Cheliabinsk

Ufa

TRANS - SIBERIAN

Saratov

Orenburg

Aktiubinsk

0   150
Miles

Astrakhan

Kazalinsk

Aral
Sea

Caucasus

Pero

Caspian Sea

Khiva

Baku

Krasnovodsk

Bukhara

Ashkhabad

Merv

Kushk

Railways completed by **1914**, important instruments of Russian imperial control

The Turkestan-Siberian (Turksib) railway, opened **1930**, an important instrument of Russian colonization and Soviet control

P E R S I A

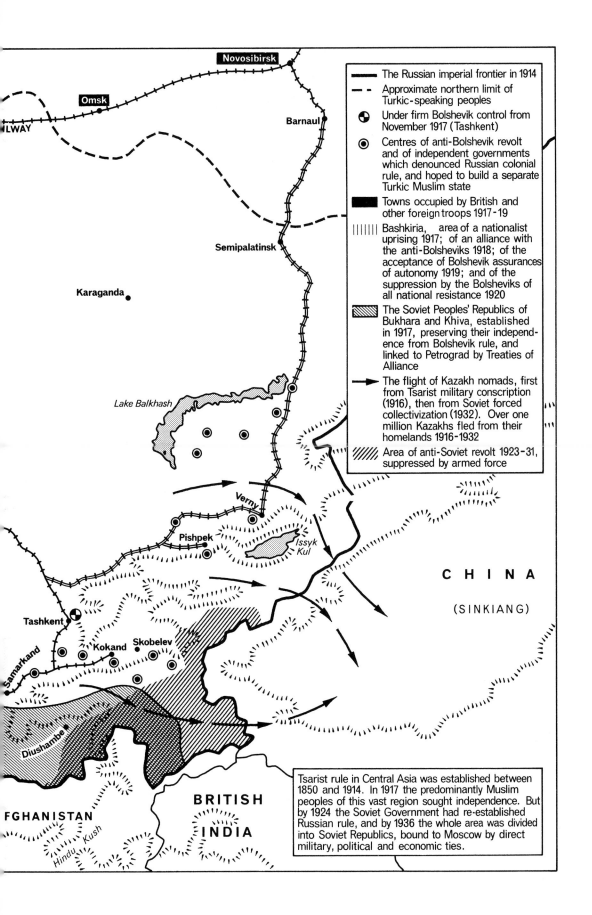

Novosibirsk

Omsk

ILWAY

Barnaul

The Russian imperial frontier in 1914

Approximate northern limit of Turkic-speaking peoples

Under firm Bolshevik control from November 1917 (Tashkent)

Centres of anti-Bolshevik revolt and of independent governments which denounced Russian colonial rule, and hoped to build a separate Turkic Muslim state

Towns occupied by British and other foreign troops 1917-19

Bashkiria, area of a nationalist uprising 1917; of an alliance with the anti-Bolsheviks 1918; of the acceptance of Bolshevik assurances of autonomy 1919; and of the suppression by the Bolsheviks of all national resistance 1920

The Soviet Peoples' Republics of Bukhara and Khiva, established in 1917, preserving their independence from Bolshevik rule, and linked to Petrograd by Treaties of Alliance

The flight of Kazakh nomads, first from Tsarist military conscription (1916), then from Soviet forced collectivization (1932). Over one million Kazakhs fled from their homelands 1916-1932

Area of anti-Soviet revolt 1923-31, suppressed by armed force

Semipalatinsk

Karaganda

Lake Balkhash

Verny

Pishpek

Issyk Kul

C H I N A

(SINKIANG)

Tashkent

Samarkand

Kokand

Skobelev

Diushambe

B R I T I S H

FGHANISTAN

INDIA

Hindu Kush

Tsarist rule in Central Asia was established between 1850 and 1914. In 1917 the predominantly Muslim peoples of this vast region sought independence. But by 1924 the Soviet Government had re-established Russian rule, and by 1936 the whole area was divided into Soviet Republics, bound to Moscow by direct military, political and economic ties.

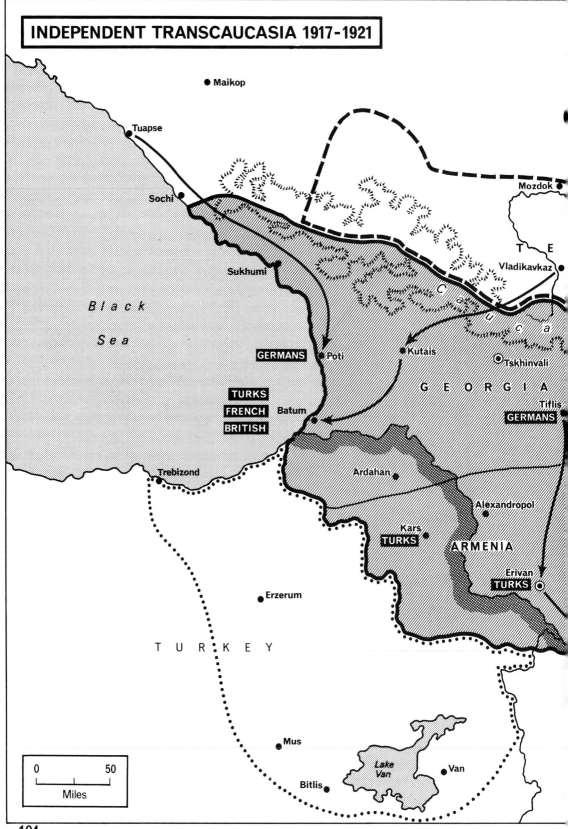

INDEPENDENT TRANSCAUCASIA 1917-1921

● Maikop

● Tuapse

● Sochi

● Sukhumi

Mozdok ●

T   E

Vladikavkaz ●

Black

Sea

GERMANS ● Poti

● Kutais

⊙ Tskhinvali

G E O R G I A

Tiflis
GERMANS

TURKS
FRENCH   Batum
BRITISH

● Trebizond

Ardahan ●

Alexandropol ●

Kars ●
TURKS

A R M E N I A

● Erzerum

Erivan
TURKS ⊙

T U R K E Y

● Mus

Lake
Van
● Van

0   50

● Bitlis

Miles

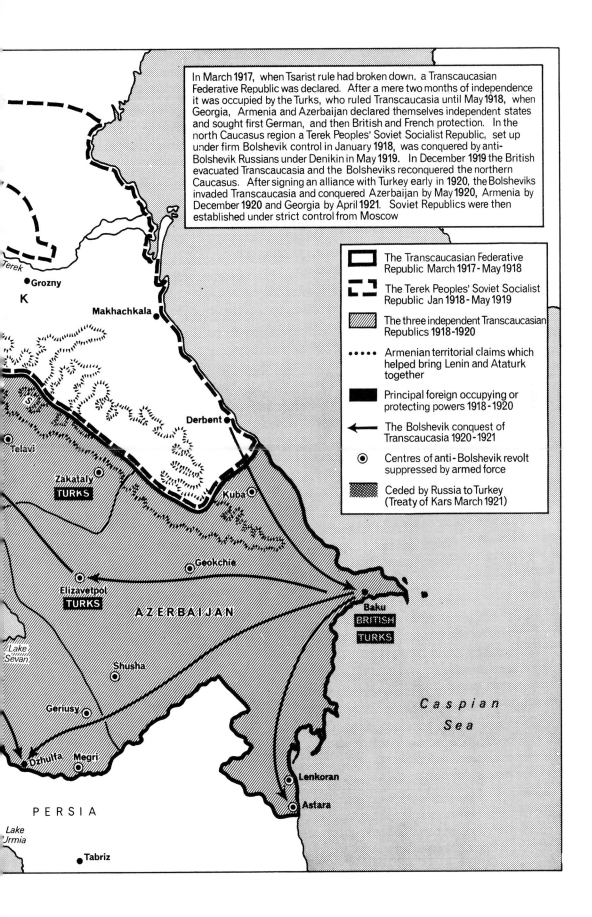

In March 1917, when Tsarist rule had broken down, a Transcaucasian Federative Republic was declared. After a mere two months of independence it was occupied by the Turks, who ruled Transcaucasia until May 1918, when Georgia, Armenia and Azerbaijan declared themselves independent states and sought first German, and then British and French protection. In the north Caucasus region a Terek Peoples' Soviet Socialist Republic, set up under firm Bolshevik control in January 1918, was conquered by anti-Bolshevik Russians under Denikin in May 1919. In December 1919 the British evacuated Transcaucasia and the Bolsheviks reconquered the northern Caucasus. After signing an alliance with Turkey early in 1920, the Bolsheviks invaded Transcaucasia and conquered Azerbaijan by May 1920, Armenia by December 1920 and Georgia by April 1921. Soviet Republics were then established under strict control from Moscow

The Transcaucasian Federative Republic March 1917 - May 1918

The Terek Peoples' Soviet Socialist Republic Jan 1918 - May 1919

The three independent Transcaucasian Republics 1918-1920

Armenian territorial claims which helped bring Lenin and Ataturk together

Principal foreign occupying or protecting powers 1918-1920

The Bolshevik conquest of Transcaucasia 1920-1921

Centres of anti-Bolshevik revolt suppressed by armed force

Ceded by Russia to Turkey (Treaty of Kars March 1921)

Terek

Grozny

K

Makhachkala

Telavi

Zakataly
TURKS

Derbent

Kuba

Geokchie

Elizavetpol
TURKS

AZERBAIJAN

Baku
BRITISH
TURKS

Lake
Sevan

Shusha

Caspian
Sea

Geriusy

Dzhulfa   Megri

Lenkoran

PERSIA

Astara

Lake
Urmia

Tabriz

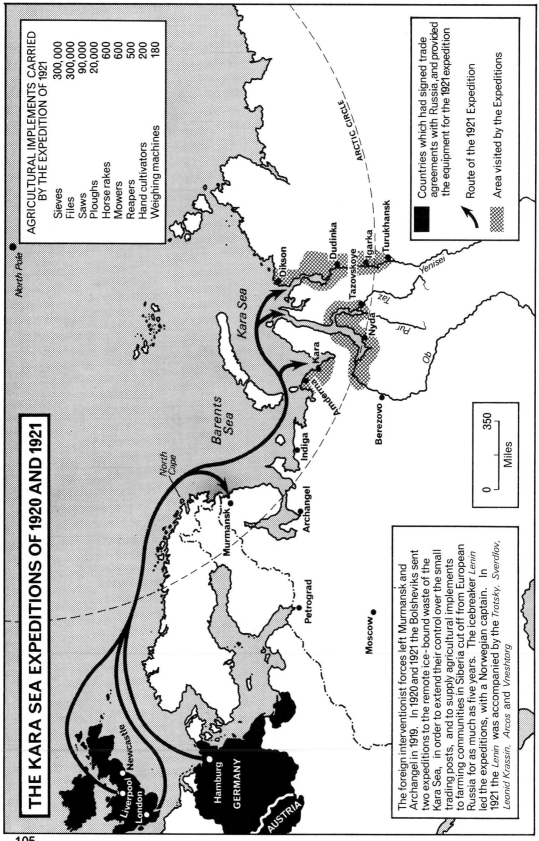

THE KARA SEA EXPEDITIONS OF 1920 AND 1921

AGRICULTURAL IMPLEMENTS CARRIED
BY THE EXPEDITION OF 1921

Sieves	300,000
Files	300,000
Saws	90,000
Ploughs	20,000
Horse rakes	600
Mowers	600
Reapers	500
Hand cultivators	200
Weighing machines	180

Countries which had signed trade agreements with Russia, and provided the equipment for the 1921 expedition

Route of the 1921 Expedition

Area visited by the Expeditions

ARCTIC CIRCLE

North Pole

Turukhansk
Igarka
Tazovskoye
Dudinka
Dikson
Nyda
Taz
Yenisei
Pur
Ob
Kara
Amderma
Berezovo
Indiga
Archangel
North Cape
Murmansk
Petrograd
Moscow

Kara Sea

Barents Sea

Liverpool
Newcastle
London
Hamburg
GERMANY
AUSTRIA

0   350
Miles

The foreign interventionist forces left Murmansk and Archangel in 1919. In 1920 and 1921 the Bolsheviks sent two expeditions to the remote ice-bound waste of the Kara Sea, in order to extend their control over the small trading posts, and to supply agricultural implements to farming communities in Siberia cut off from European Russia for as much as five years. The icebreaker *Lenin* led the expeditions, with a Norwegian captain. In 1921 the *Lenin* was accompanied by the *Trotsky, Sverdlov, Leonid Krassin, Arcos* and *Vneshtorg*.

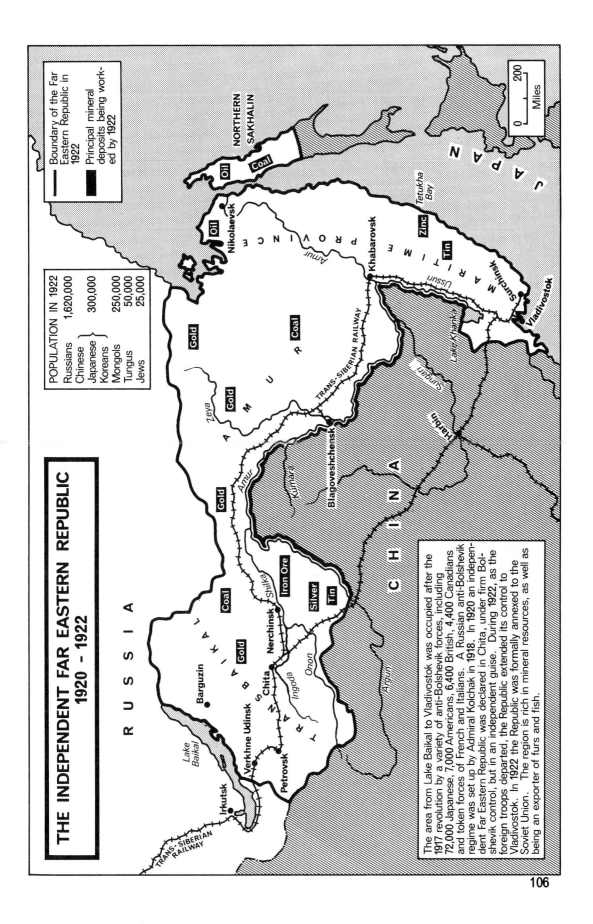

THE INDEPENDENT FAR EASTERN REPUBLIC 1920 - 1922

Boundary of the Far
Eastern Republic in
1922

Principal mineral
deposits being work-
ed by 1922

POPULATION IN 1922

Russians	1,620,000
Chinese	300,000
Japanese	250,000
Koreans	
Mongols	50,000
Tungus	25,000
Jews	

0   200
Miles

RUSSIA

JAPAN

CHINA

NORTHERN SAKHALIN

MARITIME PROVINCE

AMUR PROVINCE

Lake Baikal

Irkutsk

Verkhne Udinsk

Barguzin

Petrovsk

Chita

Nerchinsk

Blagoveshchensk

Khabarovsk

Vladivostok

Surchinsk

Nikolaevsk

Harbin

Lake Khanka

Tetukha Bay

Zeya

Amur

Kumara

Shilka

Ingoda

Onon

Argun

Ussuri

Sungari

TRANS-SIBERIAN RAILWAY

Oil

Coal

Oil

Zinc

Tin

Coal

Gold

Gold

Gold

Iron Ore

Silver

Tin

Coal

Gold

The area from Lake Baikal to Vladivostok was occupied after the
1917 revolution by a variety of anti-Bolshevik forces, including
72,000 Japanese, 7,000 Americans, 6,400 British, 4,400 Canadians
and token forces of French and Italians. A Russian anti-Bolshevik
regime was set up by Admiral Kolchak in 1918. In 1920 an independent Far Eastern Republic was declared in Chita, under firm Bolshevik control, but in an independent guise. During 1922, as the
foreign troops departed, the Republic extended its control to
Vladivostok. In 1922 the Republic was formally annexed to the
Soviet Union. The region is rich in mineral resources, as well as
being an exporter of furs and fish.

106

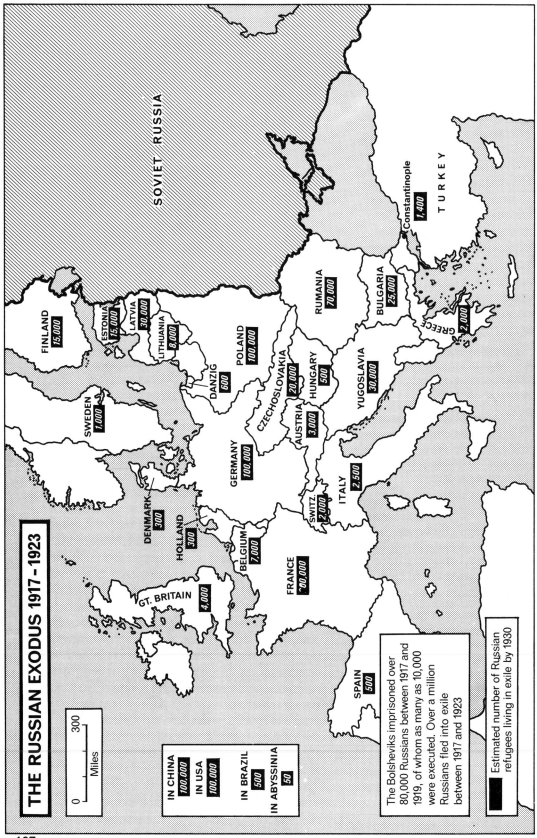

THE RUSSIAN EXODUS 1917-1923

SOVIET RUSSIA

TURKEY

Constantinople **1,400**

RUMANIA **70,000**

BULGARIA **25,000**

GREECE **2,000**

FINLAND **15,000**

ESTONIA **15,000**

LATVIA **30,000**

LITHUANIA **8,000**

POLAND **100,000**

DANZIG **600**

CZECHOSLOVAKIA **20,000**

HUNGARY **500**

SWEDEN **1,000**

AUSTRIA **3,000**

YUGOSLAVIA **30,000**

GERMANY **100,000**

ITALY **2,500**

SWITZ. **2,000**

DENMARK **300**

HOLLAND **300**

BELGIUM **7,000**

FRANCE **200,000**

GT. BRITAIN **4,000**

SPAIN **500**

300

0   Miles

IN CHINA **100,000**

IN USA **100,000**

IN BRAZIL **500**

IN ABYSSINIA **50**

The Bolsheviks imprisoned over
80,000 Russians between 1917 and
1919, of whom as many as 10,000
were executed. Over a million
Russians fled into exile
between 1917 and 1923

■ Estimated number of Russian
refugees living in exile by 1930

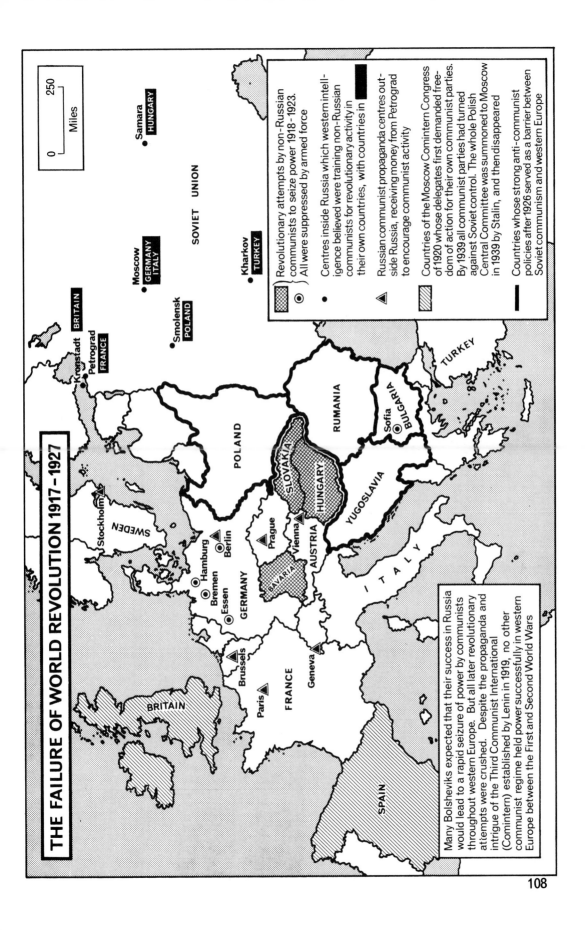

THE FAILURE OF WORLD REVOLUTION 1917–1927

Scale: 0 — 250 Miles

Legend:

- Revolutionary attempts by non-Russian communists to seize power 1918–1923. All were suppressed by armed force

- Centres inside Russia which western intelligence believed were training non-Russian communists for revolutionary activity in their own countries, with countries in

- Russian communist propaganda centres outside Russia, receiving money from Petrograd to encourage communist activity

- Countries of the Moscow Comintern Congress of 1920 whose delegates first demanded freedom of action for their own communist parties. By 1939 all communist parties had turned against Soviet control. The whole Polish Central Committee was summoned to Moscow in 1939 by Stalin, and then disappeared

- Countries whose strong anti-communist policies after 1926 served as a barrier between Soviet communism and western Europe

Many Bolsheviks expected that their success in Russia would lead to a rapid seizure of power by communists throughout western Europe. But all later revolutionary attempts were crushed. Despite the propaganda and intrigue of the Third Communist International (Comintern) established by Lenin in 1919, no other communist regime held power successfully in western Europe between the First and Second World Wars

Labels on map: Samara HUNGARY; Moscow GERMANY ITALY; Kharkov TURKEY; Smolensk POLAND; Kronstadt; Petrograd FRANCE; BRITAIN; SOVIET UNION; Stockholm; SWEDEN; POLAND; RUMANIA; SLOVAKIA; HUNGARY; Sofia BULGARIA; TURKEY; Hamburg; Berlin; Bremen; Essen; GERMANY; Prague; Vienna; AUSTRIA; BAVARIA; YUGOSLAVIA; Brussels; Paris; FRANCE; Geneva; ITALY; BRITAIN; SPAIN

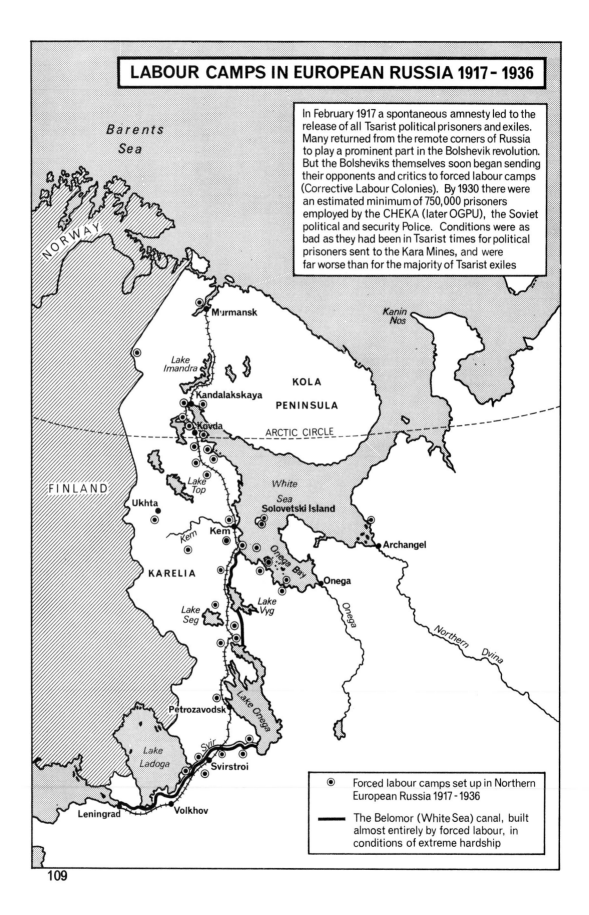

LABOUR CAMPS IN EUROPEAN RUSSIA 1917-1936

Barents Sea

NORWAY

In February 1917 a spontaneous amnesty led to the release of all Tsarist political prisoners and exiles. Many returned from the remote corners of Russia to play a prominent part in the Bolshevik revolution. But the Bolsheviks themselves soon began sending their opponents and critics to forced labour camps (Corrective Labour Colonies). By 1930 there were an estimated minimum of 750,000 prisoners employed by the CHEKA (later OGPU), the Soviet political and security Police. Conditions were as bad as they had been in Tsarist times for political prisoners sent to the Kara Mines, and were far worse than for the majority of Tsarist exiles

Murmansk

Kanin Nos

Lake Imandra

KOLA PENINSULA

Kandalakskaya

Kovda

ARCTIC CIRCLE

FINLAND

Lake Top

White Sea

Ukhta

Solovetski Island

Kem Kem

Archangel

KARELIA

Onega Bay

Onega

Lake Vyg

Onega

Lake Seg

Northern Dvina

Petrozavodsk

Lake Onega

Svir

Lake Ladoga

Svirstroi

⊙   Forced labour camps set up in Northern European Russia 1917-1936

━━   The Belomor (White Sea) canal, built almost entirely by forced labour, in conditions of extreme hardship

Leningrad   Volkhov

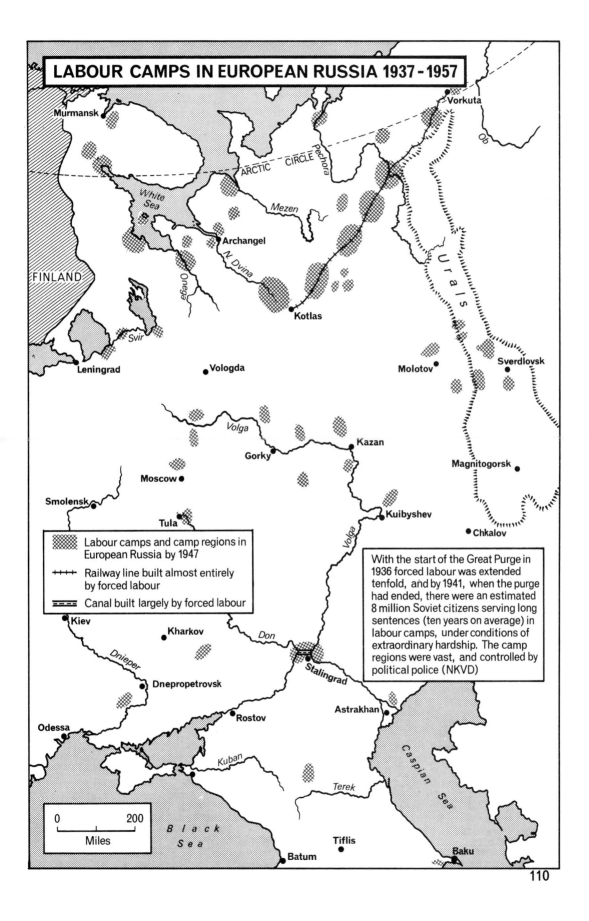

LABOUR CAMPS IN EUROPEAN RUSSIA 1937-1957

With the start of the Great Purge in 1936 forced labour was extended tenfold, and by 1941, when the purge had ended, there were an estimated 8 million Soviet citizens serving long sentences (ten years on average) in labour camps, under conditions of extraordinary hardship. The camp regions were vast, and controlled by political police (NKVD)

Labour camps and camp regions in European Russia by 1947

++++ Railway line built almost entirely by forced labour

=== Canal built largely by forced labour

0 — 200

Miles

110

LABOUR CAMPS EAST OF THE URALS 1918-1958

A revolt of camp inmates at
Igarka was suppressed in
1948. As many as 2,666
escaped towards the Urals.
They were bombed from the
air and nearly all were killed
or captured

*Barents
Sea*

**Novaya
Zemlya**

*Kara
Sea*

●**Vorkuta**

●**Moscow**

Norylsk

NORYLLAG

●**Igarka**

●**Turukhansk**

Urals

Ob

Yenisei

KRASLAG

TRANS-SIBERIAN RAILWAY

⊙**Tobolsk**

Narym
⊙

*Caspian
Sea*

Ob

Irtysh

Tomsk

Krasnoyarsk

*Aral
Sea*

KARLAG

Karaganda
⊙

⊙**Dzhezkazgan**

⊙**Kemerovo**

SIBLAG

Yenisei

*Lake
Balkhash*

Among the prisoners in the camps were peasants who ha[...]
resisted collectivization, soviet citizens who had lived
abroad for any length of time (esp. Jews), foreign
communists who had sought refuge in Moscow, inhabitan[...]
of the border lands (eg Poles, Koreans, Chinese), religiou[...]
groups, state officials suspected of "sabotage", artists,
writers, university lecturers, and leaders of minority
groups (eg Mongols, Uzbeks, Georgians). All were put t[...]
work in different ways - railway building, tree felling,
coal and gold mining, light industry and agriculture

0   200
|_____|
Miles

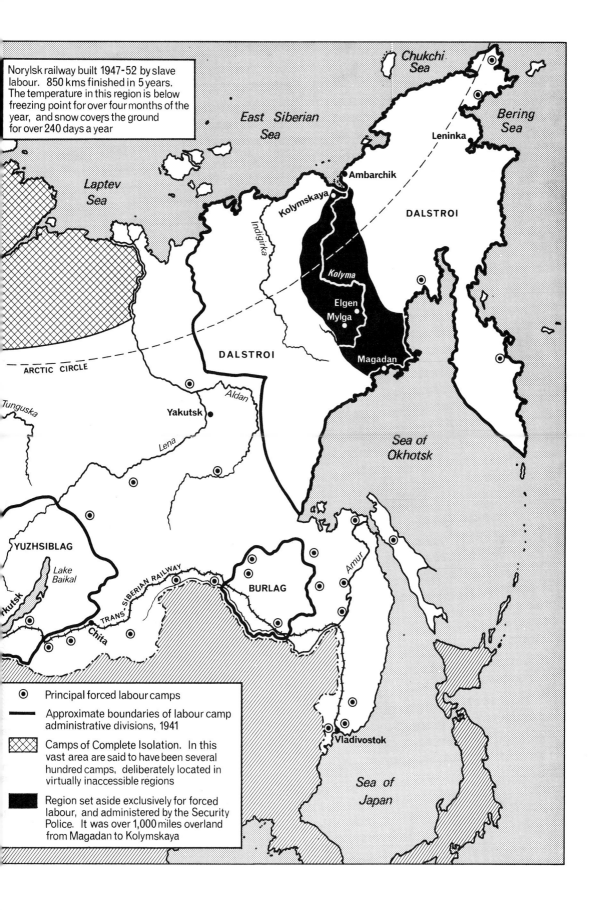

Norylsk railway built 1947-52 by slave labour. 850 kms finished in 5 years. The temperature in this region is below freezing point for over four months of the year, and snow covers the ground for over 240 days a year

Chukchi Sea

East Siberian Sea

Bering Sea

Leninka

Laptev Sea

Ambarchik

Kolymskaya

DALSTROI

Indigirka

Kolyma

Elgen
Mylga

ARCTIC CIRCLE

DALSTROI

Magadan

Tunguska

Aldan

Yakutsk

Lena

Sea of Okhotsk

YUZHSIBLAG

Lake Baikal

TRANS SIBERIAN RAILWAY

Amur

BURLAG

rkutsk

Chita

Vladivostok

Sea of Japan

⊙   Principal forced labour camps

──   Approximate boundaries of labour camp administrative divisions, 1941

▨   Camps of Complete Isolation. In this vast area are said to have been several hundred camps, deliberately located in virtually inaccessible regions

■   Region set aside exclusively for forced labour, and administered by the Security Police. It was over 1,000 miles overland from Magadan to Kolymskaya

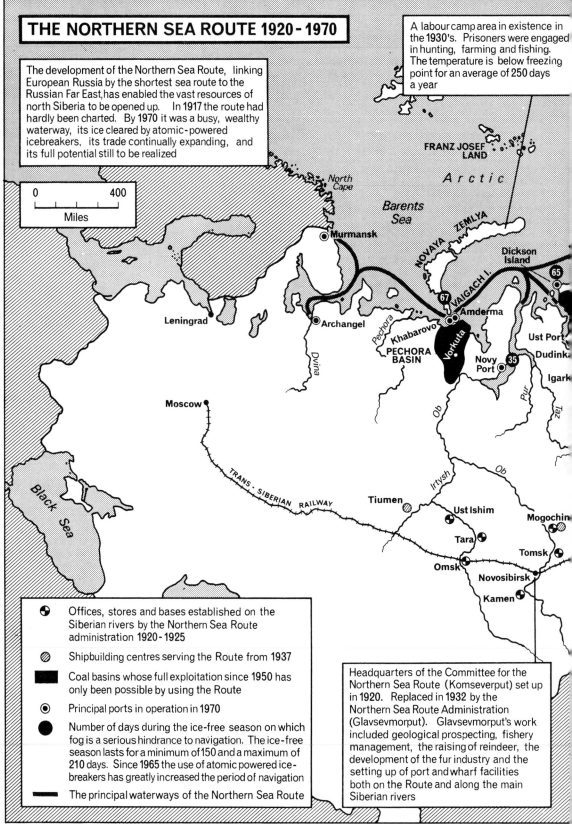

THE NORTHERN SEA ROUTE 1920 - 1970

The development of the Northern Sea Route, linking European Russia by the shortest sea route to the Russian Far East, has enabled the vast resources of north Siberia to be opened up.   In 1917 the route had hardly been charted. By 1970 it was a busy, wealthy waterway, its ice cleared by atomic-powered icebreakers, its trade continually expanding, and its full potential still to be realized

A labour camp area in existence in the 1930's. Prisoners were engaged in hunting, farming and fishing. The temperature is below freezing point for an average of 250 days a year

0   400
Miles

FRANZ JOSEF LAND

Arctic

North Cape

Barents Sea

NOVAYA ZEMLYA

Murmansk

Dickson Island

65

67 VAIGACH I.

Leningrad

Archangel

Amderma

Ust Port

Pechora

Khabarovo

Dudinka

PECHORA BASIN

Vorkuta

Novy Port

35

Igark

Dvina

Ob

Pur

Taz

Moscow

Irtysh

Ob

TRANS - SIBERIAN RAILWAY

Tiumen

Black Sea

Ust Ishim

Mogochin

Tara

Tomsk

Omsk

Novosibirsk

Kamen

Offices, stores and bases established on the Siberian rivers by the Northern Sea Route administration 1920 - 1925

Shipbuilding centres serving the Route from 1937

Coal basins whose full exploitation since 1950 has only been possible by using the Route

Principal ports in operation in 1970

Number of days during the ice-free season on which fog is a serious hindrance to navigation. The ice-free season lasts for a minimum of 150 and a maximum of 210 days. Since 1965 the use of atomic powered ice-breakers has greatly increased the period of navigation

The principal waterways of the Northern Sea Route

Headquarters of the Committee for the Northern Sea Route (Komseverput) set up in 1920. Replaced in 1932 by the Northern Sea Route Administration (Glavsevmorput). Glavsevmorput's work included geological prospecting, fishery management, the raising of reindeer, the development of the fur industry and the setting up of port and wharf facilities both on the Route and along the main Siberian rivers

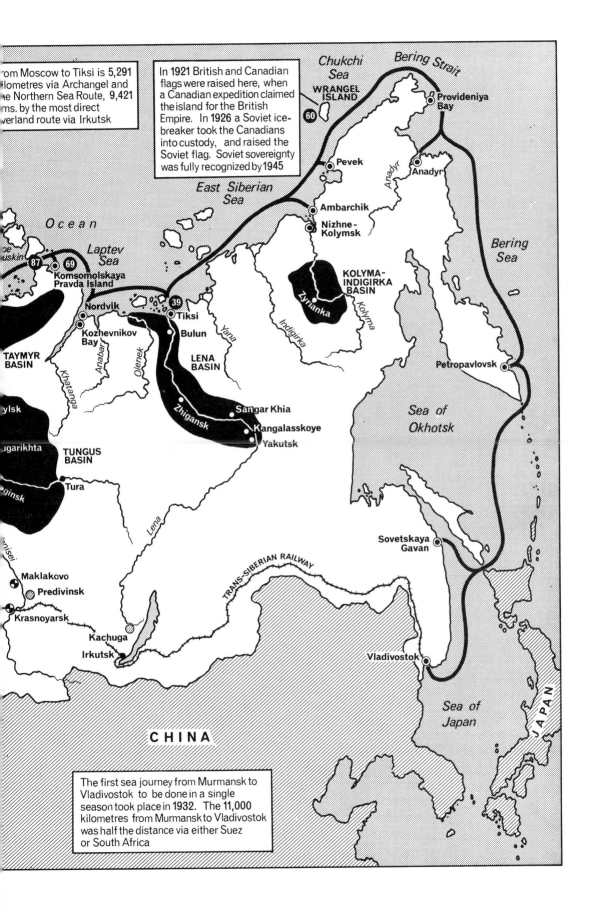

From Moscow to Tiksi is 5,291 kilometres via Archangel and the Northern Sea Route, 9,421 kms. by the most direct overland route via Irkutsk

In 1921 British and Canadian flags were raised here, when a Canadian expedition claimed the island for the British Empire. In 1926 a Soviet ice-breaker took the Canadians into custody, and raised the Soviet flag. Soviet sovereignty was fully recognized by 1945

The first sea journey from Murmansk to Vladivostok to be done in a single season took place in 1932. The 11,000 kilometres from Murmansk to Vladivostok was half the distance via either Suez or South Africa

Chukchi Sea

Bering Strait

WRANGEL ISLAND

60

Provideniya Bay

East Siberian Sea

Pevek

Anadyr

Anadyr

Ocean

Ambarchik

Nizhne-Kolymsk

Bering Sea

87   69

Laptev Sea

Komsomolskaya Pravda Island

Nordvik

Kozhevnikov Bay

39

Tiksi

Bulun

KOLYMA-INDIGIRKA BASIN

Zyrianka

Indigirka

Kolyma

TAYMYR BASIN

Khatanga

Anabar

Olenek

Yana

LENA BASIN

Petropavlovsk

ylsk

Zhigansk

Sangar Khia

Sea of Okhotsk

ugarikhta

TUNGUS BASIN

Kangalasskoye

Yakutsk

ginsk

Tura

Lena

Maklakovo

Predivinsk

Krasnoyarsk

Kachuga

Irkutsk

TRANS-SIBERIAN RAILWAY

Sovetskaya Gavan

Vladivostok

Sea of Japan

JAPAN

C H I N A

THE SOVIET UNION UNDER STALIN 1922-1953

Arct

Bare

NORWAY

North
Sea

SWEDEN

FINLAND

London

Leningrad

100

FRANCE

WEST GERMANY

Rhine

Berlin

Potsdam
1945

Warsaw

Volga

Moscow
1942
1944

200

Prague

100

AUSTRIA

Vienna

Budapest

Kiev

Kuibysh

Kharkov

Saratov

Urals

ITALY

Adriatic Sea

Danube

Belgrade

Bucharest

400

DONBASS

Sofia

Yalta
1945

Black Sea

Mediterranean Sea

GREECE

Prinkipo

Caucasus

Caspian Sea

TURKEY

0   300
Miles

Tabriz

Teheran
1943

PERSIA

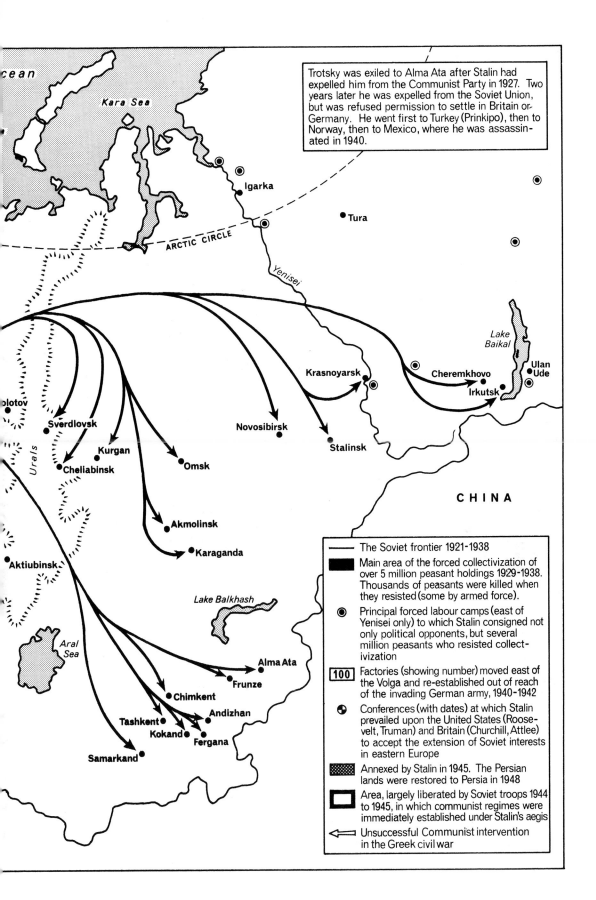

Trotsky was exiled to Alma Ata after Stalin had expelled him from the Communist Party in 1927. Two years later he was expelled from the Soviet Union, but was refused permission to settle in Britain or Germany. He went first to Turkey (Prinkipo), then to Norway, then to Mexico, where he was assassinated in 1940.

Kara Sea

cean

Igarka

Tura

ARCTIC CIRCLE

Yenisei

Lake Baikal

Krasnoyarsk

Cheremkhovo

Ulan Ude

Irkutsk

blotov

Sverdlovsk

Novosibirsk

Stalinsk

Kurgan

Cheliabinsk

Omsk

CHINA

Urals

Akmolinsk

Karaganda

Aktiubinsk

Lake Balkhash

Aral Sea

Alma Ata

Frunze

Chimkent

Andizhan

Tashkent

Kokand

Fergana

Samarkand

--- The Soviet frontier 1921-1938

■ Main area of the forced collectivization of over 5 million peasant holdings 1929-1938. Thousands of peasants were killed when they resisted (some by armed force).

◉ Principal forced labour camps (east of Yenisei only) to which Stalin consigned not only political opponents, but several million peasants who resisted collectivization

[100] Factories (showing number) moved east of the Volga and re-established out of reach of the invading German army, 1940-1942

✪ Conferences (with dates) at which Stalin prevailed upon the United States (Roosevelt, Truman) and Britain (Churchill, Attlee) to accept the extension of Soviet interests in eastern Europe

▨ Annexed by Stalin in 1945. The Persian lands were restored to Persia in 1948

▢ Area, largely liberated by Soviet troops 1944 to 1945, in which communist regimes were immediately established under Stalin's aegis

⇐ Unsuccessful Communist intervention in the Greek civil war

THE PARTITION OF POLAND 1939

The destruction of Poland was principally a German action. 1,700,000 German troops soon defeated the 600,000 Polish soldiers. German air attack destroyed the centres of the main Polish cities. The Poles hoped to make a final stand in the Pripet marsh area, but the Russian advance destroyed all chance of further Polish resistance

Baltic Sea

LITHUANIA

Königsberg

EAST

PRUSSIA

Vilna

Suvalki

Minsk

Augustov

Grodno

Lomza

Bialystok

RUSSIA

Posnan

Warsaw

Brest-
Litovsk

Pinsk

Pripet

Lodz

P O L A N D

Marshes

Lublin

Lutsk

SOVIET

Sokal

Rovno

GERMANY

Tarnov

Cracow

Yaroslav

Lvov

Przemysl

Tarnopol

SLOVAKIA

Stanislavov

Kamenets
Podolsk

HUNGARY

German advance against Poland from 3 September 1939

Russian advance against Poland from 17 September 1939

Dividing line between the German and Russian zones of occupation, agreed upon in advance by the Russo-German Pact of 23 August 1939

Annexed by the Soviet Union in October 1939

Annexed by Germany

Annexed by Lithuania

RUMANIA

0   100

Miles

114

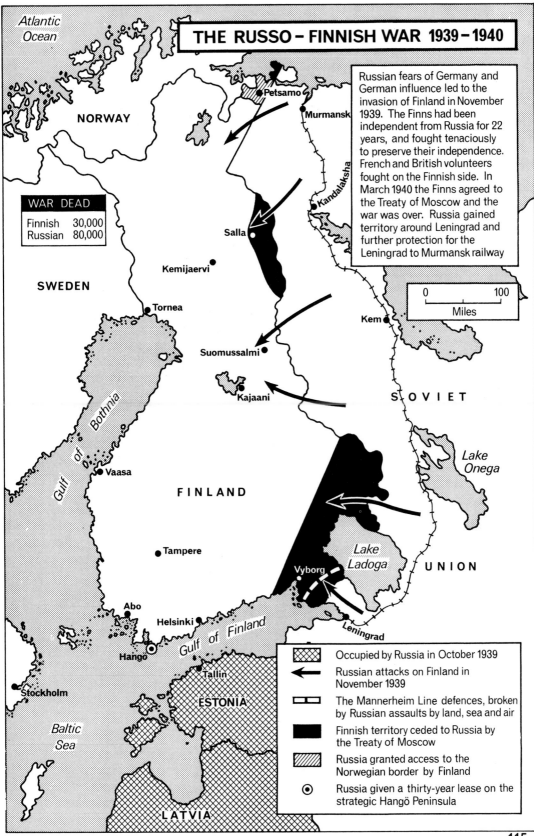

THE RUSSO – FINNISH WAR 1939 – 1940

Russian fears of Germany and German influence led to the invasion of Finland in November 1939. The Finns had been independent from Russia for 22 years, and fought tenaciously to preserve their independence. French and British volunteers fought on the Finnish side. In March 1940 the Finns agreed to the Treaty of Moscow and the war was over. Russia gained territory around Leningrad and further protection for the Leningrad to Murmansk railway

Atlantic Ocean

NORWAY

Petsamo

Murmansk

Kandalaksha

Salla

Kemijaervi

SWEDEN

Tornea

Kem

WAR DEAD
Finnish 30,000
Russian 80,000

0   100
Miles

Suomussalmi

Kajaani

S O V I E T

Lake Onega

FINLAND

Vaasa

Tampere

Lake Ladoga

U N I O N

Vyborg

Abo

Helsinki

Gulf of Finland

Leningrad

Hango

Tallin

Stockholm

ESTONIA

Baltic Sea

LATVIA

Gulf of Bothnia

Occupied by Russia in October 1939

Russian attacks on Finland in November 1939

The Mannerheim Line defences, broken by Russian assaults by land, sea and air

Finnish territory ceded to Russia by the Treaty of Moscow

Russia granted access to the Norwegian border by Finland

Russia given a thirty-year lease on the strategic Hangö Peninsula

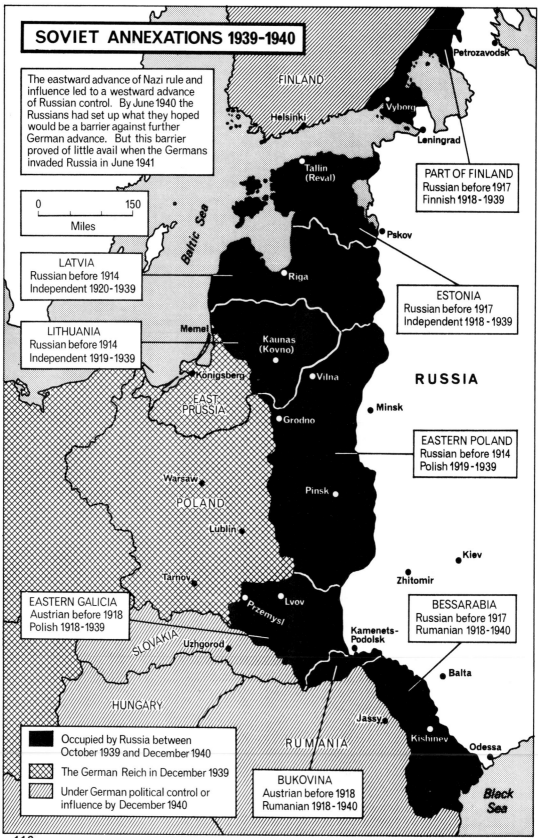

SOVIET ANNEXATIONS 1939-1940

The eastward advance of Nazi rule and influence led to a westward advance of Russian control. By June 1940 the Russians had set up what they hoped would be a barrier against further German advance. But this barrier proved of little avail when the Germans invaded Russia in June 1941

0   150
Miles

PART OF FINLAND
Russian before 1917
Finnish 1918 - 1939

LATVIA
Russian before 1914
Independent 1920 - 1939

ESTONIA
Russian before 1917
Independent 1918 - 1939

LITHUANIA
Russian before 1914
Independent 1919 - 1939

EASTERN POLAND
Russian before 1914
Polish 1919 - 1939

EASTERN GALICIA
Austrian before 1918
Polish 1918 - 1939

BESSARABIA
Russian before 1917
Rumanian 1918 - 1940

FINLAND
Helsinki
Vyborg
Leningrad
Petrozavodsk
Tallin (Reval)
Pskov
Riga
Memel
Kaunas (Kovno)
Vilna
Minsk
Königsberg
EAST PRUSSIA
Grodno
RUSSIA
Warsaw
POLAND
Pinsk
Lublin
Tarnov
Kiev
Zhitomir
Lvov
Przemysl
Kamenets-Podolsk
SLOVAKIA
Uzhgorod
Balta
HUNGARY
Jassy
Kishinev
Odessa
RUMANIA
Baltic Sea
Black Sea

BUKOVINA
Austrian before 1918
Rumanian 1918 - 1940

■ Occupied by Russia between October 1939 and December 1940

▨ The German Reich in December 1939

▨ Under German political control or influence by December 1940

116

EUROPE ON 22 JUNE 1941

Archangel

NORWAY

SWEDEN

FINLAND

Leningrad

Hango

BRITAIN

EIRE

DENMARK

Riga

Kovno

Vilna

Moscow

S O V I E T

U N I O N

London

HOLLAND

Danzig

Berlin

GREATER

Brest-Litovsk

Cologne

GERMANY

Warsaw

BELGIUM

Prague

Cracow

Lvov

FRANCE

Munich

Vienna

SLOVAKIA

Kishinev

SWITZ.

HUNGARY

Odessa

SPAIN

YUGOSLAVIA

RUMANIA

ITALY

BULGARIA

ALBANIA

TURKEY

GREECE

The German Reich on 22 June 1941,
the day of the German invasion of Russia

Countries under German rule or
influence by June 1941

Neutral countries

Great Britain, the only state at war with
Germany on 21 June 1941; and the
Soviet Union, to whom Britain
immediately offered all possible help
and alliance in the fight against Nazism

0   300

Miles

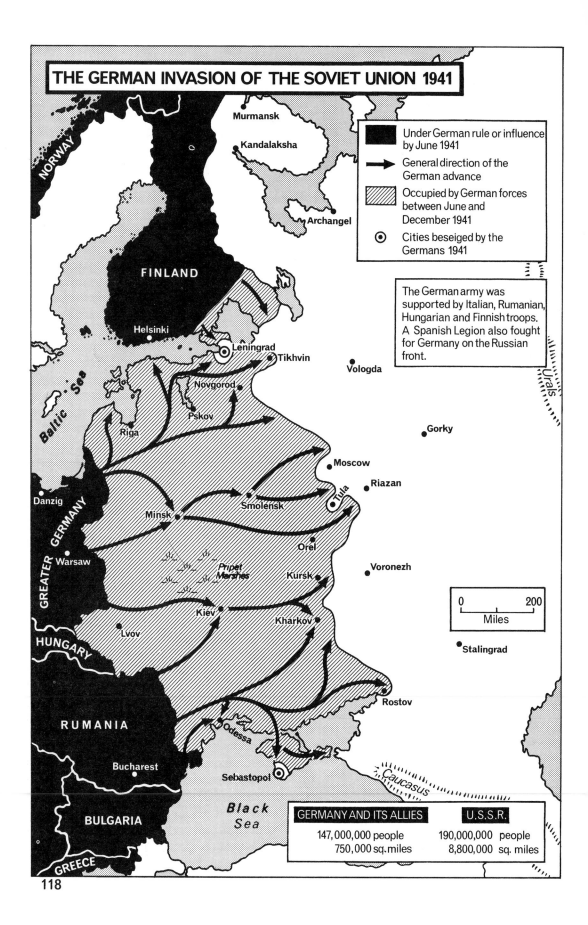

THE GERMAN INVASION OF THE SOVIET UNION 1941

Under German rule or influence by June 1941

General direction of the German advance

Occupied by German forces between June and December 1941

⊙ Cities beseiged by the Germans 1941

The German army was supported by Italian, Rumanian, Hungarian and Finnish troops. A Spanish Legion also fought for Germany on the Russian front.

NORWAY

FINLAND

Murmansk

Kandalaksha

Archangel

Helsinki

Baltic Sea

Leningrad

Tikhvin

Vologda

Novgorod

Pskov

Riga

Gorky

Moscow

Danzig

Smolensk

Riazan

Tula

GREATER GERMANY

Minsk

Orel

Warsaw

Pripet Marshes

Kursk

Voronezh

HUNGARY

Kiev

Kharkov

Lvov

Urals

0   200
Miles

Stalingrad

RUMANIA

Rostov

Odessa

Bucharest

Sebastopol

Caucasus

BULGARIA

Black Sea

GERMANY AND ITS ALLIES	U.S.S.R.
147,000,000 people	190,000,000 people
750,000 sq. miles	8,800,000 sq. miles

GREECE

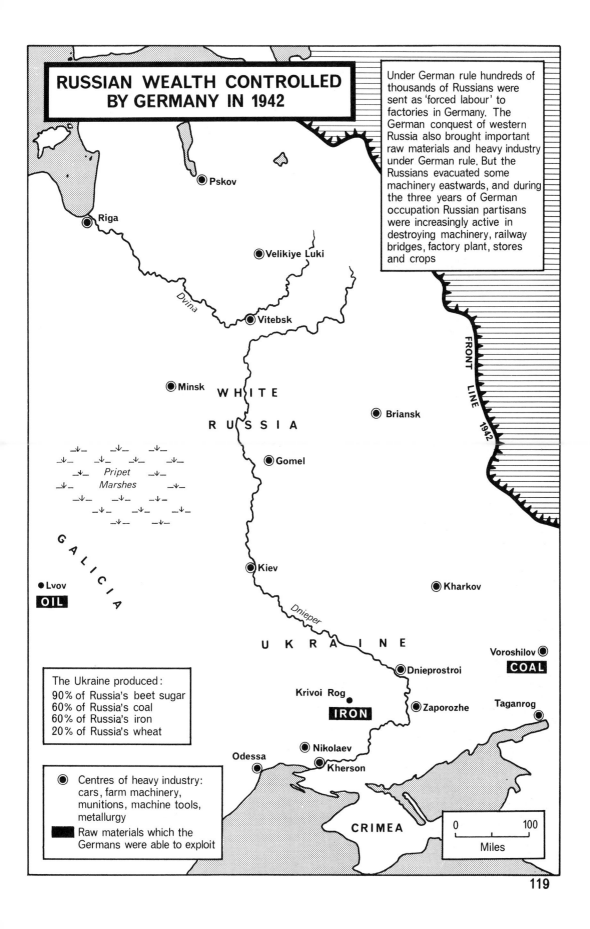

RUSSIAN WEALTH CONTROLLED BY GERMANY IN 1942

Under German rule hundreds of thousands of Russians were sent as 'forced labour' to factories in Germany. The German conquest of western Russia also brought important raw materials and heavy industry under German rule. But the Russians evacuated some machinery eastwards, and during the three years of German occupation Russian partisans were increasingly active in destroying machinery, railway bridges, factory plant, stores and crops

Pskov

Riga

Velikiye Luki

Dvina

Vitebsk

WHITE

Minsk

RUSSIA

Briansk

FRONT LINE 1942

Gomel

Pripet Marshes

GALICIA

Kiev

Dnieper

Lvov

OIL

Kharkov

UKRAINE

Voroshilov

COAL

Dnieprostroi

Krivoi Rog

IRON

Zaporozhe

Taganrog

The Ukraine produced:
90% of Russia's beet sugar
60% of Russia's coal
60% of Russia's iron
20% of Russia's wheat

Odessa

Nikolaev

Kherson

◉ Centres of heavy industry: cars, farm machinery, munitions, machine tools, metallurgy

■ Raw materials which the Germans were able to exploit

CRIMEA

0   100

Miles

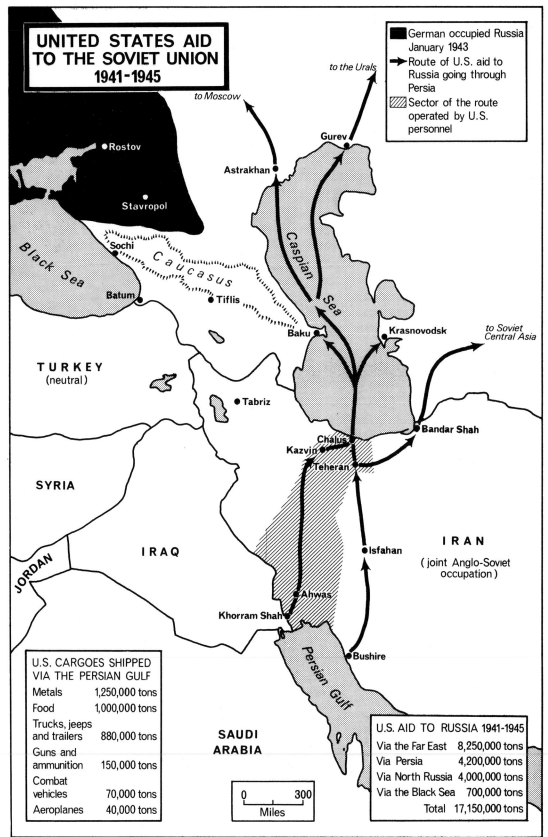

UNITED STATES AID TO THE SOVIET UNION 1941-1945

■ German occupied Russia January 1943

➤ Route of U.S. aid to Russia going through Persia

▨ Sector of the route operated by U.S. personnel

to the Urals

to Moscow

Gurev

Astrakhan

●Rostov

Stavropol

Caspian Sea

Sochi

C a u c a s u s

Batum

●Tiflis

Baku

Krasnovodsk

to Soviet Central Asia

Black Sea

T U R K E Y
(neutral)

●Tabriz

Bandar Shah

Chalus

Kazvin●
●Teheran

SYRIA

I R A N

(joint Anglo-Soviet occupation)

●Isfahan

I R A Q

JORDAN

Ahwas

Khorram Shah●

●Bushire

Persian Gulf

SAUDI ARABIA

U.S. CARGOES SHIPPED VIA THE PERSIAN GULF

Metals	1,250,000 tons
Food	1,000,000 tons
Trucks, jeeps and trailers	880,000 tons
Guns and ammunition	150,000 tons
Combat vehicles	70,000 tons
Aeroplanes	40,000 tons

0   300
Miles

U.S. AID TO RUSSIA 1941-1945

Via the Far East	8,250,000 tons
Via Persia	4,200,000 tons
Via North Russia	4,000,000 tons
Via the Black Sea	700,000 tons
Total	17,150,000 tons

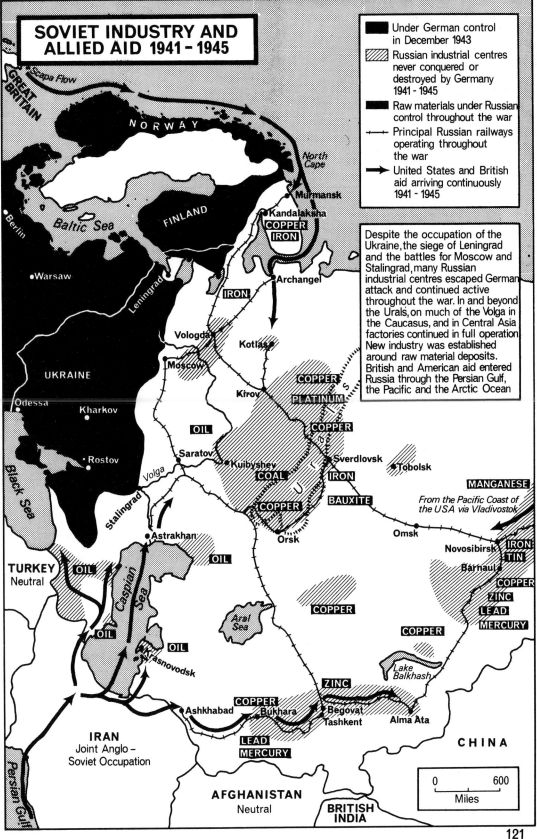

SOVIET INDUSTRY AND ALLIED AID 1941 - 1945

Under German control in December 1943

Russian industrial centres never conquered or destroyed by Germany 1941 - 1945

Raw materials under Russian control throughout the war

Principal Russian railways operating throughout the war

United States and British aid arriving continuously 1941 - 1945

Despite the occupation of the Ukraine, the siege of Leningrad and the battles for Moscow and Stalingrad, many Russian industrial centres escaped German attack and continued active throughout the war. In and beyond the Urals, on much of the Volga in the Caucasus, and in Central Asia factories continued in full operation. New industry was established around raw material deposits. British and American aid entered Russia through the Persian Gulf, the Pacific and the Arctic Ocean

GREAT BRITAIN

Scapa Flow

NORWAY

North Cape

Murmansk

Kandalaksha
COPPER
IRON

Baltic Sea

FINLAND

Berlin

Warsaw

Leningrad

Archangel

IRON

Vologda

Kotlas

Moscow

UKRAINE

Kirov

COPPER
PLATINUM

COPPER

Odessa

Kharkov

OIL

Saratov

Kuibyshev

Sverdlovsk

Tobolsk

COAL

IRON

MANGANESE

From the Pacific Coast of the USA via Vladivostok

Rostov

Volga

Stalingrad

COPPER

Orsk

BAUXITE

Omsk

Novosibirsk

IRON
TIN

Black Sea

Astrakhan

OIL

Barnaul

COPPER

ZINC
LEAD
MERCURY

TURKEY
Neutral

OIL

Caspian Sea

OIL

Aral Sea

COPPER

COPPER

OIL

OIL

Krasnovodsk

Lake Balkhash

ZINC

Ashkhabad

COPPER
Bukhara

Begovat
Tashkent

Alma Ata

CHINA

IRAN
Joint Anglo – Soviet Occupation

LEAD
MERCURY

0   600

Miles

AFGHANISTAN
Neutral

BRITISH INDIA

Persian Gulf

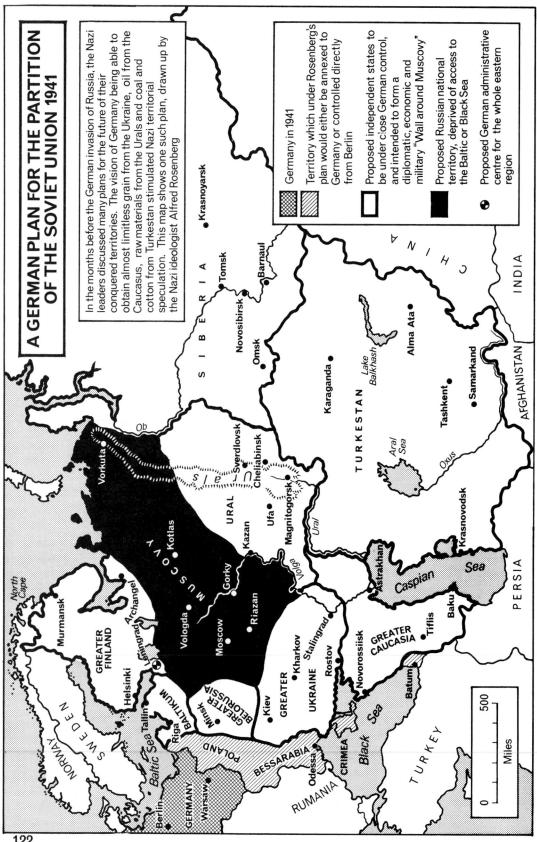

A GERMAN PLAN FOR THE PARTITION OF THE SOVIET UNION 1941

In the months before the German invasion of Russia, the Nazi leaders discussed many plans for the future of their conquered territories. The vision of Germany being able to obtain almost limitless grain from the Ukraine, oil from the Caucasus, raw materials from the Urals and coal and cotton from Turkestan stimulated Nazi territorial speculation. This map shows one such plan, drawn up by the Nazi ideologist Alfred Rosenberg

Germany in 1941

Territory which under Rosenberg's plan would either be annexed to Germany or controlled directly from Berlin

Proposed independent states to be under close German control, and intended to form a diplomatic, economic and military "Wall around Muscovy"

Proposed Russian national territory, deprived of access to the Baltic or Black Sea

Proposed German administrative centre for the whole eastern region

Krasnoyarsk

Tomsk

Barnaul

SIBERIA

Novosibirsk

Omsk

CHINA

Lake Balkhash

Alma Ata

Karaganda

Samarkand

TURKESTAN

Tashkent

Aral Sea

Ob

Vorkuta

Sverdlovsk

Cheliabinsk

Urals

URAL

Ufa

Magnitogorsk

Kazan

Oxus

AFGHANISTAN

INDIA

Kotlas

MUSCOVY

Ural

Krasnovodsk

North Cape

Archangel

Volga

Astrakhan

Caspian Sea

Murmansk

Leningrad

Gorky

Riazan

Baku

GREATER FINLAND

Vologda

Moscow

GREATER CAUCASIA

Tiflis

PERSIA

Helsinki

Tallinn

BALTIKUM

Minsk

GREATER BELORUSSIA

Kharkov

Stalingrad

Rostov

Novorossiisk

Batum

SWEDEN

Riga

Kiev

GREATER UKRAINE

Black Sea

NORWAY

Baltic Sea

POLAND

Odessa

CRIMEA

TURKEY

Berlin

Warsaw

GERMANY

BESSARABIA

RUMANIA

0   500
Miles

122

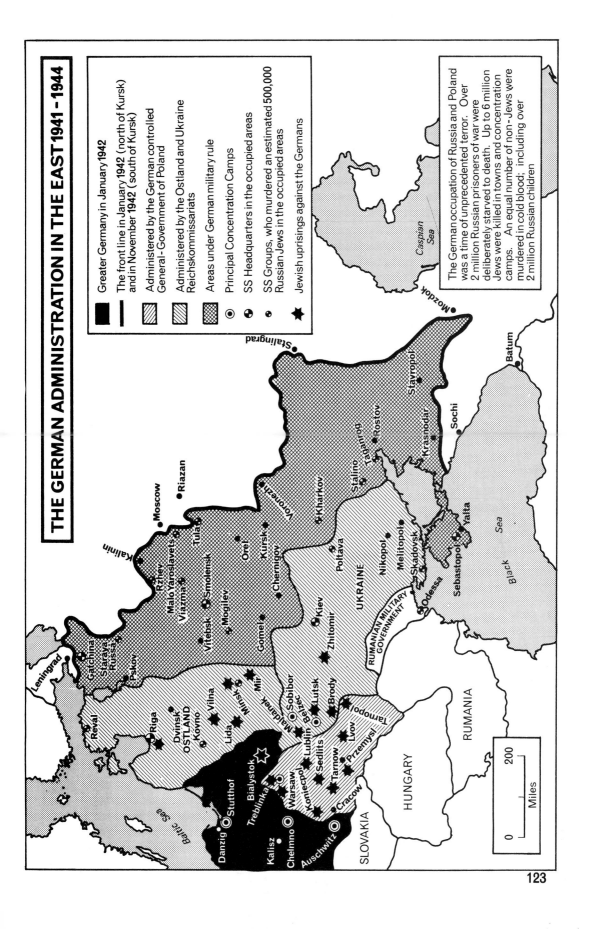

THE GERMAN ADMINISTRATION IN THE EAST 1941 - 1944

Greater Germany in January 1942

The front line in January 1942 (north of Kursk) and in November 1942 (south of Kursk)

Administered by the German controlled General - Government of Poland

Administered by the Ostland and Ukraine Reichskommissariats

Areas under German military rule

Principal Concentration Camps

SS Headquarters in the occupied areas

SS Groups, who murdered an estimated 500,000 Russian Jews in the occupied areas

Jewish uprisings against the Germans

The German occupation of Russia and Poland was a time of unprecedented terror. Over 2 million Russian prisoners of war were deliberately starved to death. Up to 6 million Jews were killed in towns and concentration camps. An equal number of non - Jews were murdered in cold blood; including over 2 million Russian children

Leningrad
Reval
Gatchina
Staraya
Russa
Pskov
Riga
Dvinsk
Kovno
OSTLAND
Vilna
Lida
Malodeczno
Minsk
Mir
Bialystok
Treblinka
Warsaw
Koniecpol
Sedlits
Sobibor
Lublin
Belzec
Lutsk
Brody
Tarnopol
Lvov
Przemysl
Tarnow
Cracow
Danzig
Stutthof
Kalisz
Chelmno
Auschwitz

SLOVAKIA
HUNGARY
RUMANIA

Kalinin
Rzhev
Malo Yaroslavets
Viazma
Vitebsk
Mogilev
Gomel
Chernigov
Kiev
Zhitomir
Moscow
Riazan
Tula
Orel
Kursk
Poltava
Nikopol
Melitopol
Skadovsk
Odessa
Sebastopol
Yalta

UKRAINE
RUMANIAN MILITARY GOVERNMENT

Voronezh
Kharkov
Stalino
Taganrog
Rostow
Krasnodar
Sochi
Stavropol
Stalingrad
Mozdok
Batum

Caspian Sea
Black Sea
Baltic Sea

0   200
Miles

123

GERMAN PLANS AND CONQUESTS IN 1942

Despite fierce German efforts, Moscow was not captured in 1941. The Germans planned a more southerly attack for 1942, hoping to capture Stalingrad, drive north along the Volga, and cut off Moscow from the east. This plan failed, as did the one to capture the oil fields of the Caucasus

Gorky

Volga

● **Moscow**

● Kazan

● **Riazan**

Smolensk

● **Kuibyshev**

Briansk ●

Orel ●

Volga

Kursk ●

● **Voronezh**

Saratov ●

Don

● **Kiev**

Kharkov ●

Stalingrad

Volga

Stalino ●

Taganrog ●

Rostov

Astrakhan ●

Caspian Sea

Armavir ●

Sebastopol ●

Maikop ●

Grozny ●

Black   Sea

C a u c a s u s

Batum ●

Tiflis ●

Baku

Under German control by June 1942

The objectives of the German General Staff

Hitler's First Plan

Hitler's Second Plan

Russian territory actually conquered by Germany between June and December of 1942. This included the Maikop oilfields, but not the larger oilfields of Baku or Grozny

TURKEY

0   100
Miles

124

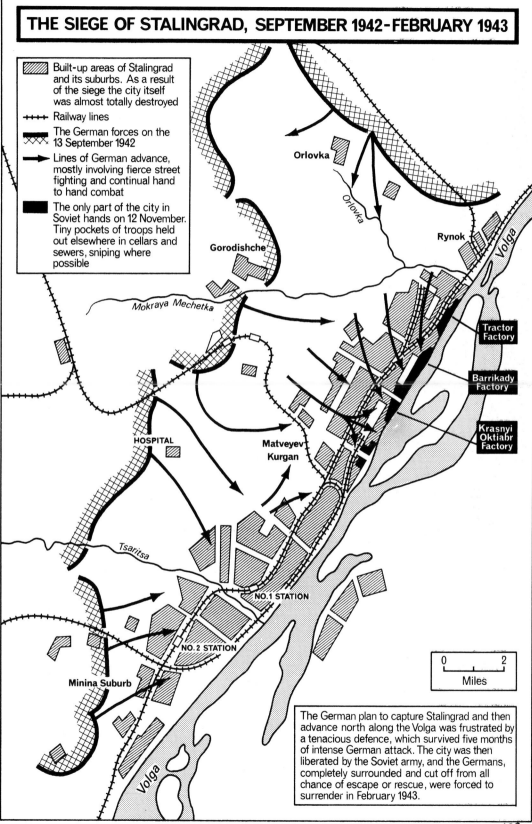

THE SIEGE OF STALINGRAD, SEPTEMBER 1942 - FEBRUARY 1943

Built-up areas of Stalingrad and its suburbs. As a result of the siege the city itself was almost totally destroyed

Railway lines

The German forces on the 13 September 1942

Lines of German advance, mostly involving fierce street fighting and continual hand to hand combat

The only part of the city in Soviet hands on 12 November. Tiny pockets of troops held out elsewhere in cellars and sewers, sniping where possible

Orlovka

Orlovka

Rynok

Volga

Gorodishche

Mokraya Mechetka

Tractor Factory

Barrikady Factory

Krasnyi Oktiabr Factory

HOSPITAL

Matveyev Kurgan

Tsaritsa

NO.1 STATION

NO.2 STATION

Minina Suburb

Volga

0   2
Miles

The German plan to capture Stalingrad and then advance north along the Volga was frustrated by a tenacious defence, which survived five months of intense German attack. The city was then liberated by the Soviet army, and the Germans, completely surrounded and cut off from all chance of escape or rescue, were forced to surrender in February 1943.

125

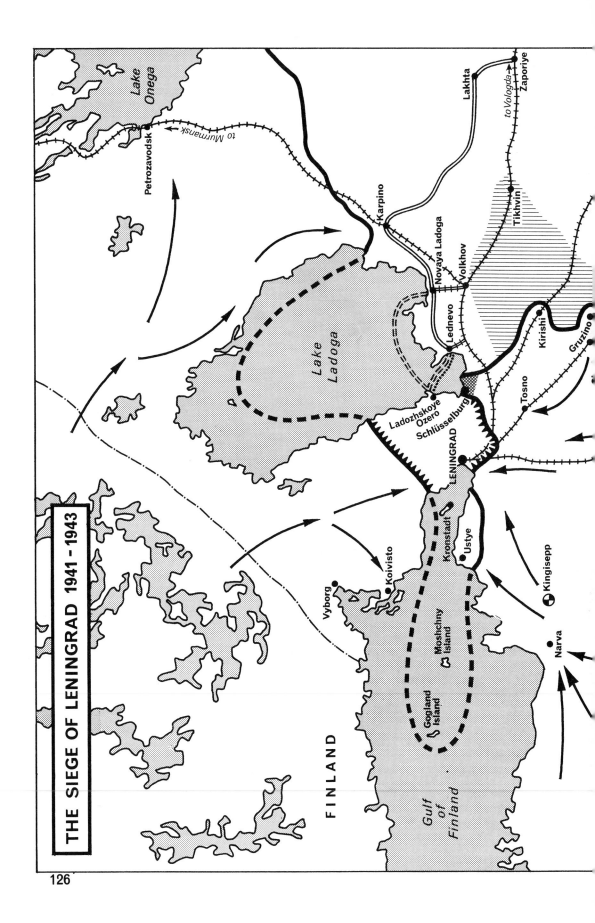

THE SIEGE OF LENINGRAD 1941 - 1943

Lake Onega

to Murmansk

Petrozavodsk

Karpino

Lakhta

Tikhvin

to Vologda

Zaporiye

Novaya Ladoga

Volkhov

Lednevo

Lake Ladoga

Kirishi

Gruzino

Ladozhskoye Ozero

Schlüsselburg

Tosno

LENINGRAD

Koivisto

Kronstadt

Ustye

Kingisepp

Vyborg

Moshchny Island

Gogland Island

Narva

FINLAND

Gulf of Finland

126

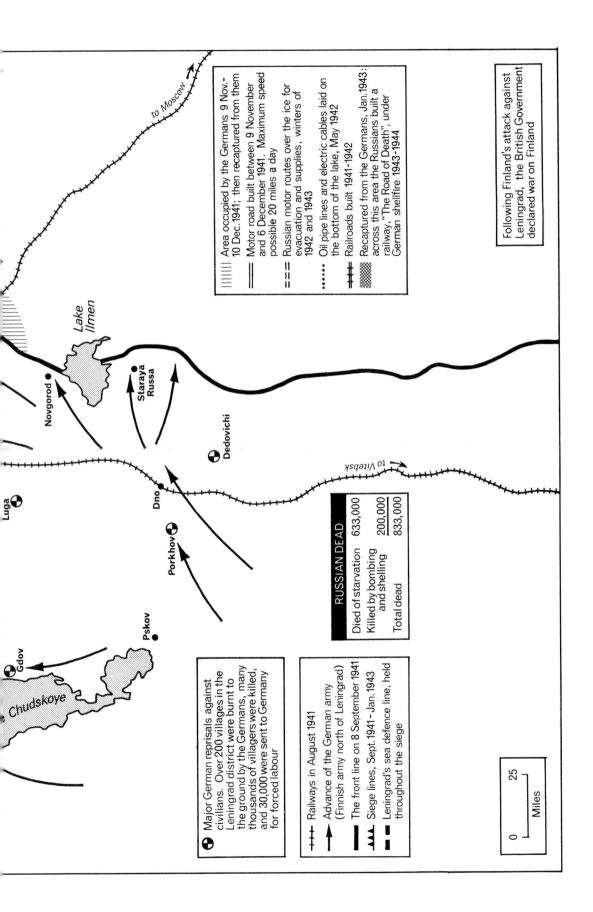

Lake
Ilmen

Novgorod

Staraya
Russa

Dedovichi

to Moscow

to Vitebsk

Dno

Luga

Porkhov

Gdov

Chudskoye

Pskov

Legend:

||||| Area occupied by the Germans 9 Nov.-
10 Dec.1941; then recaptured from them

=== Motor road built between 9 November
and 6 December 1941. Maximum speed
possible 20 miles a day

=== Russian motor routes over the ice for
evacuation and supplies, winters of
1942 and 1943

······ Oil pipe lines and electric cables laid on
the bottom of the lake, May 1942

╫╫╫ Railroads built 1941-1942

▨▨ Recaptured from the Germans, Jan.1943:
across this area the Russians built a
railway, "The Road of Death", under
German shellfire 1943-1944

Following Finland's attack against
Leningrad, the British Government
declared war on Finland

RUSSIAN DEAD	
Died of starvation	633,000
Killed by bombing and shelling	200,000
Total dead	833,000

◕ Major German reprisals against
civilians. Over 200 villages in the
Leningrad district were burnt to
the ground by the Germans, many
thousands of villagers were killed,
and 30,000 were sent to Germany
for forced labour

+++ Railways in August 1941

↑ Advance of the German army
(Finnish army north of Leningrad)

▮ The front line on 8 September 1941

▲▲▲ Siege lines, Sept. 1941 - Jan. 1943

▬ Leningrad's sea defence line, held
throughout the siege

0   25
|———|
Miles

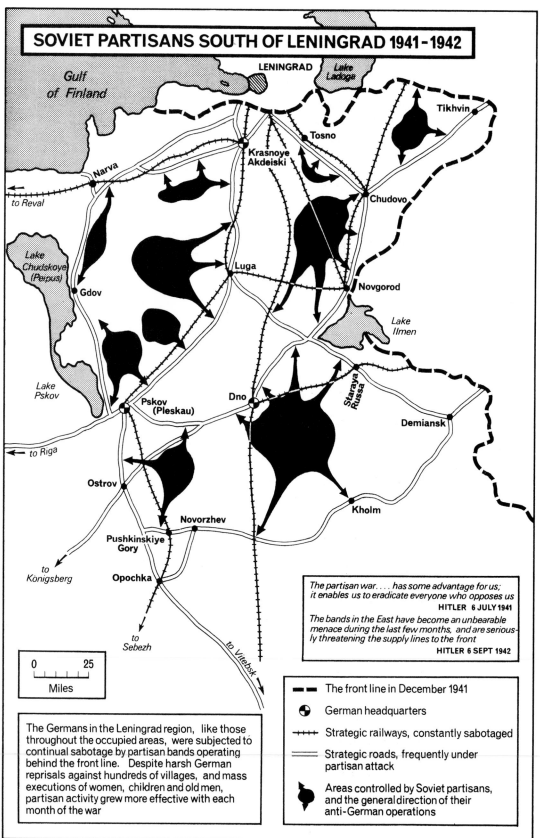

SOVIET PARTISANS SOUTH OF LENINGRAD 1941-1942

Gulf
of Finland

LENINGRAD

Lake Ladoga

Tikhvin

Narva

to Reval

Krasnoye Akdeiski

Tosno

Chudovo

Lake Chudskoye (Peipus)

Gdov

Luga

Novgorod

Lake Ilmen

Lake Pskov

Pskov (Pleskau)

Dno

Staraya Russa

Demiansk

to Riga

Ostrov

Novorzhev

Kholm

Pushkinskiye Gory

to Königsberg

Opochka

to Sebezh

to Vitebsk

*The partisan war . . . . has some advantage for us;
it enables us to eradicate everyone who opposes us*
HITLER 6 JULY 1941

*The bands in the East have become an unbearable
menace during the last few months, and are serious-
ly threatening the supply lines to the front*
HITLER 6 SEPT 1942

0   25
Miles

- - -   The front line in December 1941

German headquarters

+++++   Strategic railways, constantly sabotaged

Strategic roads, frequently under
partisan attack

Areas controlled by Soviet partisans,
and the general direction of their
anti-German operations

The Germans in the Leningrad region, like those
throughout the occupied areas, were subjected to
continual sabotage by partisan bands operating
behind the front line. Despite harsh German
reprisals against hundreds of villages, and mass
executions of women, children and old men,
partisan activity grew more effective with each
month of the war

127

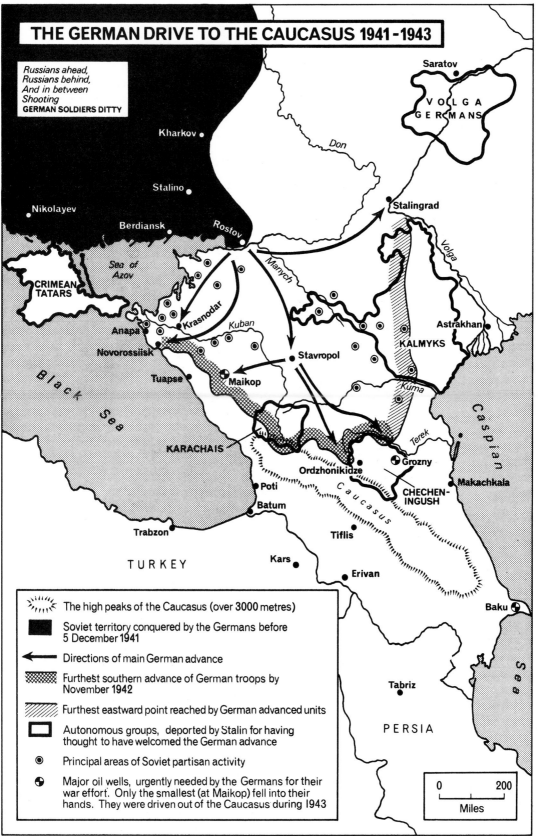

THE GERMAN DRIVE TO THE CAUCASUS 1941-1943

Russians ahead,
Russians behind,
And in between
Shooting
GERMAN SOLDIERS DITTY

Saratov

VOLGA GERMANS

Kharkov

Don

Stalino

Nikolayev

Berdiansk

Rostov

Stalingrad

Sea of Azov

Manych

Volga

CRIMEAN TATARS

Krasnodar

Kuban

Astrakhan

Anapa

KALMYKS

Novorossiisk

Stavropol

Kuma

Tuapse

Maikop

Black Sea

KARACHAIS

Terek

Grozny

Poti

Ordzhonikidze

Batum

CHECHEN-INGUSH

Makachkala

Trabzon

Caucasus

Tiflis

Caspian Sea

TURKEY

Kars

Erivan

Baku

Legend:

- ⌇⌇⌇ The high peaks of the Caucasus (over 3000 metres)
- ◼ Soviet territory conquered by the Germans before 5 December 1941
- ← Directions of main German advance
- ▨ Furthest southern advance of German troops by November 1942
- ⧅ Furthest eastward point reached by German advanced units
- ▭ Autonomous groups, deported by Stalin for having thought to have welcomed the German advance
- ◉ Principal areas of Soviet partisan activity
- ⊕ Major oil wells, urgently needed by the Germans for their war effort. Only the smallest (at Maikop) fell into their hands. They were driven out of the Caucasus during 1943

Tabriz

PERSIA

0   200
Miles

128

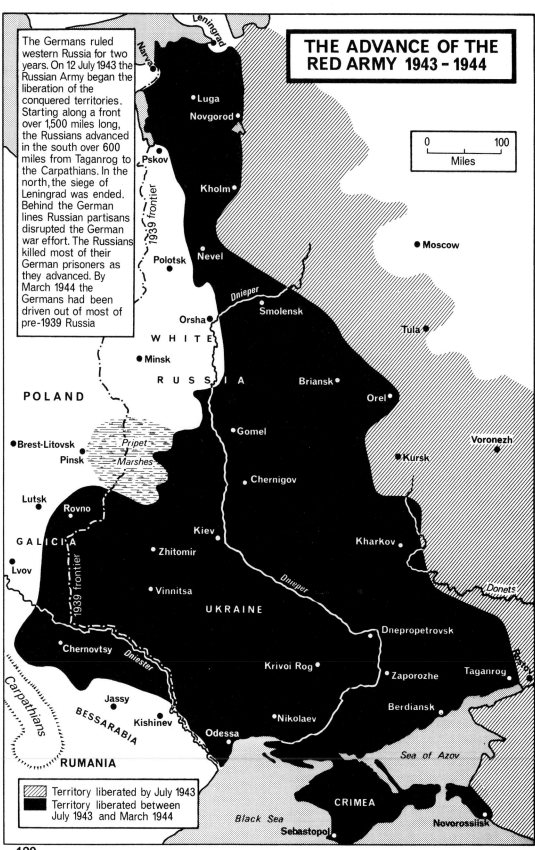

THE ADVANCE OF THE RED ARMY 1943 – 1944

The Germans ruled western Russia for two years. On 12 July 1943 the Russian Army began the liberation of the conquered territories. Starting along a front over 1,500 miles long, the Russians advanced in the south over 600 miles from Taganrog to the Carpathians. In the north, the siege of Leningrad was ended. Behind the German lines Russian partisans disrupted the German war effort. The Russians killed most of their German prisoners as they advanced. By March 1944 the Germans had been driven out of most of pre-1939 Russia

0   100
Miles

Leningrad

Narva

• Luga
Novgorod •

Pskov

1939 frontier

Kholm •

Nevel

• Moscow

Polotsk •

Dnieper

Orsha •

Smolensk

Tula •

WHITE

• Minsk

R U S S I A

Briansk •

POLAND

Orel •

• Gomel

Voronezh •

• Brest-Litovsk
Pinsk •

Pripet
Marshes

Chernigov •

• Kursk

Lutsk •

• Rovno

G A L I C I A

Kiev •

Kharkov •

Lvov •

• Zhitomir

1939 frontier

• Vinnitsa

Dnieper

U K R A I N E

Donets

Dnepropetrovsk •

• Chernovtsy

Dniester

Krivoi Rog •

• Zaporozhe

Taganrog

Don

Carpathians

Jassy •

BESSARABIA

Kishinev •

• Nikolaev

Berdiansk •

Odessa •

RUMANIA

Sea of Azov

Territory liberated by July 1943
Territory liberated between
July 1943 and March 1944

CRIMEA

Black Sea

Novorossiisk •

Sebastopol •

129

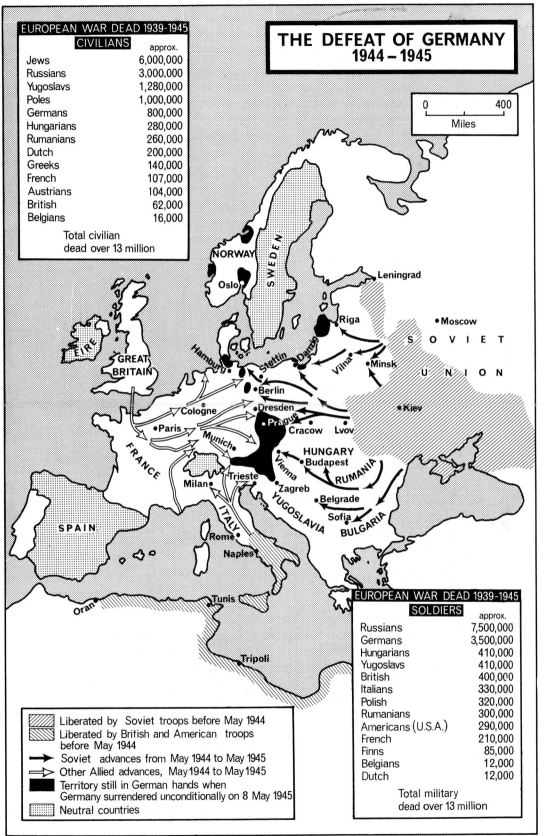

THE DEFEAT OF GERMANY 1944–1945

EUROPEAN WAR DEAD 1939-1945

CIVILIANS approx.

Jews	6,000,000
Russians	3,000,000
Yugoslavs	1,280,000
Poles	1,000,000
Germans	800,000
Hungarians	280,000
Rumanians	260,000
Dutch	200,000
Greeks	140,000
French	107,000
Austrians	104,000
British	62,000
Belgians	16,000

Total civilian
dead over 13 million

0   400
Miles

EUROPEAN WAR DEAD 1939-1945

SOLDIERS approx.

Russians	7,500,000
Germans	3,500,000
Hungarians	410,000
Yugoslavs	410,000
British	400,000
Italians	330,000
Polish	320,000
Rumanians	300,000
Americans (U.S.A.)	290,000
French	210,000
Finns	85,000
Belgians	12,000
Dutch	12,000

Total military
dead over 13 million

Liberated by Soviet troops before May 1944
Liberated by British and American troops before May 1944
Soviet advances from May 1944 to May 1945
Other Allied advances, May 1944 to May 1945
Territory still in German hands when Germany surrendered unconditionally on 8 May 1945
Neutral countries

NORWAY · Oslo · SWEDEN · Leningrad · Moscow · Riga · SOVIET UNION · Hamburg · Stettin · Danzig · Vilna · Minsk · EIRE · GREAT BRITAIN · Berlin · Dresden · Kiev · Cologne · Prague · Paris · Cracow · Lvov · Munich · HUNGARY · Budapest · FRANCE · Vienna · RUMANIA · Trieste · Milan · Zagreb · ITALY · YUGOSLAVIA · Belgrade · SPAIN · Sofia · BULGARIA · Rome · Naples · Oran · Tunis · Tripoli

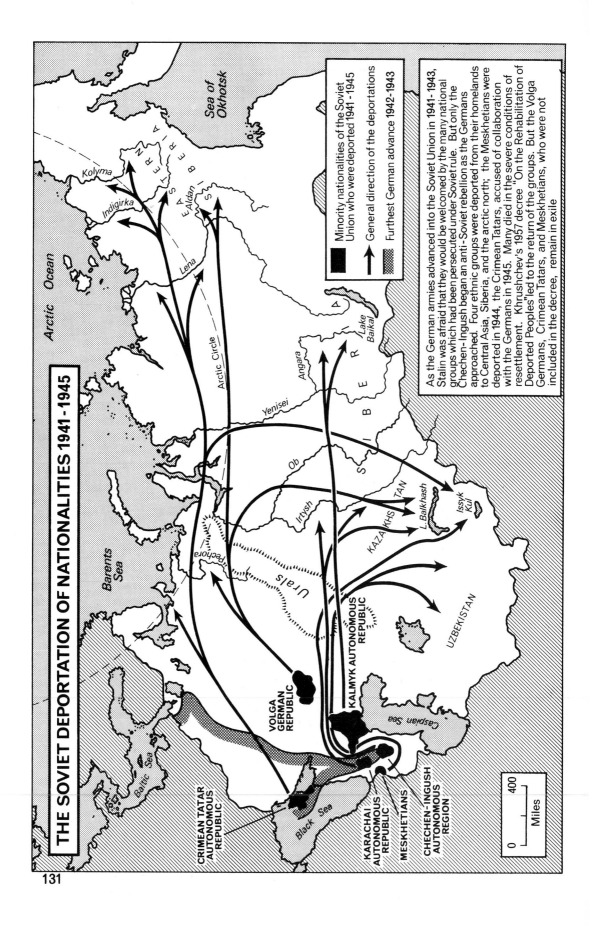

THE SOVIET DEPORTATION OF NATIONALITIES 1941 - 1945

Sea of Okhotsk

EASTERN SIBERIA

Kolyma

Indigirka

Lena

Aldan

Arctic Circle

Arctic Ocean

Barents Sea

Baltic Sea

Black Sea

Caspian Sea

Pechora

Urals

Ob

Irtysh

Yenisei

Angara

Lake Baikal

SIBERIA

KAZAKHS TAN

L. Balkhash

Issyk Kul

UZBEKISTAN

VOLGA GERMAN REPUBLIC

KALMYK AUTONOMOUS REPUBLIC

CRIMEAN TATAR AUTONOMOUS REPUBLIC

KARACHAI AUTONOMOUS REPUBLIC

MESKHETIANS

CHECHEN-INGUSH AUTONOMOUS REGION

Minority nationalities of the Soviet Union who were deported 1941 - 1945

General direction of the deportations

Furthest German advance 1942-1943

As the German armies advanced into the Soviet Union in 1941-1943, Stalin was afraid that they would be welcomed by the many national groups which had been persecuted under Soviet rule. But only the Chechen-Ingush began an anti-Soviet rebellion as the Germans approached. Four ethnic groups were deported from their homelands to Central Asia, Siberia, and the arctic north; the Meskhetians were deported in 1944, the Crimean Tatars, accused of collaboration with the Germans in 1945. Many died in the severe conditions of resettlement. Khrushchev's 1957 decree "On the Rehabilitation of Deported Peoples" led to the return of the groups. But the Volga Germans, Crimean Tatars, and Meskhetians, who were not included in the decree, remain in exile

0   400

Miles

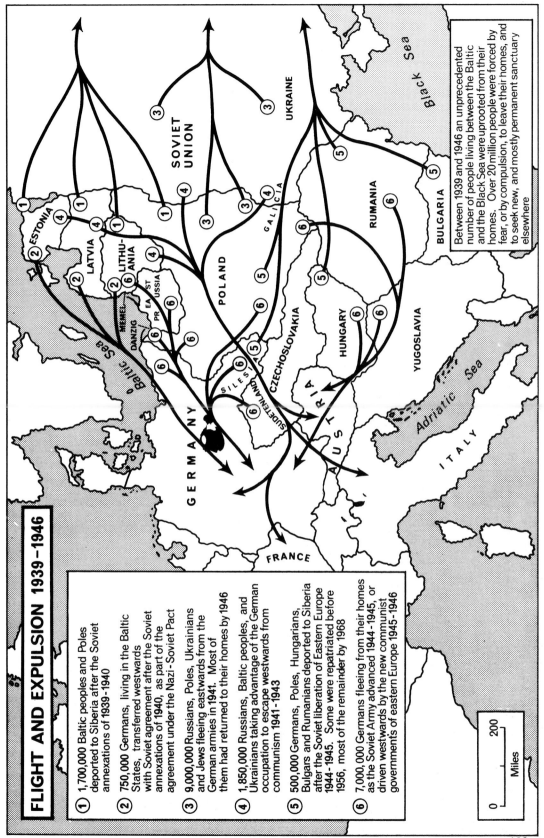

FLIGHT AND EXPULSION 1939–1946

① 1,700,000 Baltic peoples and Poles deported to Siberia after the Soviet annexations of 1939-1940

② 750,000 Germans, living in the Baltic States, transferred westwards with Soviet agreement after the Soviet annexations of 1940, as part of the agreement under the Nazi-Soviet Pact

③ 9,000,000 Russians, Poles, Ukrainians and Jews fleeing eastwards from the German armies in 1941. Most of them had returned to their homes by 1946

④ 1,850,000 Russians, Baltic peoples, and Ukrainians taking advantage of the German occupation to escape westwards from communism 1941-1943

⑤ 500,000 Germans, Poles, Hungarians, Bulgars and Rumanians deported to Siberia after the Soviet liberation of Eastern Europe 1944-1945. Some were repatriated before 1956, most of the remainder by 1968

⑥ 7,000,000 Germans fleeing from their homes as the Soviet Army advanced 1944-1945, or driven westwards by the new communist governments of eastern Europe 1945-1946

Between 1939 and 1946 an unprecedented number of people living between the Baltic and the Black Sea were uprooted from their homes. Over 20 million people were forced by fear, or by compulsion, to leave their homes, and to seek new, and mostly permanent sanctuary elsewhere

0   200
Miles

THE SOVIET UNION IN EASTERN EUROPE 1945 – 1948

Legend:

- Territory annexed by Russia 1939-1940, and re-incorporated in Russia in 1945
- Former German and Czechoslovak territory annexed by Russia in 1945
- States liberated by the Soviet army, and in which Communist regimes came to power between 1945 and 1948
- Russian occupation zones in Austria (evacuated 1950) and Germany
- British, French and American occupation zones
- The 'Iron Curtain' in 1948

FINLAND

North Sea

SWEDEN

Baltic Sea

Vyborg

Leningrad

Reval

ESTONIA

Pskov

Riga

LATVIA

Memel

LITHUANIA

Königsberg

Kovno

Vilna

EAST

PRUSSIA

Minsk

Bremen

Stettin

annexed by Poland from Germany

Bialystok

S O V I E T

Berlin

Posnan

Warsaw

Pinsk

G E R M A N Y

Erfurt

POLAND

U N I O N

Bonn

Dresden

SILESIA

Breslau

Nuremburg

Cracow

GALICIA

Lvov

Prague

Przemysl

Chernovtsy

FRANCE

CZECHOSLOVAKIA

Uzhgorod

Jassy

Kishinev

Munich

Vienna

BESSARABIA

A U S T R I A

Budapest

SWITZ.

HUNGARY

Trieste

RUMANIA

ITALY

Belgrade

Bucharest

YUGOSLAVIA

Adriatic Sea

Black Sea

Sofia

BULGARIA

ALBANIA

Tirana

GREECE

Ægean Sea

TURKEY

The Russian liberation of Eastern Europe was quickly followed by the establishment of communist regimes, and an 'Iron Curtain' from the Baltic to the Adriatic. Communist rule brought national subservience to Russian policy, and the subordination of personal liberty. The cities of Berlin and Vienna were divided into Russian, British, French and American sectors

0   200
Miles

THE SOVIET UNION IN EASTERN EUROPE 1949-1968

0 — 200 Miles

FINLAND

Vyborg
Leningrad

Tallin
(Reval)

SWEDEN

North Sea

Baltic Sea

Riga

Klaypeda
(Memel)

Kaliningrad

SOVIET

UNION

Rostock
Gdansk

East Berlin
Szczecin

EAST GERMANY
Posnan

Warsaw

POLAND

Halle
Lodz

Dresden
Wroclaw
Lublin

Kiev

WEST GERMANY
Prague
CZECHOSLOVAKIA
Cracow

Przemysl

Lvov

FRANCE
Brno
Kosice

Bratislava

SWITZ.
AUSTRIA
Debrecen

Györ
Budapest

HUNGARY
Jassy

Cluj

Odessa

Zagreb
Pécs

RUMANIA

Rijeka
Arad

Adriatic Sea

YUGOSLAVIA
Constanza

Belgrade
Bucharest

ITALY
Split
Nish

Varna

Kotor
BULGARIA
Black Sea

ALBANIA
Sofia
Burgas

Tirana

Durres
TURKEY

Vlone

GREECE
Aegean Sea

— Frontiers of communist states since 1945

▨ Only European communist state entirely free from Soviet direction of foreign, economic and domestic policy since 1949

▧ Only communist state within the Soviet bloc pursuing a relatively independent foreign policy since 1968

▨ Only communist state in Europe aligned with China and refusing all contact with the Soviet Union since 1961

☐ Only European communist state to accept Soviet guidance with equanimity

■ Principal areas of anti-Soviet protest and revolt 1953-1968, crushed by Soviet military intervention (East Germany, Hungary, Czechoslovakia) and by strong political pressure (Poland)

134

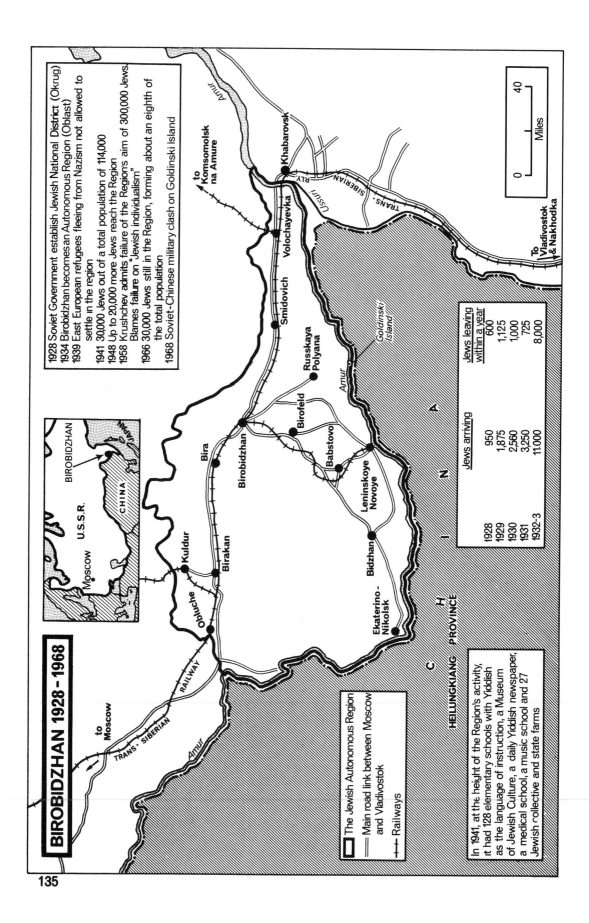

BIROBIDZHAN 1928 – 1968

1928 Soviet Government establish Jewish National District (Okrug)
1934 Birobidzhan becomes an Autonomous Region (Oblast)
1939 East European refugees fleeing from Nazism not allowed to settle in the region
1941 30,000 Jews out of a total population of 114,000
1948 Up to 20,000 more Jews reach the Region
1958 Krushchev admits failure of the Region's aim of 300,000 Jews. Blames failure on "Jewish individualism"
1966 30,000 Jews still in the Region, forming about an eighth of the total population
1968 Soviet-Chinese military clash on Goldinski Island

BIROBIDZHAN
MOSCOW
U.S.S.R.
CHINA

to Moscow
TRANS - SIBERIAN   RAILWAY
Amur

Kuldur
Bira
Birakan
Obluche
Birobidzhan
Birofeld
Russkaya Polyana
Babstovo
Leninskoye Novoye
Bidzhan
Ekaterino - Nikolsk

Smidovich
Volochayevka
to Komsomolsk na Amure
Khabarovsk
Amur
TRANS - SIBERIAN   RLY.
USSURI

Goldinski Island

C   H   I   N   A

HEILUNGKIANG   PROVINCE

To Vladivostok & Nakhodka

	Jews arriving	Jews leaving within a year
1928	950	600
1929	1,875	1,125
1930	2,560	1,000
1931	3,250	725
1932-3	11,000	8,000

☐ The Jewish Autonomous Region
═══ Main road link between Moscow and Vladivostok
┼┼┼ Railways

In 1941, at the height of the Region's activity, it had 128 elementary schools with Yiddish as the language of instruction, a Museum of Jewish Culture, a daily Yiddish newspaper, a medical school, a music school and 27 Jewish collective and state farms

0   40
Miles

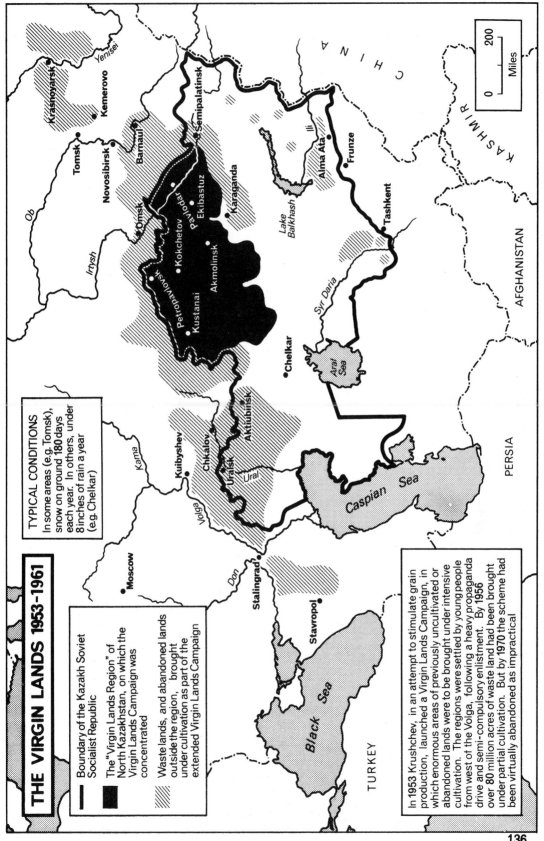

THE VIRGIN LANDS 1953-1961

Boundary of the Kazakh Soviet Socialist Republic

The "Virgin Lands Region" of North Kazakhstan, on which the Virgin Lands Campaign was concentrated

Waste lands, and abandoned lands outside the region, brought under cultivation as part of the extended Virgin Lands Campaign

TYPICAL CONDITIONS
In some areas (e.g. Tomsk), snow on ground 180 days each year. In others, under 8 inches of rain a year (e.g. Chelkar)

In 1953 Krushchev, in an attempt to stimulate grain production, launched a Virgin Lands Campaign, in which enormous areas of previously uncultivated or abandoned lands were to be brought under intensive cultivation. The regions were settled by young people from west of the Volga, following a heavy propaganda drive and semi-compulsory enlistment. By 1956 over 80 million acres of waste land had been brought under partial cultivation. But by 1970 the scheme had been virtually abandoned as impractical

CHINA

KASHMIR

AFGHANISTAN

PERSIA

TURKEY

Krasnoyarsk

Kemerovo

Tomsk

Novosibirsk

Barnaul

Semipalatinsk

Omsk

Ekibastuz

Pavlodar

Kokchetov

Karaganda

Akmolinsk

Petropavlovsk

Kustanai

Alma Ata

Frunze

Tashkent

Lake Balkhash

Chelkar

Aral Sea

Kuibyshev

Chkalov

Aktiubinsk

Uralsk

Moscow

Stalingrad

Stavropol

Caspian Sea

Black Sea

Yenisei

Ob

Irtysh

Ili

Syr Daria

Kama

Ural

Volga

Don

0   200
Miles

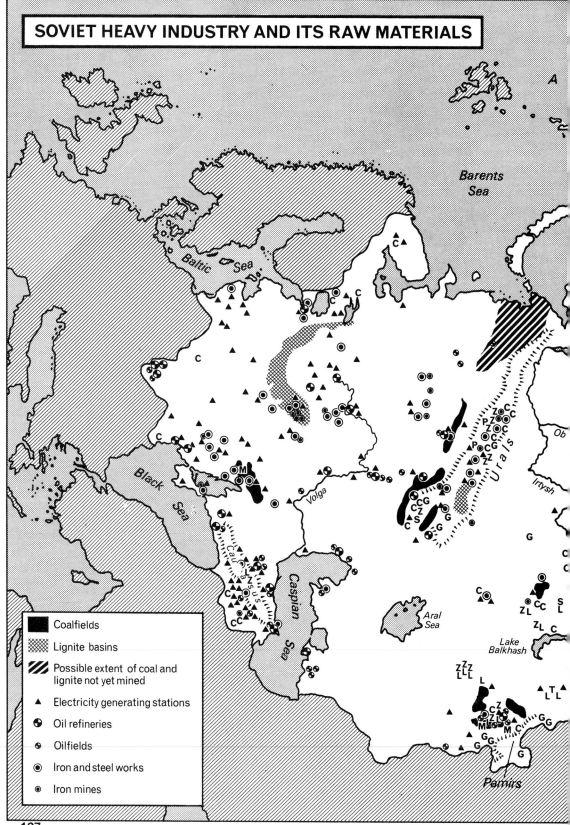

SOVIET HEAVY INDUSTRY AND ITS RAW MATERIALS

Barents Sea

Baltic Sea

Black Sea

Caspian Sea

Aral Sea

Lake Balkhash

Volga

Urals

Ob

Irtysh

Caucasus

Pemirs

Coalfields

Lignite basins

Possible extent of coal and lignite not yet mined

▲ Electricity generating stations

Oil refineries

Oilfields

Iron and steel works

Iron mines

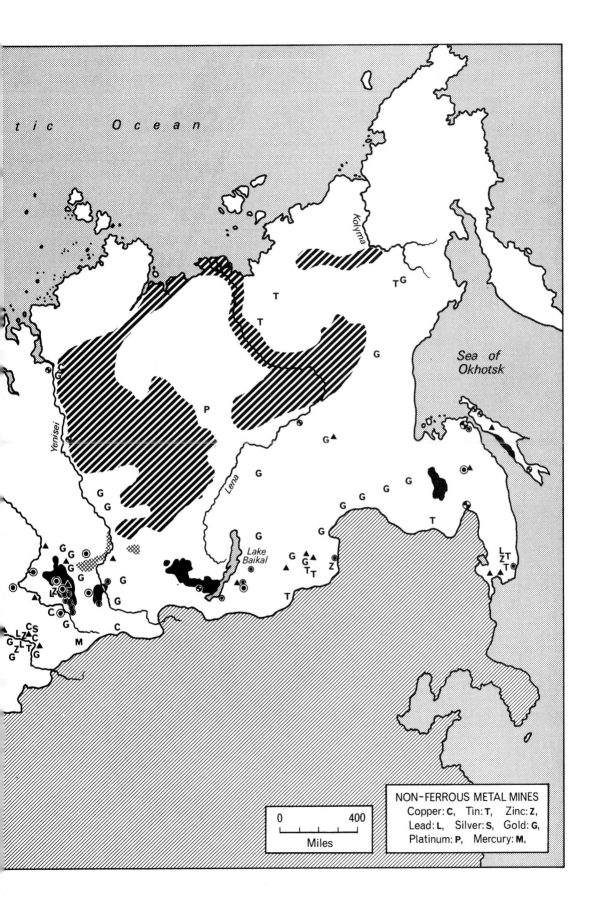

tic   O c e a n

Kolyma

Sea of
Okhotsk

T G

T

T

G

G

P

Yenisei

Lena

G

G

G

G G G

Lake
Baikal

G

G

T

G

G G ▲
G
T T

Z

T

T

G G
G ▲
G G
G
C
G

C

M

L Z
G Z L T
G

C S
▲ C
▲

L Z T
Z T

0   400
Miles

NON-FERROUS METAL MINES
Copper: **C**, Tin: **T**,   Zinc: **Z**,
Lead: **L**, Silver: **S**, Gold: **G**,
Platinum: **P**, Mercury: **M**,

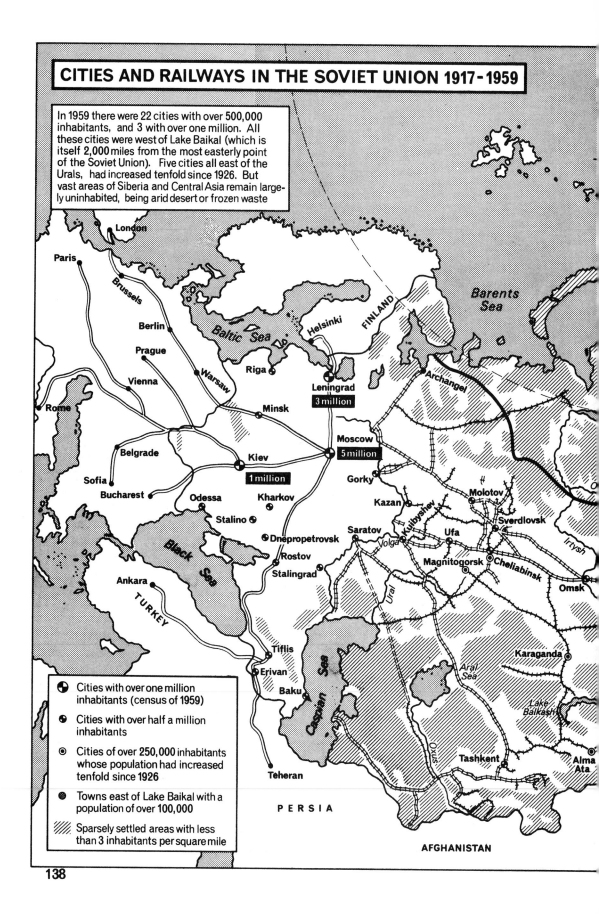

CITIES AND RAILWAYS IN THE SOVIET UNION 1917-1959

In 1959 there were 22 cities with over 500,000 inhabitants, and 3 with over one million. All these cities were west of Lake Baikal (which is itself 2,000 miles from the most easterly point of the Soviet Union). Five cities all east of the Urals, had increased tenfold since 1926. But vast areas of Siberia and Central Asia remain largely uninhabited, being arid desert or frozen waste

London

Paris

Brussels

Berlin

Prague

Vienna

Warsaw

Riga

Helsinki

FINLAND

Barents Sea

Baltic Sea

Leningrad
3 million

Archangel

Rome

Minsk

Belgrade

Kiev
1 million

Moscow
5 million

Gorky

Molotov

Sofia

Bucharest

Odessa

Kharkov

Kazan

Kuibyshev

Sverdlovsk

Stalino

Dnepropetrovsk

Saratov

Ufa

Magnitogorsk

Cheliabinsk

Irtysh

Rostov

Stalingrad

Volga

Ural

Omsk

Ankara

TURKEY

Black Sea

Karaganda

Aral Sea

Lake Balkash

Tiflis

Caspian Sea

Erivan

Baku

Oxus

Tashkent

Alma Ata

Teheran

PERSIA

AFGHANISTAN

Legend:

- ⊕ Cities with over one million inhabitants (census of 1959)
- ◓ Cities with over half a million inhabitants
- ◉ Cities of over 250,000 inhabitants whose population had increased tenfold since 1926
- ● Towns east of Lake Baikal with a population of over 100,000
- ⫽⫽ Sparsely settled areas with less than 3 inhabitants per square mile

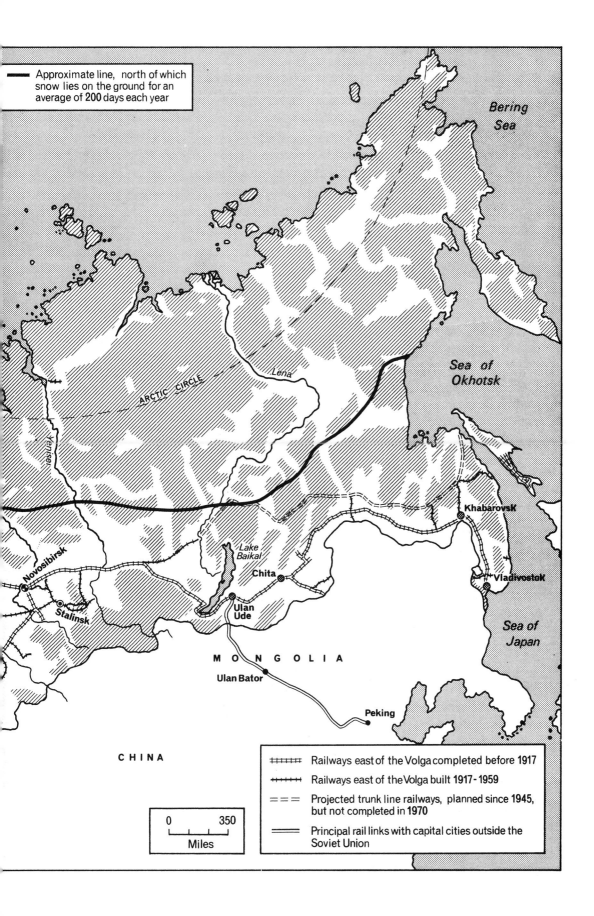

Approximate line, north of which snow lies on the ground for an average of **200** days each year

Bering Sea

Sea of Okhotsk

ARCTIC CIRCLE

Lena

Yenisei

Khabarovsk

Novosibirsk

Lake Baikal

Chita

Stalinsk

Ulan Ude

Vladivostok

Sea of Japan

M O N G O L I A

Ulan Bator

Peking

C H I N A

0   350
Miles

┼┼┼┼┼ Railways east of the Volga completed before **1917**

┼┼┼┼┼ Railways east of the Volga built **1917-1959**

=== Projected trunk line railways, planned since **1945**, but not completed in **1970**

═══ Principal rail links with capital cities outside the Soviet Union

THE CHANGING NAMES OF SOVIET CITIES 1917-1961

● Petrograd
Leningrad

● Königsberg
Kaliningrad

Tver
Kalinin ●

Viatka
Kirov

Nizhnii-Novgorod
Gorky ●

Volga

Bobriki ●
Stalinogorsk

Stavropol
Toliatti ●

Pokrovsk
Engels ●

Ekaterin-enstadt ●
Marx

Elizavetgrad ●
Kirovo

Yuzovo
Stalino ●

Lugansk ●
Voroshilov

Chistiakovo
Torez ●

Tsaritsyn
Stalingrad ●

Mariupol ●
Zhdanov

Don

Ekaterinodar
Krasnodar ●

Stavropol
Voroshilovsk ●

Black Sea

Caspian Sea

Vladikavkaz ●
Ordzhonikidze

Alexandropol ●
Leninakan

Elizavetpol ●
Kirovabad

Between **1930** and his death in **1953** Stalin
was commemorated in over a thousand place
names including: Stalina, Stalino, Stalinsk,
Stalinskii, Stalinskaya, Stalinskoye,
Stalinogorsk, Stalingrad and Stalinabad.
Since **1953** all have been renamed; the last
two as Dushanbe and Volgograd

●   Towns founded before 1917, which changed
their names after 1917

▬   New names chosen since 1917 (some have already
reverted to their original name e.g. Perm)

139

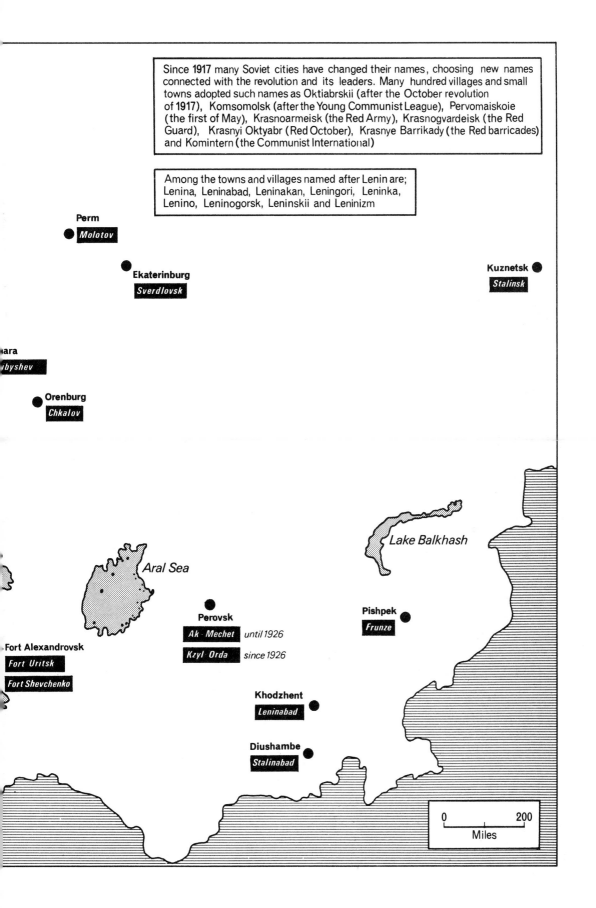

Since 1917 many Soviet cities have changed their names, choosing new names connected with the revolution and its leaders. Many hundred villages and small towns adopted such names as Oktiabrskii (after the October revolution of 1917), Komsomolsk (after the Young Communist League), Pervomaiskoie (the first of May), Krasnoarmeisk (the Red Army), Krasnogvardeisk (the Red Guard), Krasnyi Oktyabr (Red October), Krasnye Barrikady (the Red barricades) and Komintern (the Communist International)

Among the towns and villages named after Lenin are; Lenina, Leninabad, Leninakan, Leningori, Leninka, Lenino, Leninogorsk, Leninskii and Leninizm

Perm
Molotov

Ekaterinburg
Sverdlovsk

Kuznetsk
Stalinsk

ara
ibyshev

Orenburg
Chkalov

Lake Balkhash

Aral Sea

Perovsk
Ak - Mechet   until 1926
Kzyl - Orda   since 1926

Pishpek
Frunze

Fort Alexandrovsk
Fort Uritsk
Fort Shevchenko

Khodzhent
Leninabad

Diushambe
Stalinabad

0   200
Miles

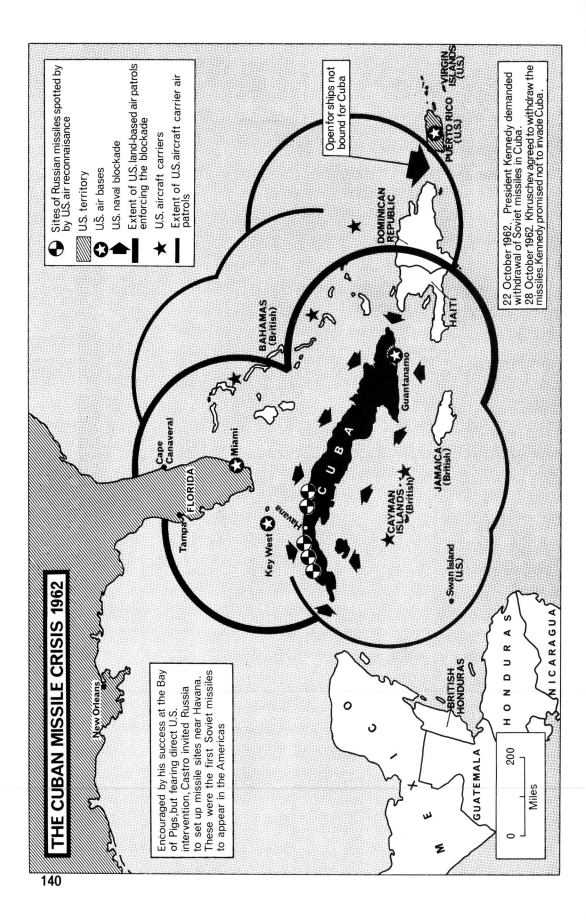

THE CUBAN MISSILE CRISIS 1962

Legend:

⊕ Sites of Russian missiles spotted by U.S. air reconnaissance

▨ U.S. territory

★ U.S. air bases

◆ U.S. naval blockade

▬ Extent of U.S. land-based air patrols enforcing the blockade

★ U.S. aircraft carriers

Extent of U.S. aircraft carrier air patrols

Encouraged by his success at the Bay of Pigs, but fearing direct U.S. intervention, Castro invited Russia to set up missile sites near Havana. These were the first Soviet missiles to appear in the Americas

Open for ships not bound for Cuba

22 October 1962. President Kennedy demanded withdrawal of Soviet missiles in Cuba.

28 October 1962. Khruschev agreed to withdraw the missiles. Kennedy promised not to invade Cuba.

New Orleans

FLORIDA

Tampa

Cape Canaveral

Miami

Key West

CUBA

Havana

Guantanamo

BAHAMAS (British)

CAYMAN ISLANDS (British)

JAMAICA (British)

Swan Island (U.S.)

DOMINICAN REPUBLIC

HAITI

PUERTO RICO (U.S.)

VIRGIN ISLANDS (U.S.)

MEXICO

GUATEMALA

BRITISH HONDURAS

HONDURAS

NICARAGUA

0   200

Miles

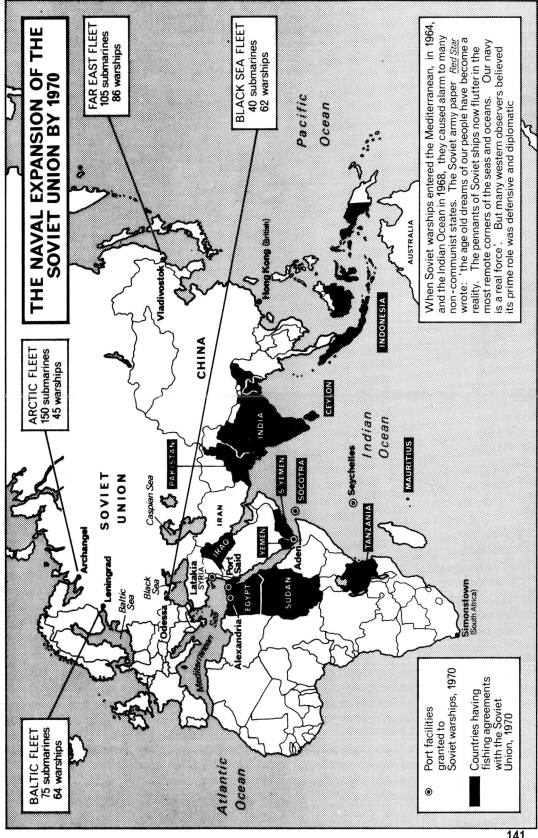

THE NAVAL EXPANSION OF THE SOVIET UNION BY 1970

ARCTIC FLEET
150 submarines
45 warships

BALTIC FLEET
75 submarines
64 warships

FAR EAST FLEET
105 submarines
86 warships

BLACK SEA FLEET
40 submarines
62 warships

When Soviet warships entered the Mediterranean, in 1964, and the Indian Ocean in 1968, they caused alarm to many non-communist states. The Soviet army paper *Red Star* wrote: 'the age old dreams of our people have become a reality. The pennants of Soviet ships now flutter in the most remote corners of the seas and oceans. Our navy is a real force'. But many western observers believed its prime role was defensive and diplomatic

⦿ Port facilities
granted to
Soviet warships, 1970

▉ Countries having
fishing agreements
with the Soviet
Union, 1970

Atlantic Ocean

Pacific Ocean

Indian Ocean

SOVIET UNION

CHINA

INDIA

IRAN

IRAQ

EGYPT

SUDAN

AUSTRALIA

INDONESIA

Vladivostok

Archangel

Leningrad

Baltic Sea

Odessa

Black Sea

Caspian Sea

Latakia
SYRIA

Port Said

Alexandria

Mediterranean

YEMEN

S YEMEN

Aden

SOCOTRA

PAKISTAN

CEYLON

Seychelles

TANZANIA

MAURITIUS

Hong Kong (British)

Simonstown
(South Africa)

141

THE SOVIET UNION AND CHINA 1860-1970

The Chinese Communist Party was founded in 1921. But the Soviet Union preferred to support the Kuomintang under Chiang Kai Shek, to which it gave substantial military aid to establish its power 1923-1927, and to fight the Japanese 1937-1941 (when Stalin formed a Non-Aggression pact with Japan). In 1945 Soviet troops drove the Japanese from Northern China. In 1949 the Chinese Communists came to power. From a policy of considerable Soviet aid to China in the 1950's, the two nations became increasingly hostile. By 1960 the rift was open, and soon led to armed skirmishes on the frontier

TANNU TUVA

1914   Russian protectorate

1921   Independent "Peoples' Republic" allied with the Soviet Union

1944   Annexed by the Soviet Union

SINKIANG

1760-1920   Chinese

1921-1949   Under Soviet influence and partial occupation

Since 1949   Chinese. Heavily colonized by Chinese settlers

SOVIET UNION

TANNU TUVA

Irkutsk

MONGO

Lake Balkhash

Alma Ata

Tashkent

Urumchi

Hami

Kashgar

SINKIANG

Lop Nor

Yarkand

Khotan

AFGHANISTAN

Kabul

Gilgit

KASHMIR

C H I

PAKISTAN

Lahore

INDIA

TIBET

Lhasa

NEPAL

SIKKIM

BHUTAN

INDIA

INDIA

BURMA

EAST PAKISTAN

Territory annexed by Russia 1858-1860

⊙   Communist Party cells established under Moscow's instructions 1920-1924 and urged to collaborate with the Kuomintang (nationalists)

Soviet air units defending Kuomintang strongholds against Japan 1941

→   Soviet military advances across China in the war against Japan 1945

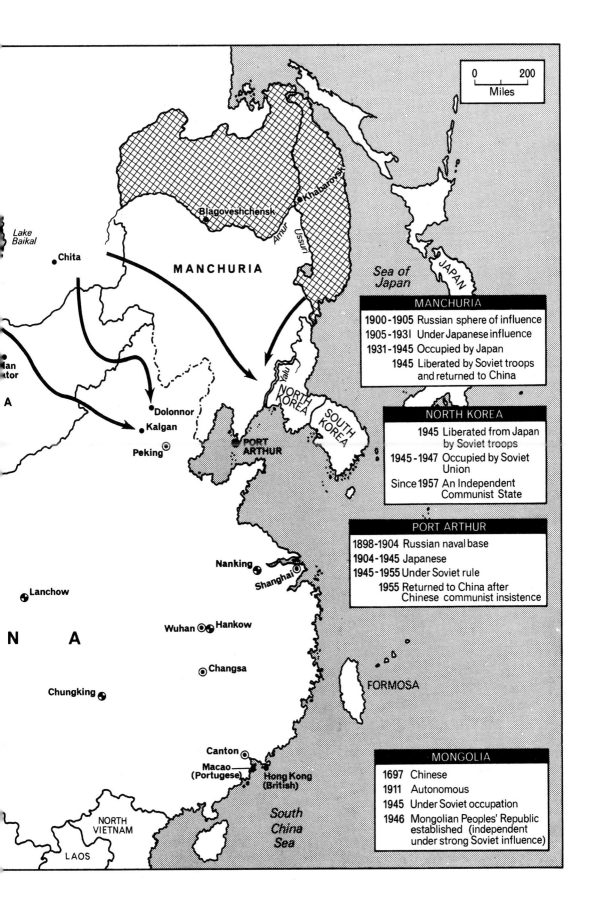

Lake
Baikal

Chita

MANCHURIA

Blagoveshchensk

Khabarovsk

Amur

Ussuri

Sea of
Japan

JAPAN

an
tor

A

Dolonnor

Kalgan

Peking

NORTH
KOREA

SOUTH
KOREA

Yalu

PORT
ARTHUR

Nanking

Shanghai

Lanchow

N   A

Wuhan   Hankow

Changsa

Chungking

FORMOSA

Canton

Macao
(Portugese)

Hong Kong
(British)

NORTH
VIETNAM

LAOS

South
China
Sea

0	200
Miles	

MANCHURIA

1900-1905	Russian sphere of influence
1905-1931	Under Japanese influence
1931-1945	Occupied by Japan
1945	Liberated by Soviet troops and returned to China

NORTH KOREA

1945	Liberated from Japan by Soviet troops
1945-1947	Occupied by Soviet Union
Since 1957	An Independent Communist State

PORT ARTHUR

1898-1904	Russian naval base
1904-1945	Japanese
1945-1955	Under Soviet rule
1955	Returned to China after Chinese communist insistence

MONGOLIA

1697	Chinese
1911	Autonomous
1945	Under Soviet occupation
1946	Mongolian Peoples' Republic established (independent under strong Soviet influence)

THE SOVIET-CHINESE BORDERLANDS 1970

——————	The Soviet-Chinese border
—·—·—	Other international borders
+++++++	Soviet, Mongolian and Chinese railways in the border area
▨	Land over 2000 metres (6562 feet)
⊕	Main airfields

S O V I E T

Caspian Sea

Aral Sea

to Moscow

Omsk

TRANS - SIBERIAN RAILWAY

Novosibirsk ⊕

Achinsk

Karaganda ⊕

Barnaul

Krasnoyarsk ⊕

Rubtsovsk

Biisk

Abakan

Semipalatinsk ⊕

Leninogorsk

Lake Balkash

Aktogai

Lake Zaisan

Lake Markakol

PERSIA

Tashkent ⊕

Lugovoi

Urdzhar

Samarkand

Frunze

Panfilov

L. Alakol

Tahcheng

Ulyungur Nor

Diushambe

R. Nachu

Alma Ata ⊕

Osh

Dzhalal Abad

Issyk Kul

Ebi Nor

Kuldja

M O

AFGHANISTAN

Kashgar

Aksu

Urumchi ⊕

Lop Nor

PAKISTAN

KASHMIR

Lanchow

INDIA

C H I N

0	250

Miles

143

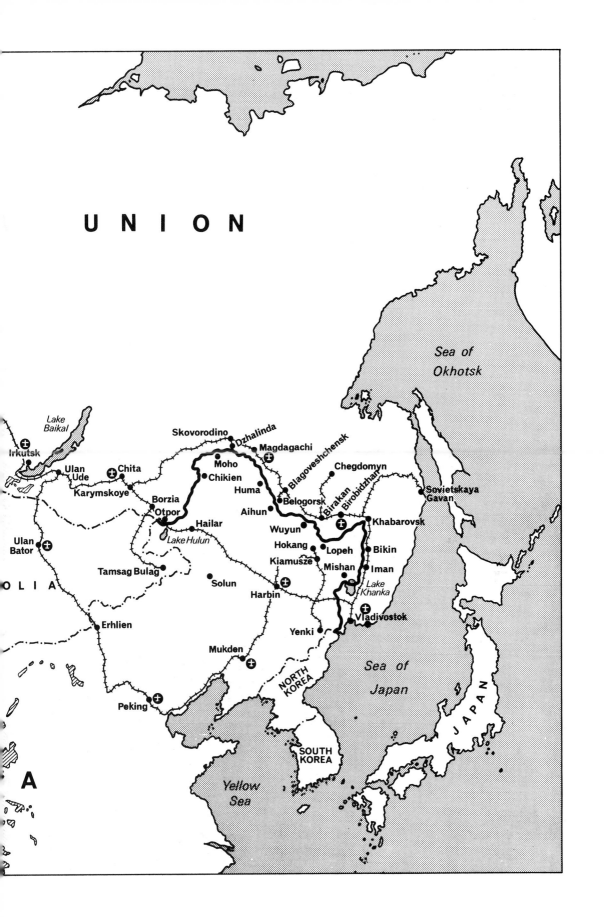

THE REPUBLICS AND AUTONOMOUS REGIONS OF THE SOVIET UNION IN 1970

North Sea

Arctic

LATVIAN S.S.R.

ESTONIA S.S.R.

North Cape

Baltic Sea

Karelian A.S.S.R.

LITHUANIA S.S.R.

Nenets N.O.

Part of the RSFSR

BELORUSSIAN S.S.R.

Komi A.S.S.R.

R U S S I A N

UKRAINIAN S.S.R.

Moscow

Yamal Nenets N.O.

Mary A.S.S.R.

Chuvash A.S.S.R.

Komi-Permyak N.O.

MOLDAVIAN S.S.R.

Khanty-Mansi N.O.

Mordovian A.S.S.R.

Udmurt A.S.S.R.

Black Sea

Tatar A.S.S.R.

S O V I E T

Bashkir A.S.S.R.

Adyge A.O.

Abkhaz A.S.S.R.
N.Ossetian A.O.
S.Ossetian A.O.

Cherkess A.O.

Dagestan A.S.S.R.

Adzhar A.S.S.R.

Kara-Kalpak A.S.S.R.

GEORGIAN S.S.R.

Caspian Sea

ARMENIAN S.S.R.

Nakhichevan A.S.S.R.

AZERBAIDZAN S.S.R.

Nagorno-Karabakh A.O.

KIRGIZ S.S.R.

TURKMEN S.S.R.

Gorno-Badakhshan A

0   400
Miles

UZBEK S.S.R.

TADZHIK S.S.R.

144

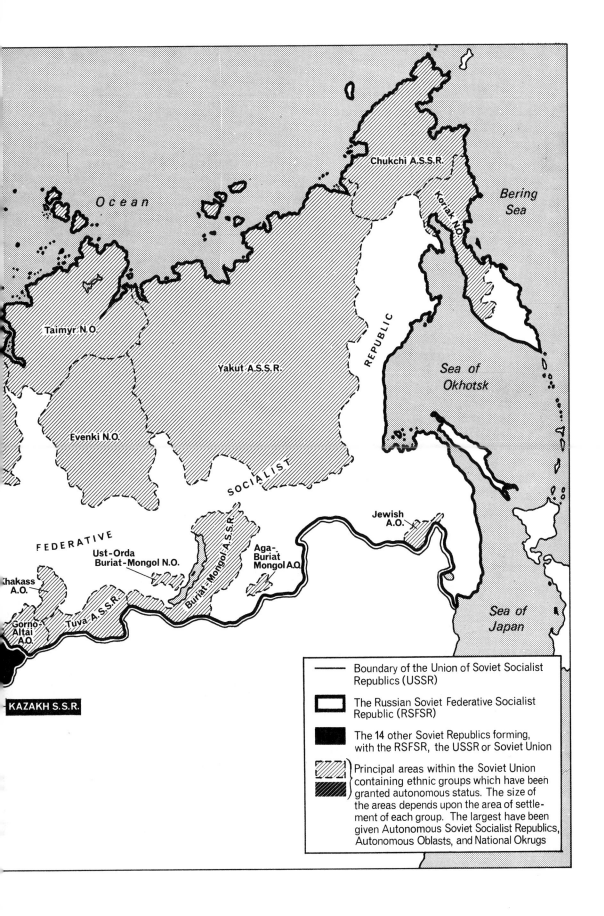

O c e a n

Bering
Sea

Chukchi A.S.S.R.

Korak N.O.

Taimyr N.O.

REPUBLIC

Sea of
Okhotsk

Yakut A.S.S.R.

Evenki N.O.

S O C I A L I S T

Jewish
A.O.

F E D E R A T I V E

Ust-Orda
Buriat-Mongol N.O.

Buriat-Mongol A.S.S.R.

Aga-
Buriat
Mongol A.O.

Khakass
A.O.

Tuva A.S.S.R.

Sea of
Japan

Gorno-
Altai
A.O.

KAZAKH S.S.R.

———	Boundary of the Union of Soviet Socialist Republics (USSR)
☐	The Russian Soviet Federative Socialist Republic (RSFSR)
■	The **14** other Soviet Republics forming, with the RSFSR, the USSR or Soviet Union
▨ ▧	Principal areas within the Soviet Union containing ethnic groups which have been granted autonomous status. The size of the areas depends upon the area of settlement of each group. The largest have been given Autonomous Soviet Socialist Republics, Autonomous Oblasts, and National Okrugs

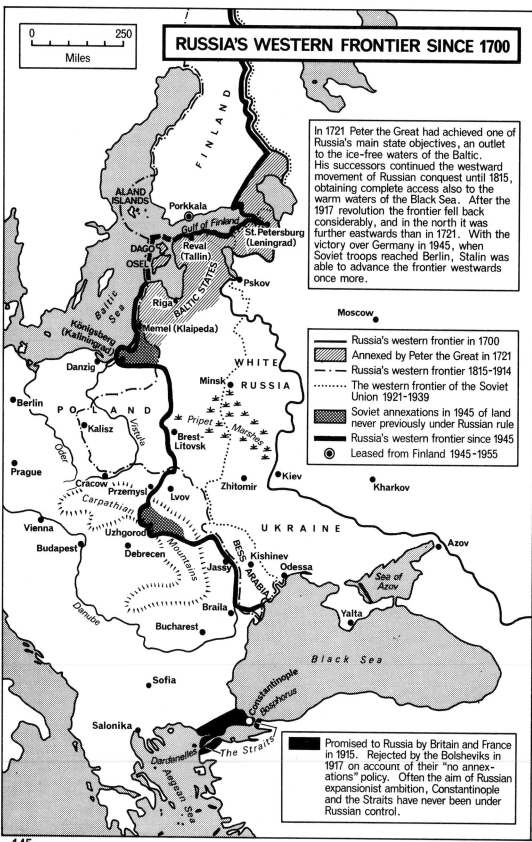

RUSSIA'S WESTERN FRONTIER SINCE 1700

In 1721 Peter the Great had achieved one of Russia's main state objectives, an outlet to the ice-free waters of the Baltic. His successors continued the westward movement of Russian conquest until 1815, obtaining complete access also to the warm waters of the Black Sea. After the 1917 revolution the frontier fell back considerably, and in the north it was further eastwards than in 1721. With the victory over Germany in 1945, when Soviet troops reached Berlin, Stalin was able to advance the frontier westwards once more.

Russia's western frontier in 1700

Annexed by Peter the Great in 1721

Russia's western frontier 1815-1914

The western frontier of the Soviet Union 1921-1939

Soviet annexations in 1945 of land never previously under Russian rule

Russia's western frontier since 1945

Leased from Finland 1945-1955

Promised to Russia by Britain and France in 1915. Rejected by the Bolsheviks in 1917 on account of their "no annexations" policy. Often the aim of Russian expansionist ambition, Constantinople and the Straits have never been under Russian control.

145

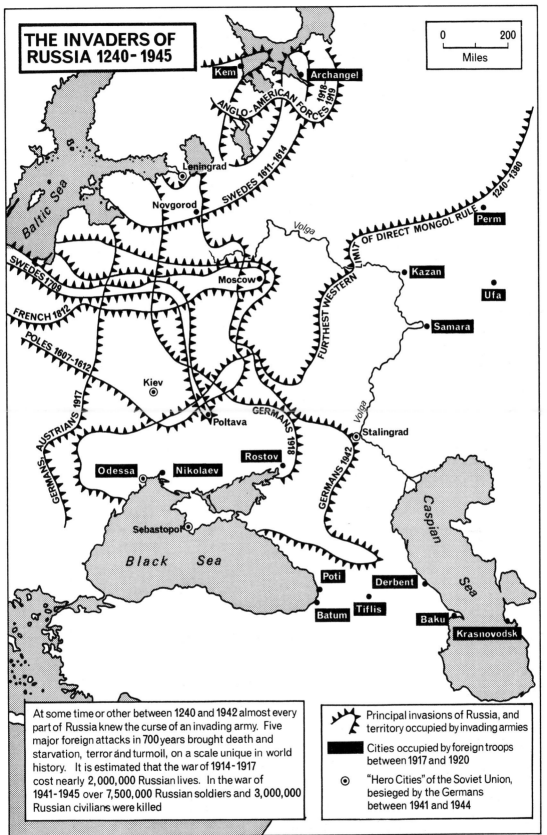

THE INVADERS OF RUSSIA 1240-1945

0 ——— 200
Miles

Kem

Archangel
1918-1919

ANGLO-AMERICAN FORCES

Leningrad

SWEDES 1611-1614

Novgorod

Baltic Sea

Volga

1240-1380

LIMIT OF DIRECT MONGOL RULE

Perm

Kazan

Ufa

SWEDES 1709

Moscow

FURTHEST WESTERN

Samara

FRENCH 1812

POLES 1607-1612

Kiev

AUSTRIANS 1917

GERMANS

Poltava

GERMANS 1918

Volga

Stalingrad

GERMANS 1942

Rostov

Odessa

Nikolaev

Caspian Sea

Sebastopol

Black Sea

Poti

Derbent

Batum

Tiflis

Baku

Krasnovodsk

At some time or other between 1240 and 1942 almost every
part of Russia knew the curse of an invading army. Five
major foreign attacks in 700 years brought death and
starvation, terror and turmoil, on a scale unique in world
history. It is estimated that the war of 1914-1917
cost nearly 2,000,000 Russian lives. In the war of
1941-1945 over 7,500,000 Russian soldiers and 3,000,000
Russian civilians were killed

Principal invasions of Russia, and
territory occupied by invading armies

Cities occupied by foreign troops
between 1917 and 1920

⊙ "Hero Cities" of the Soviet Union,
besieged by the Germans
between 1941 and 1944

GREAT POWER CONFRONTATION AND CONCILIATION, 1972-1986

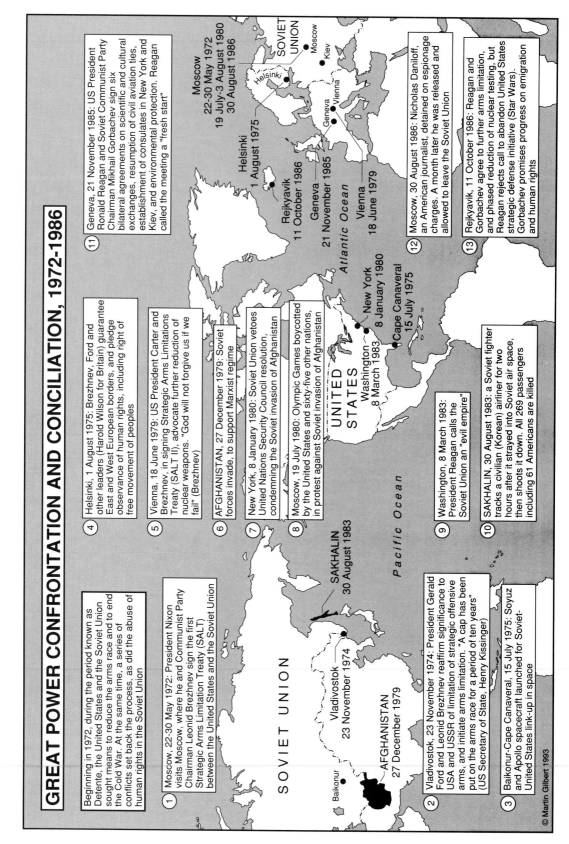

Beginning in 1972, during the period known as Detente, the United States and the Soviet Union sought means to reduce the arms race and to end the Cold War. At the same time, a series of conflicts set back the process, as did the abuse of human rights in the Soviet Union

1. Moscow, 22-30 May 1972: President Nixon visits Moscow, where he and Communist Party Chairman Leonid Brezhnev sign the first Strategic Arms Limitation Treaty (SALT) between the United States and the Soviet Union

2. Vladivostok, 23 November 1974: President Gerald Ford and Leonid Brezhnev reaffirm significance to USA and USSR of limitation of strategic offensive arms, and initiate arms limitation. "A cap has been put on the arms race for a period of ten years" (US Secretary of State, Henry Kissinger)

3. Baikonur-Cape Canaveral, 15 July 1975: Soyuz and Apollo spacecraft launched for Soviet-United States link-up in space

4. Helsinki, 1 August 1975: Brezhnev, Ford and other leaders (Harold Wilson for Britain) guarantee East and West European borders, and pledge observance of human rights, including right of free movement of peoples

5. Vienna, 18 June 1979: US President Carter and Brezhnev, in signing Strategic Arms Limitations Treaty (SALT II), advocate further reduction of nuclear weapons. "God will not forgive us if we fail" (Brezhnev)

6. AFGHANISTAN, 27 December 1979: Soviet forces invade, to support Marxist regime

7. New York, 8 January 1980: Soviet Union vetoes United Nations Security Council resolution, condemning the Soviet invasion of Afghanistan

8. Moscow, 19 July 1980: Olympic Games boycotted by the United States and sixty-five other nations, in protest against Soviet invasion of Afghanistan

9. Washington, 8 March 1983: President Reagan calls the Soviet Union an "evil empire"

10. SAKHALIN, 30 August 1983: a Soviet fighter tracks a civilian (Korean) airliner for two hours after it strayed into Soviet air space, then shoots it down. All 269 passengers including 61 Americans are killed

11. Geneva, 21 November 1985: US President Ronald Reagan and Soviet Communist Party Chairman Mikhail Gorbachev sign six bilateral agreements on scientific and cultural exchanges, resumption of civil aviation ties, establishment of consulates in New York and Kiev, and environmental protection. Reagan called the meeting a "fresh start"

12. Moscow, 30 August 1986: Nicholas Daniloff, an American journalist, detained on espionage charges. A month later he was released and allowed to leave the Soviet Union

13. Reijkyavik, 11 October 1986: Reagan and Gorbachev agree to further arms limitation, and phased reduction of nuclear testing, but Reagan rejects call to abandon United States strategic defense initiative (Star Wars). Gorbachev promises progress on emigration and human rights

SOVIET UNION

UNITED STATES

Atlantic Ocean

Pacific Ocean

Moscow
22-30 May 1972
19 July-3 August 1980
30 August 1986

Helsinki
1 August 1975

Reijkyavik
11 October 1986

Geneva
21 November 1985

Vienna
18 June 1979

New York
8 January 1980

Washington
8 March 1983

Cape Canaveral
15 July 1975

Moscow
Kiev

Helsinki
Geneva
Vienna

SAKHALIN
30 August 1983

Vladivostok
23 November 1974

AFGHANISTAN
27 December 1979

Baikonur

© Martin Gilbert 1993

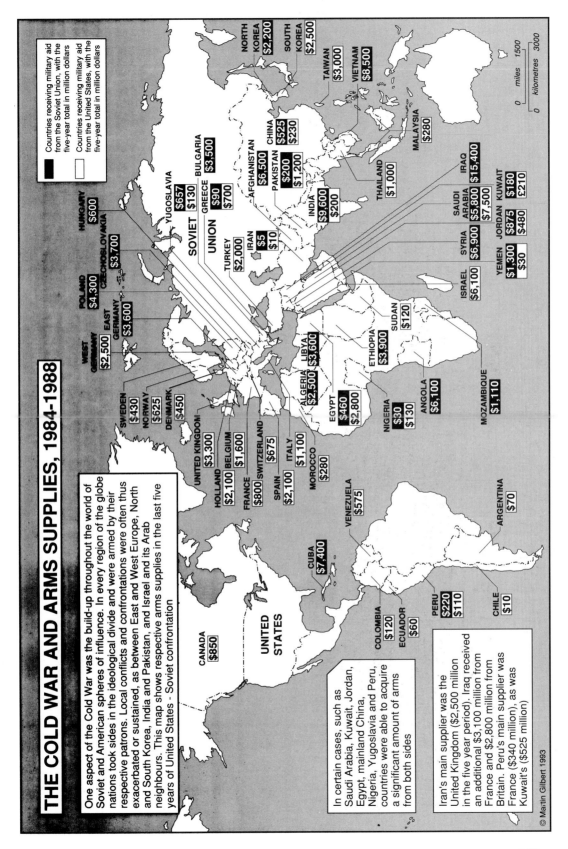

THE COLD WAR AND ARMS SUPPLIES, 1984-1988

One aspect of the Cold War was the build-up throughout the world of Soviet and American spheres of influence. In every region of the globe nations took sides in the ideological divide and were armed by their respective patrons. Local conflicts and confrontations were often thus exacerbated or sustained, as between East and West Europe, North and South Korea, India and Pakistan, and Israel and its Arab neighbours. This map shows respective arms supplies in the last five years of United States - Soviet confrontation

In certain cases, such as Saudi Arabia, Kuwait, Jordan, Egypt, mainland China, Nigeria, Yugoslavia and Peru, countries were able to acquire a significant amount of arms from both sides

Iran's main supplier was the United Kingdom ($2,500 million in the five year period). Iraq received an additional $3,100 million from France and $2,800 million from Britain. Peru's main supplier was France ($340 million), as was Kuwait's ($525 million)

Countries receiving military aid from the Soviet Union, with the five-year total in million dollars

Countries receiving military aid from the United States, with the five-year total in million dollars

0 miles 1500
0 kilometres 3000

CANADA $850

UNITED STATES

CUBA $7,400

COLOMBIA $120
ECUADOR $60
PERU $220 / $110
CHILE $10
VENEZUELA $575
ARGENTINA $70

SWEDEN $430
NORWAY $625
DENMARK $450
UNITED KINGDOM $3,300
HOLLAND $2,100
BELGIUM $1,600
FRANCE $800
SWITZERLAND $675
SPAIN $2,100
ITALY $1,100
MOROCCO $280

WEST GERMANY $2,500
EAST GERMANY $3,600
POLAND $4,300
CZECHOSLOVAKIA $3,700
HUNGARY $600
YUGOSLAVIA $657 / $130
BULGARIA $3,500
GREECE $90
TURKEY $700 / $2,000
IRAN $5 / $10

SOVIET UNION

ALGERIA $2,500
LIBYA $3,600
EGYPT $460 / $2,800
NIGERIA $30 / $130
ANGOLA $6,100
SUDAN $120
ETHIOPIA $3,900
MOZAMBIQUE $1,110

ISRAEL $6,100
SYRIA $6,900
YEMEN $1,300 / $30
JORDAN $875 / $480
SAUDI ARABIA $5,800 / $7,500
KUWAIT $180 / £210
IRAQ $15,400

AFGHANISTAN $6,500
PAKISTAN $200 / $1,200
INDIA $9,600 / $200
CHINA $525 / $230
THAILAND $1,000
MALAYSIA $280

NORTH KOREA $2,200
SOUTH KOREA $2,500
TAIWAN $3,000
VIETNAM $8,500

© Martin Gilbert 1993

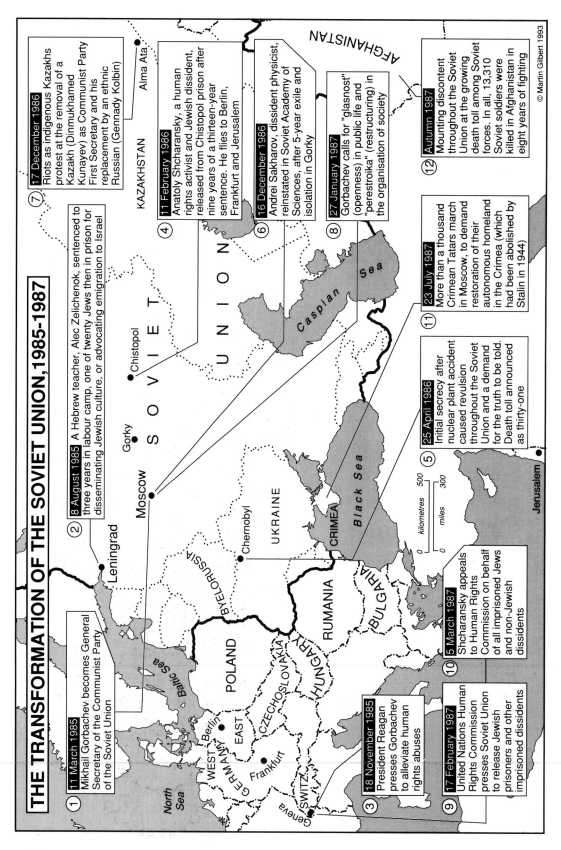

THE TRANSFORMATION OF THE SOVIET UNION, 1985-1987

© Martin Gilbert 1993

① **11 March 1985**
Mikhail Gorbachev becomes General Secretary of the Communist Party of the Soviet Union

② **8 August 1985** A Hebrew teacher, Alec Zelichenok, sentenced to three years in labour camp, one of twenty Jews then in prison for disseminating Jewish culture, or advocating emigration to Israel

③ **18 November 1985**
President Reagan presses Gorbachev to alleviate human rights abuses

④ **11 February 1986**
Anatoly Shcharansky, a human rights activist and Jewish dissident, released from Chistopol prison after nine years of a thirteen-year sentence. He flies to Berlin, Frankfurt and Jerusalem

⑤ **25 April 1986**
Initial secrecy after nuclear plant accident caused revulsion throughout the Soviet Union and a demand for the truth to be told. Death toll announced as thirty-one

⑥ **16 December 1986**
Andrei Sakharov, dissident physicist, reinstated in Soviet Academy of Sciences, after 5-year exile and isolation in Gorky

⑦ **17 December 1986**
Riots as indigenous Kazakhs protest at the removal of a Kazakh (Dinmukhamed Kunayev) as Communist Party First Secretary and his replacement by an ethnic Russian (Gennady Kolbin)

⑧ **27 January 1987**
Gorbachev calls for "glasnost" (openness) in public life and "perestroika" (restructuring) in the organisation of society

⑨ **17 February 1987**
United Nations Human Rights Commission presses Soviet Union to release Jewish prisoners and other imprisoned dissidents

⑩ **5 March 1987**
Shcharansky appeals to Human Rights Commission on behalf of all imprisoned Jews and non-Jewish dissidents

⑪ **23 July 1987**
More than a thousand Crimean Tatars march in Moscow, to demand restoration of their autonomous homeland in the Crimea (which had been abolished by Stalin in 1944)

⑫ **Autumn 1987**
Mounting discontent throughout the Soviet Union at the growing death toll among Soviet forces. In all, 13,310 Soviet soldiers were killed in Afghanistan in eight years of fighting

149

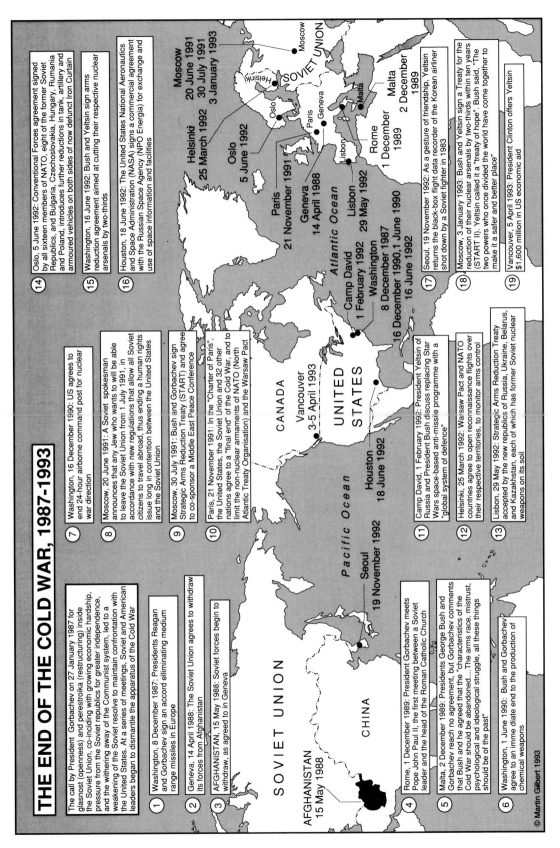

THE END OF THE COLD WAR, 1987-1993

The call by President Gorbachev on 27 January 1987 for glasnost (openness) and perestroika (restructuring) inside the Soviet Union, co-inciding with growing economic hardship, pressure from the Soviet republics for greater independence, and the withering away of the Communist system, led to a weakening of the Soviet resolve to maintain confrontation with the United States. At a series of meetings, Soviet and American leaders resolve to dismantle the apparatus of the Cold War

1. Washington, 8 December 1987: Presidents Reagan and Gorbachev sign an accord elliminating medium range missiles in Europe

2. Geneva, 14 April 1988: The Soviet Union agrees to withdraw its forces from Afghanistan

3. AFGHANISTAN, 15 May 1988: Soviet forces begin to withdraw, as agreed to in Geneva

4. Rome, 1 December 1989: President Gorbachev meets Pope John Paul II, the first meeting between a Soviet leader and the head of the Roman Catholic Church

5. Malta, 2 December 1989: Presidents George Bush and Gorbachev reach no agreement, but Gorbachev comments that Bush and he agreed that the "characteristics of the Cold War should be abandoned....The arms race, mistrust, psychological and ideological struggle, all these things should be of the past"

6. Washington, 1 June 1990: Bush and Gorbachev agree to an imme diate end to the production of chemical weapons

7. Washington, 16 December 1990: US agrees to end 24-hour airborne command post for nuclear war direction

8. Moscow, 20 June 1991: A Soviet spokesman announces that any Jew who wants to will be able to leave the Soviet Union from 1 July 1991, in accordance with new regulations that allow all Soviet citizens to travel abroad, thus ending a human rights issue long in contention between the United States and the Soviet Union

9. Moscow, 30 July 1991: Bush and Gorbachev sign Strategic Arms Reduction Treaty (START) and agree to co-sponsor a Middle East Peace Conference

10. Paris, 21 November 1991: In the "Charter of Paris", the United States, the Soviet Union and 32 other nations agree to a "final end" of the Cold War, and to limit the non-nuclear armaments of NATO (North Atlantic Treaty Organisation) and the Warsaw Pact

11. Camp David, 1 February 1992: President Yeltsin of Russia and President Bush discuss replacing Star Wars space-based anti-missile programme with a "global system of defence"

12. Helsinki, 25 March 1992: Warsaw Pact and NATO countries agree to open reconnaissance flights over their respective territories, to monitor arms control

13. Lisbon, 29 May 1992: Strategic Arms Reduction Treaty accepted by the new republics of Russia, Ukraine, Belarus, and Kazakhstan, each of which has former Soviet nuclear weapons on its soil

14. Oslo, 5 June 1992: Conventional Forces agreement signed by all sixteen members of NATO, eight of the former Soviet Republics, and Bulgaria, Czechoslovakia, Hungary, Rumania and Poland, introduces further reductions in tank, artillery and armoured vehicles on both sides of now defunct Iron Curtain

15. Washington, 16 June 1992: Bush and Yeltsin sign arms reduction agreement aimed at cutting their respective nuclear arsenals by two-thirds

16. Houston, 18 June 1992: The United States National Aeronautics and Space Administration (NASA) signs a commercial agreement with the Russian Space Agency (NPO Energia) for exchange and use of space information and facilities

17. Seoul, 19 November 1992: As a gesture of friendship, Yeltsin returns the black-box flight data recorder of the Korean airliner shot down by a Soviet fighter in 1983

18. Moscow, 3 January 1993: Bush and Yeltsin sign a Treaty for the reduction of their nuclear arsenals by two-thirds within ten years (START II). Yeltsin called it a "treaty of hope". Bush said, "The two powers who once divided the world have come together to make it a safer and better place"

19. Vancouver, 5 April 1993: President Clinton offers Yeltsin $1,600 million in US economic aid

© Martin Gilbert 1993

150

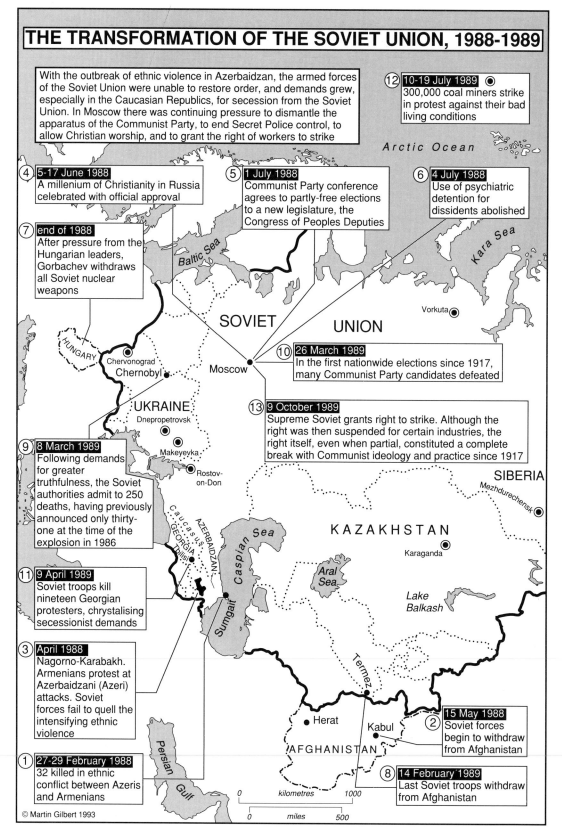

THE TRANSFORMATION OF THE SOVIET UNION, 1988-1989

With the outbreak of ethnic violence in Azerbaidzan, the armed forces of the Soviet Union were unable to restore order, and demands grew, especially in the Caucasian Republics, for secession from the Soviet Union. In Moscow there was continuing pressure to dismantle the apparatus of the Communist Party, to end Secret Police control, to allow Christian worship, and to grant the right of workers to strike

⑫ 10-19 July 1989 ◉
300,000 coal miners strike in protest against their bad living conditions

④ 5-17 June 1988
A millenium of Christianity in Russia celebrated with official approval

⑤ 1 July 1988
Communist Party conference agrees to partly-free elections to a new legislature, the Congress of Peoples Deputies

⑥ 4 July 1988
Use of psychiatric detention for dissidents abolished

⑦ end of 1988
After pressure from the Hungarian leaders, Gorbachev withdraws all Soviet nuclear weapons

⑩ 26 March 1989
In the first nationwide elections since 1917, many Communist Party candidates defeated

⑬ 9 October 1989
Supreme Soviet grants right to strike. Although the right was then suspended for certain industries, the right itself, even when partial, constituted a complete break with Communist ideology and practice since 1917

⑨ 8 March 1989
Following demands for greater truthfulness, the Soviet authorities admit to 250 deaths, having previously announced only thirty-one at the time of the explosion in 1986

⑪ 9 April 1989
Soviet troops kill nineteen Georgian protesters, chrystalising secessionist demands

③ April 1988
Nagorno-Karabakh. Armenians protest at Azerbaidzani (Azeri) attacks. Soviet forces fail to quell the intensifying ethnic violence

② 15 May 1988
Soviet forces begin to withdraw from Afghanistan

① 27-29 February 1988
32 killed in ethnic conflict between Azeris and Armenians

⑧ 14 February 1989
Last Soviet troops withdraw from Afghanistan

Arctic Ocean

Kara Sea

Baltic Sea

SOVIET   UNION

Vorkuta ◉

Moscow

HUNGARY

Chervonograd ◉
Chernobyl ◉

UKRAINE
Dnepropetrovsk ◉

Makeyevka ◉

Rostov-
on-Don ◉

SIBERIA
Mezhdurechensk ◉

Caucasus
GEORGIA
Tbilisi
AZERBAIDZAN
Caspian Sea

KAZAKHSTAN

Karaganda ◉

Aral
Sea

Lake
Balkash

Sumgait

Termez

Herat
Kabul

AFGHANISTAN

Persian Gulf

0   kilometres   1000

0   miles   500

151

THE COLLAPSE OF COMMUNISM IN EASTERN EUROPE, 1989

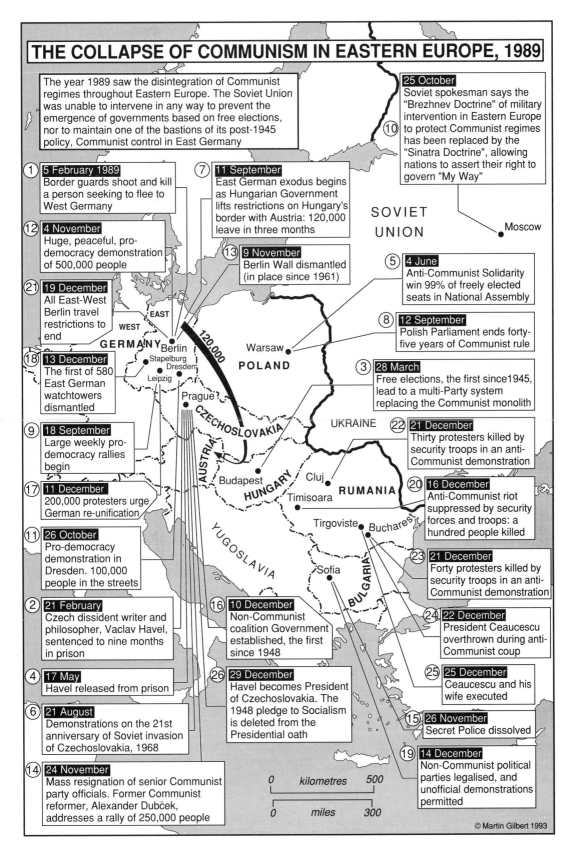

The year 1989 saw the disintegration of Communist regimes throughout Eastern Europe. The Soviet Union was unable to intervene in any way to prevent the emergence of governments based on free elections, nor to maintain one of the bastions of its post-1945 policy, Communist control in East Germany

25 October
(10) Soviet spokesman says the "Brezhnev Doctrine" of military intervention in Eastern Europe to protect Communist regimes has been replaced by the "Sinatra Doctrine", allowing nations to assert their right to govern "My Way"

(1) **5 February 1989**
Border guards shoot and kill a person seeking to flee to West Germany

(7) **11 September**
East German exodus begins as Hungarian Government lifts restrictions on Hungary's border with Austria: 120,000 leave in three months

SOVIET UNION

Moscow

(12) **4 November**
Huge, peaceful, pro-democracy demonstration of 500,000 people

(13) **9 November**
Berlin Wall dismantled (in place since 1961)

(5) **4 June**
Anti-Communist Solidarity win 99% of freely elected seats in National Assembly

(21) **19 December**
All East-West Berlin travel restrictions to end

EAST
WEST
GERMANY Berlin
Stapelburg
Dresden
Leipzig
Prague
120,000
Warsaw
POLAND

(8) **12 September**
Polish Parliament ends forty-five years of Communist rule

(18) **13 December**
The first of 580 East German watchtowers dismantled

(3) **28 March**
Free elections, the first since 1945, lead to a multi-Party system replacing the Communist monolith

(9) **18 September**
Large weekly pro-democracy rallies begin

CZECHOSLOVAKIA
AUSTRIA

UKRAINE

(22) **21 December**
Thirty protesters killed by security troops in an anti-Communist demonstration

(17) **11 December**
200,000 protesters urge German re-unification

Budapest
HUNGARY
Cluj
Timisoara
RUMANIA

(20) **16 December**
Anti-Communist riot suppressed by security forces and troops: a hundred people killed

(11) **26 October**
Pro-democracy demonstration in Dresden. 100,000 people in the streets

YUGOSLAVIA

Tirgoviste
Bucharest
Sofia
BULGARIA

(23) **21 December**
Forty protesters killed by security troops in an anti-Communist demonstration

(2) **21 February**
Czech dissident writer and philosopher, Vaclav Havel, sentenced to nine months in prison

(16) **10 December**
Non-Communist coalition Government established, the first since 1948

(24) **22 December**
President Ceaucescu overthrown during anti-Communist coup

(4) **17 May**
Havel released from prison

(26) **29 December**
Havel becomes President of Czechoslovakia. The 1948 pledge to Socialism is deleted from the Presidential oath

(25) **25 December**
Ceaucescu and his wife executed

(6) **21 August**
Demonstrations on the 21st anniversary of Soviet invasion of Czechoslovakia, 1968

(15) **26 November**
Secret Police dissolved

(19) **14 December**
Non-Communist political parties legalised, and unofficial demonstrations permitted

(14) **24 November**
Mass resignation of senior Communist party officials. Former Communist reformer, Alexander Dubček, addresses a rally of 250,000 people

0   kilometres   500

0   miles   300

© Martin Gilbert 1993

152

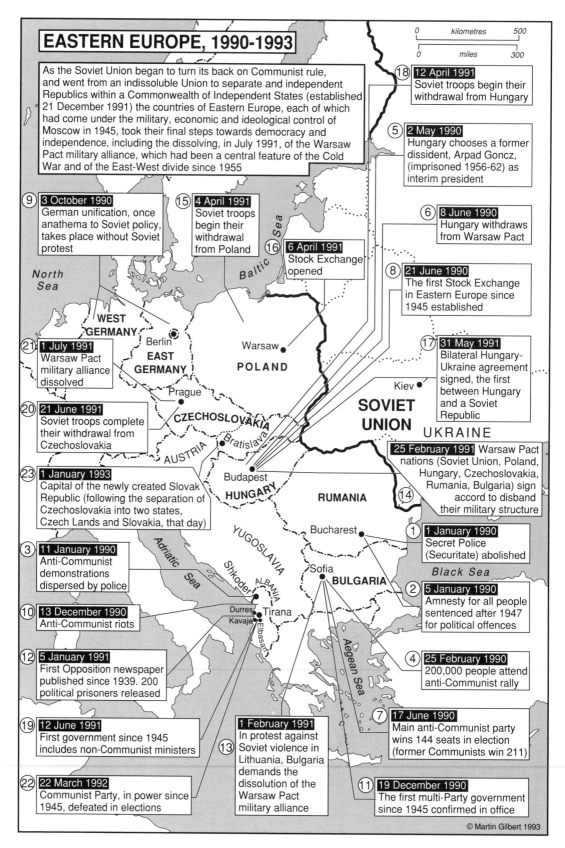

EASTERN EUROPE, 1990-1993

As the Soviet Union began to turn its back on Communist rule, and went from an indissoluble Union to separate and independent Republics within a Commonwealth of Independent States (established 21 December 1991) the countries of Eastern Europe, each of which had come under the military, economic and ideological control of Moscow in 1945, took their final steps towards democracy and independence, including the dissolving, in July 1991, of the Warsaw Pact military alliance, which had been a central feature of the Cold War and of the East-West divide since 1955

18 **12 April 1991**
Soviet troops begin their withdrawal from Hungary

5 **2 May 1990**
Hungary chooses a former dissident, Arpad Goncz, (imprisoned 1956-62) as interim president

6 **8 June 1990**
Hungary withdraws from Warsaw Pact

9 **3 October 1990**
German unification, once anathema to Soviet policy, takes place without Soviet protest

15 **4 April 1991**
Soviet troops begin their withdrawal from Poland

16 **6 April 1991**
Stock Exchange opened

8 **21 June 1990**
The first Stock Exchange in Eastern Europe since 1945 established

17 **31 May 1991**
Bilateral Hungary-Ukraine agreement signed, the first between Hungary and a Soviet Republic

21 **1 July 1991**
Warsaw Pact military alliance dissolved

20 **21 June 1991**
Soviet troops complete their withdrawal from Czechoslovakia

23 **1 January 1993**
Capital of the newly created Slovak Republic (following the separation of Czechoslovakia into two states, Czech Lands and Slovakia, that day)

25 February 1991 Warsaw Pact nations (Soviet Union, Poland, Hungary, Czechoslovakia, Rumania, Bulgaria) sign accord to disband their military structure
14

3 **11 January 1990**
Anti-Communist demonstrations dispersed by police

1 **1 January 1990**
Secret Police (Securitate) abolished

10 **13 December 1990**
Anti-Communist riots

2 **5 January 1990**
Amnesty for all people sentenced after 1947 for political offences

12 **5 January 1991**
First Opposition newspaper published since 1939. 200 political prisoners released

4 **25 February 1990**
200,000 people attend anti-Communist rally

19 **12 June 1991**
First government since 1945 includes non-Communist ministers

1 February 1991
In protest against Soviet violence in Lithuania, Bulgaria demands the dissolution of the Warsaw Pact military alliance
13

7 **17 June 1990**
Main anti-Communist party wins 144 seats in election (former Communists win 211)

22 **22 March 1992**
Communist Party, in power since 1945, defeated in elections

11 **19 December 1990**
The first multi-Party government since 1945 confirmed in office

Map labels: North Sea, Baltic Sea, WEST GERMANY, EAST GERMANY, Berlin, POLAND, Warsaw, Prague, CZECHOSLOVAKIA, Bratislava, AUSTRIA, Budapest, HUNGARY, SOVIET UNION, UKRAINE, Kiev, RUMANIA, Bucharest, YUGOSLAVIA, Adriatic Sea, Shkoder, ALBANIA, Durres, Kavaje, Elbasan, Tirana, Sofia, BULGARIA, Black Sea, Aegean Sea

0 — kilometres — 500
0 — miles — 300

© Martin Gilbert 1993

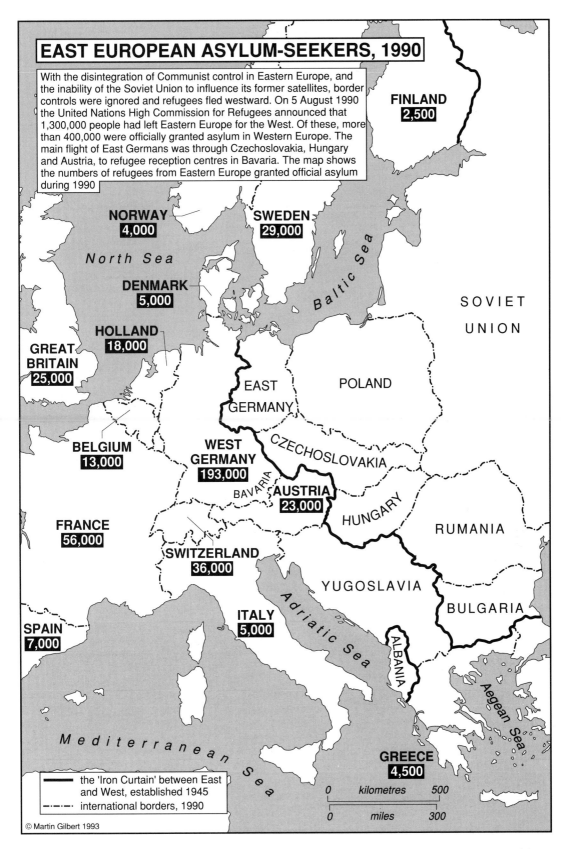

EAST EUROPEAN ASYLUM-SEEKERS, 1990

With the disintegration of Communist control in Eastern Europe, and the inability of the Soviet Union to influence its former satellites, border controls were ignored and refugees fled westward. On 5 August 1990 the United Nations High Commission for Refugees announced that 1,300,000 people had left Eastern Europe for the West. Of these, more than 400,000 were officially granted asylum in Western Europe. The main flight of East Germans was through Czechoslovakia, Hungary and Austria, to refugee reception centres in Bavaria. The map shows the numbers of refugees from Eastern Europe granted official asylum during 1990

FINLAND 2,500

NORWAY 4,000

SWEDEN 29,000

North Sea

Baltic Sea

SOVIET UNION

DENMARK 5,000

HOLLAND 18,000

GREAT BRITAIN 25,000

POLAND

EAST GERMANY

BELGIUM 13,000

WEST GERMANY 193,000

CZECHOSLOVAKIA

BAVARIA

AUSTRIA 23,000

HUNGARY

RUMANIA

FRANCE 56,000

SWITZERLAND 36,000

YUGOSLAVIA

BULGARIA

Adriatic Sea

SPAIN 7,000

ITALY 5,000

ALBANIA

Aegean Sea

Mediterranean Sea

GREECE 4,500

the 'Iron Curtain' between East and West, established 1945
international borders, 1990

0 — kilometres — 500

0 — miles — 300

© Martin Gilbert 1993

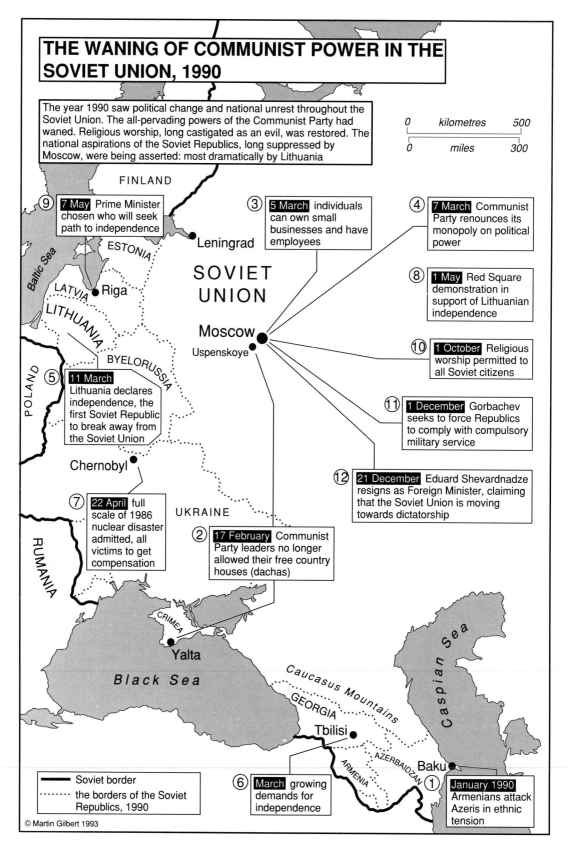

THE WANING OF COMMUNIST POWER IN THE SOVIET UNION, 1990

The year 1990 saw political change and national unrest throughout the Soviet Union. The all-pervading powers of the Communist Party had waned. Religious worship, long castigated as an evil, was restored. The national aspirations of the Soviet Republics, long suppressed by Moscow, were being asserted: most dramatically by Lithuania

0   kilometres   500

0   miles   300

FINLAND

⑨ **7 May** Prime Minister chosen who will seek path to independence

Leningrad

Baltic Sea

ESTONIA

LATVIA   Riga

LITHUANIA

POLAND

③ **5 March** individuals can own small businesses and have employees

④ **7 March** Communist Party renounces its monopoly on political power

SOVIET UNION

⑧ **1 May** Red Square demonstration in support of Lithuanian independence

Moscow

Uspenskoye

⑩ **1 October** Religious worship permitted to all Soviet citizens

BYELORUSSIA

⑤ **11 March** Lithuania declares independence, the first Soviet Republic to break away from the Soviet Union

⑪ **1 December** Gorbachev seeks to force Republics to comply with compulsory military service

Chernobyl

⑫ **21 December** Eduard Shevardnadze resigns as Foreign Minister, claiming that the Soviet Union is moving towards dictatorship

⑦ **22 April** full scale of 1986 nuclear disaster admitted, all victims to get compensation

UKRAINE

RUMANIA

② **17 February** Communist Party leaders no longer allowed their free country houses (dachas)

CRIMEA

Yalta

Black Sea

Caucasus Mountains

Caspian Sea

GEORGIA

Tbilisi

AZERBAIDZAN

ARMENIA

Baku

— Soviet border

.... the borders of the Soviet Republics, 1990

⑥ **March** growing demands for independence

① **January 1990** Armenians attack Azeris in ethnic tension

© Martin Gilbert 1993

155

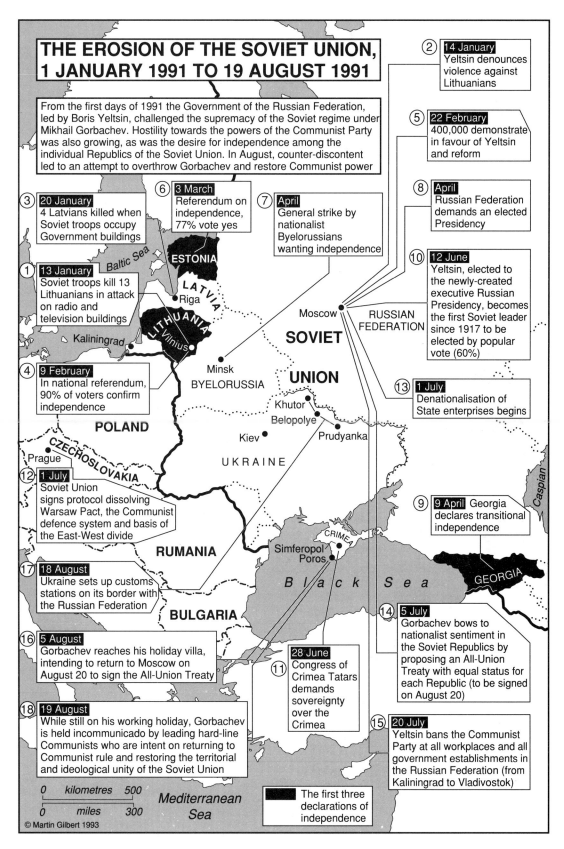

THE EROSION OF THE SOVIET UNION, 1 JANUARY 1991 TO 19 AUGUST 1991

From the first days of 1991 the Government of the Russian Federation, led by Boris Yeltsin, challenged the supremacy of the Soviet regime under Mikhail Gorbachev. Hostility towards the powers of the Communist Party was also growing, as was the desire for independence among the individual Republics of the Soviet Union. In August, counter-discontent led to an attempt to overthrow Gorbachev and restore Communist power

② **14 January** Yeltsin denounces violence against Lithuanians

⑤ **22 February** 400,000 demonstrate in favour of Yeltsin and reform

⑧ **April** Russian Federation demands an elected Presidency

③ **20 January** 4 Latvians killed when Soviet troops occupy Government buildings

⑥ **3 March** Referendum on independence, 77% vote yes

⑦ **April** General strike by nationalist Byelorussians wanting independence

⑩ **12 June** Yeltsin, elected to the newly-created executive Russian Presidency, becomes the first Soviet leader since 1917 to be elected by popular vote (60%)

① **13 January** Soviet troops kill 13 Lithuanians in attack on radio and television buildings

④ **9 February** In national referendum, 90% of voters confirm independence

⑬ **1 July** Denationalisation of State enterprises begins

⑫ **1 July** Soviet Union signs protocol dissolving Warsaw Pact, the Communist defence system and basis of the East-West divide

⑨ **9 April** Georgia declares transitional independence

⑰ **18 August** Ukraine sets up customs stations on its border with the Russian Federation

⑯ **5 August** Gorbachev reaches his holiday villa, intending to return to Moscow on August 20 to sign the All-Union Treaty

⑪ **28 June** Congress of Crimea Tatars demands sovereignty over the Crimea

⑭ **5 July** Gorbachev bows to nationalist sentiment in the Soviet Republics by proposing an All-Union Treaty with equal status for each Republic (to be signed on August 20)

⑱ **19 August** While still on his working holiday, Gorbachev is held incommunicado by leading hard-line Communists who are intent on returning to Communist rule and restoring the territorial and ideological unity of the Soviet Union

⑮ **20 July** Yeltsin bans the Communist Party at all workplaces and all government establishments in the Russian Federation (from Kaliningrad to Vladivostok)

ESTONIA
LATVIA
Riga
LITHUANIA
Vilnius
Kaliningrad
Baltic Sea

Moscow
SOVIET
UNION
RUSSIAN FEDERATION

Minsk
BYELORUSSIA
Khutor
Belopolye
Kiev
Prudyanka
UKRAINE

POLAND
CZECHOSLOVAKIA
Prague
RUMANIA
BULGARIA

Simferopol
Poros
CRIMEA
B l a c k   S e a
GEORGIA
Caspian

Mediterranean Sea

0   kilometres   500
0   miles   300

■ The first three declarations of independence

© Martin Gilbert 1993

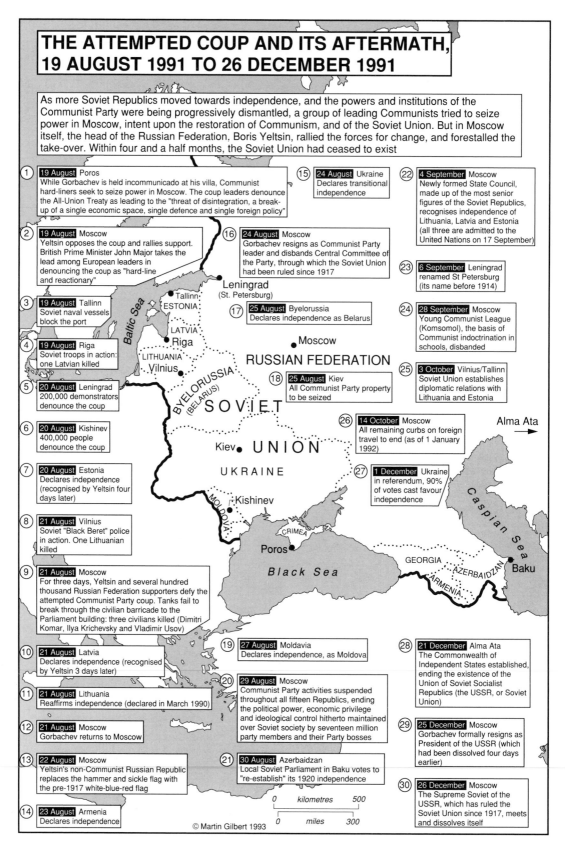

THE ATTEMPTED COUP AND ITS AFTERMATH, 19 AUGUST 1991 TO 26 DECEMBER 1991

As more Soviet Republics moved towards independence, and the powers and institutions of the Communist Party were being progressively dismantled, a group of leading Communists tried to seize power in Moscow, intent upon the restoration of Communism, and of the Soviet Union. But in Moscow itself, the head of the Russian Federation, Boris Yeltsin, rallied the forces for change, and forestalled the take-over. Within four and a half months, the Soviet Union had ceased to exist

1. **19 August** Poros
While Gorbachev is held incommunicado at his villa, Communist hard-liners seek to seize power in Moscow. The coup leaders denounce the All-Union Treaty as leading to the "threat of disintegration, a break-up of a single economic space, single defence and single foreign policy"

2. **19 August** Moscow
Yeltsin opposes the coup and rallies support. British Prime Minister John Major takes the lead among European leaders in denouncing the coup as "hard-line and reactionary"

3. **19 August** Tallinn
Soviet naval vessels block the port

4. **19 August** Riga
Soviet troops in action: one Latvian killed

5. **20 August** Leningrad
200,000 demonstrators denounce the coup

6. **20 August** Kishinev
400,000 people denounce the coup

7. **20 August** Estonia
Declares independence (recognised by Yeltsin four days later)

8. **21 August** Vilnius
Soviet "Black Beret" police in action. One Lithuanian killed

9. **21 August** Moscow
For three days, Yeltsin and several hundred thousand Russian Federation supporters defy the attempted Communist Party coup. Tanks fail to break through the civilian barricade to the Parliament building: three civilians killed (Dimitri Komar, Ilya Krichevsky and Vladimir Usov)

10. **21 August** Latvia
Declares independence (recognised by Yeltsin 3 days later)

11. **21 August** Lithuania
Reaffirms independence (declared in March 1990)

12. **21 August** Moscow
Gorbachev returns to Moscow

13. **22 August** Moscow
Yeltsin's non-Communist Russian Republic replaces the hammer and sickle flag with the pre-1917 white-blue-red flag

14. **23 August** Armenia
Declares independence

15. **24 August** Ukraine
Declares transitional independence

16. **24 August** Moscow
Gorbachev resigns as Communist Party leader and disbands Central Committee of the Party, through which the Soviet Union had been ruled since 1917

17. **25 August** Byelorussia
Declares independence as Belarus

18. **25 August** Kiev
All Communist Party property to be seized

19. **27 August** Moldavia
Declares independence, as Moldova

20. **29 August** Moscow
Communist Party activities suspended throughout all fifteen Republics, ending the political power, economic privilege and ideological control hitherto maintained over Soviet society by seventeen million party members and their Party bosses

21. **30 August** Azerbaidzan
Local Soviet Parliament in Baku votes to "re-establish" its 1920 independence

22. **4 September** Moscow
Newly formed State Council, made up of the most senior figures of the Soviet Republics, recognises independence of Lithuania, Latvia and Estonia (all three are admitted to the United Nations on 17 September)

23. **6 September** Leningrad
renamed St Petersburg (its name before 1914)

24. **28 September** Moscow
Young Communist League (Komsomol), the basis of Communist indoctrination in schools, disbanded

25. **3 October** Vilnius/Tallinn
Soviet Union establishes diplomatic relations with Lithuania and Estonia

26. **14 October** Moscow
All remaining curbs on foreign travel to end (as of 1 January 1992)

27. **1 December** Ukraine
in referendum, 90% of votes cast favour independence

28. **21 December** Alma Ata
The Commonwealth of Independent States established, ending the existence of the Union of Soviet Socialist Republics (the USSR, or Soviet Union)

29. **25 December** Moscow
Gorbachev formally resigns as President of the USSR (which had been dissolved four days earlier)

30. **26 December** Moscow
The Supreme Soviet of the USSR, which has ruled the Soviet Union since 1917, meets and dissolves itself

Tallinn
ESTONIA
LATVIA
Riga
LITHUANIA
Vilnius
Baltic Sea
Leningrad (St. Petersburg)
Moscow
RUSSIAN FEDERATION
BYELORUSSIA (BELARUS)
SOVIET
Kiev UNION
UKRAINE
MOLDOVA
Kishinev
CRIMEA
Poros
Black Sea
GEORGIA
ARMENIA
AZERBAIDZAN
Baku
Caspian Sea
Alma Ata

| 0 | kilometres | 500 |
| 0 | miles | 300 |

© Martin Gilbert 1993

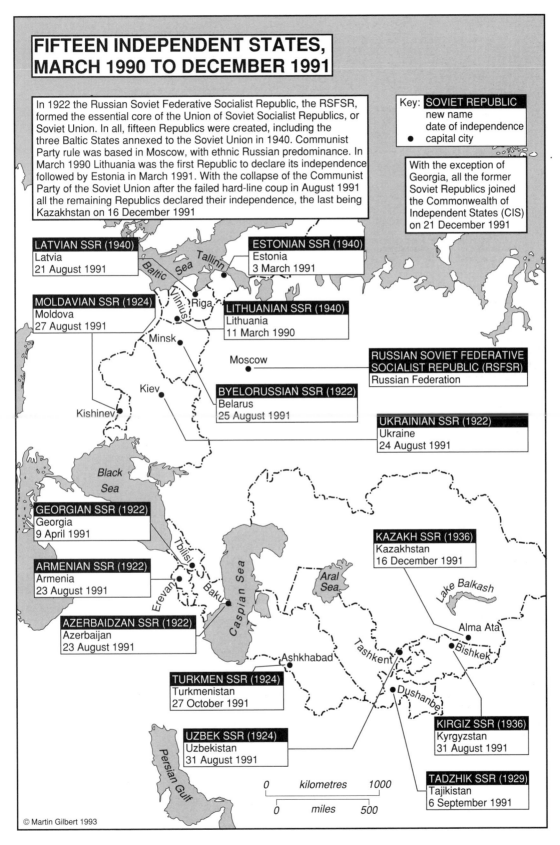

FIFTEEN INDEPENDENT STATES, MARCH 1990 TO DECEMBER 1991

In 1922 the Russian Soviet Federative Socialist Republic, the RSFSR, formed the essential core of the Union of Soviet Socialist Republics, or Soviet Union. In all, fifteen Republics were created, including the three Baltic States annexed to the Soviet Union in 1940. Communist Party rule was based in Moscow, with ethnic Russian predominance. In March 1990 Lithuania was the first Republic to declare its independence followed by Estonia in March 1991. With the collapse of the Communist Party of the Soviet Union after the failed hard-line coup in August 1991 all the remaining Republics declared their independence, the last being Kazakhstan on 16 December 1991

Key: **SOVIET REPUBLIC**
new name
date of independence
• capital city

With the exception of Georgia, all the former Soviet Republics joined the Commonwealth of Independent States (CIS) on 21 December 1991

LATVIAN SSR (1940)
Latvia
21 August 1991

ESTONIAN SSR (1940)
Estonia
3 March 1991

MOLDAVIAN SSR (1924)
Moldova
27 August 1991

LITHUANIAN SSR (1940)
Lithuania
11 March 1990

RUSSIAN SOVIET FEDERATIVE SOCIALIST REPUBLIC (RSFSR)
Russian Federation

BYELORUSSIAN SSR (1922)
Belarus
25 August 1991

UKRAINIAN SSR (1922)
Ukraine
24 August 1991

GEORGIAN SSR (1922)
Georgia
9 April 1991

KAZAKH SSR (1936)
Kazakhstan
16 December 1991

ARMENIAN SSR (1922)
Armenia
23 August 1991

AZERBAIDZAN SSR (1922)
Azerbaijan
23 August 1991

TURKMEN SSR (1924)
Turkmenistan
27 October 1991

KIRGIZ SSR (1936)
Kyrgyzstan
31 August 1991

UZBEK SSR (1924)
Uzbekistan
31 August 1991

TADZHIK SSR (1929)
Tajikistan
6 September 1991

Tallinn
Baltic Sea
Vilnius
Riga
Minsk
Moscow
Kiev
Kishinev
Black Sea
Tbilisi
Erevan
Baku
Caspian Sea
Aral Sea
Lake Balkash
Alma Ata
Bishkek
Ashkhabad
Tashkent
Dushanbe
Persian Gulf

0   kilometres   1000
0   miles   500

© Martin Gilbert 1993

158

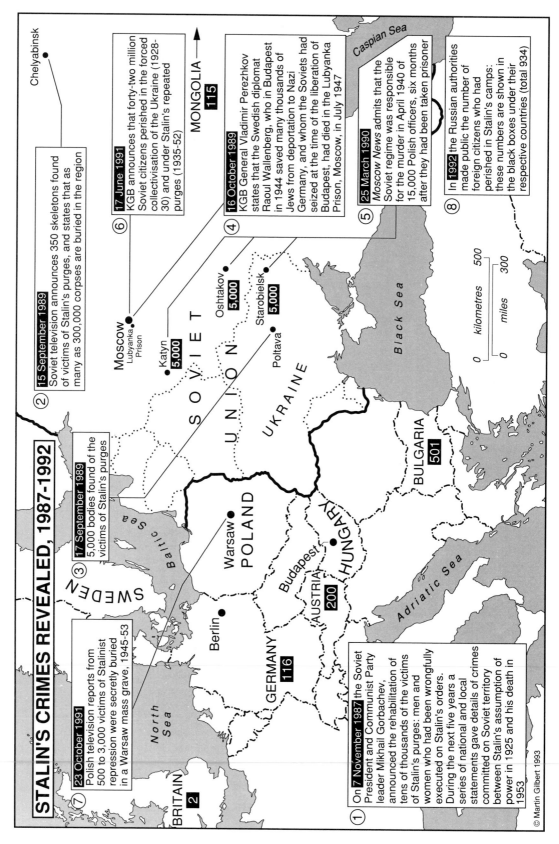

STALIN'S CRIMES REVEALED, 1987-1992

② **15 September 1989**
Soviet television announces 350 skeletons found of victims of Stalin's purges, and states that as many as 300,000 corpses are buried in the region

⑥ **17 June 1991**
KGB announces that forty-two million Soviet citizens perished in the forced collectivisation of the Ukraine (1928-30) and under Stalin's repeated purges (1935-52)

④ **16 October 1989**
KGB General Vladimir Perezhkov states that the Swedish diplomat Raoul Wallenberg, who in Budapest in 1944 saved many thousands of Jews from deportation to Nazi Germany, and whom the Soviets had seized at the time of the liberation of Budapest, had died in the Lubyanka Prison, Moscow, in July 1947

⑤ **25 March 1990**
Moscow News admits that the Soviet regime was responsible for the murder in April 1940 of 15,000 Polish officers, six months after they had been taken prisoner

⑧ In **1992** the Russian authorities made public the number of foreign citizens who had perished in Stalin's camps: these numbers are shown in the black boxes under their respective countries (total 934)

③ **17 September 1989**
5,000 bodies found of the victims of Stalin's purges

⑦ **23 October 1991**
Polish television reports from 500 to 3,000 victims of Stalinist repression were secretly buried in a Warsaw mass grave, 1945-53

① On **7 November 1987** the Soviet President and Communist Party leader Mikhail Gorbachev, announced the rehabilitation of tens of thousands of the victims of Stalin's purges: men and women who had been wrongfully executed on Stalin's orders. During the next five years a series of national and local statements gave details of crimes committed on Soviet territory between Stalin's assumption of power in 1925 and his death in 1953

Chelyabinsk

MONGOLIA **115**

Caspian Sea

Moscow
Lubyanka Prison

Katyn **5,000**

Oshtakov **5,000**

Starobielsk **5,000**

Poltava

S O V I E T   U N I O N

UKRAINE

Black Sea

Baltic Sea

SWEDEN

North Sea

Warsaw
POLAND

Berlin

GERMANY **116**

AUSTRIA **200**

Budapest
HUNGARY

BULGARIA **501**

Adriatic Sea

BRITAIN **2**

0   kilometres   500

0   miles   300

© Martin Gilbert 1993

159

THE COMMONWEALTH OF INDEPENDENT STATES, 1992

(9) 7 February Yeltsin and Mitterand sign Franco-Russian Treaty

(26) 9 November Yeltsin and Major sign Anglo-Russian Treaty

(1) Established on 21 December 1991, the Commonwealth of Independent States had a stormy first year, but its structure survived, and it was gradually accepted by the international community, to which its member States appealed at different times for economic help, and with which its members began to establish bilateral working relationships at diplomatic and economic levels

(3) 8 January 1992 European Community (under Britain's presidency) agrees on 2 December 1991, to emergency food aid worth $263 million. Russia accepts this on 8 January 1992

(23) 25 July Eleven members of the Commonwealth of Independent States combined to send a "Unified Team" to the Olympic Games in Barcelona, winning the largest number of Gold Medals (45) as against the United States (37), the recently united East and West Germany (33), and China (16)

(10) 10 February 'Operation Provide Hope', the United States airlift to the CIS, begins. Fifty-four flights in all, with 17,000 tons of food and medical supplies (left over from the Gulf War)

(4) 13 January Poland and Lithuania recognise existing borders and agree to non-interference in internal affairs

(5) 14 January Estonia and Russia establish diplomatic relations

(15) 2 March Polish-Belarus diplomatic relations established. Belarus agrees to set up Polish language schools for its Polish minority

(17) 6 March Trade links inaugurated

(8) 1 February The Commonwealth of Independent States agrees to withdraw all its troops, principally Russians, from the Baltic Republics

(21) 22 April Exposing the scale of former Soviet deception, Ukraine declares that between **6,000** and **8,000** people died as a result of the nuclear plant explosion in 1986

(6) 16 January Hungary and Moldova establish diplomatic relations (Moldova's first)

(12) 21 February Yeltsin agrees to re-establish a German National District on the Volga (abolished by Stalin in the 1930s)

(7) 29 January Ukraine signs barter deal with Iran: gas and oil from Ukraine in return for chemicals, concrete and steel piping

(13) 24 February 3 dead when construction battalion riots suppressed

(24) 3 August Russia and Ukraine agree to divide the former Soviet Black Sea Fleet after three years joint control

(20) 28 March 18 dead in fighting between pro- and anti-Russia factions. Five thousand flee to the Odessa region

(22) 15 May Mutual Security Treaty signed (Russia, Kazakhstan, Armenia, Turkmenistan, Uzbekistan and Tajikistan), recognising each others borders and pledging common defence against aggression

(25) 14-16 August 50 dead as secessionist Abkhazians fight Georgians **26 August.** Georgians set up interim government over Abkhazians (250,00 Georgians and 160,000 Abkhazians live in region)

(2) 6 January 113 killed since late December in civil war

(14) 25 February Azeris claim 1,000 killed by Armenians

(18) 9 March Last Russian troops evacuated from Armenian enclave of Nagorno-Karabakh, after 3 soldiers killed

(17) 15 March Armenian-Azerbaijan truce signed

(27) 23 December Thousands of Tajiks flee into Afghanistan during fighting between local Tajik ex-Communist and Islamic forces

(11) 17 February The six Muslim Republics of the CIS join the Muslim trading group, the Economic Co-operation Organisation

(16) 4 March Joint Turkmenistan-Iran Chamber of Commerce established

0 kilometres 1000

0 miles 500

160

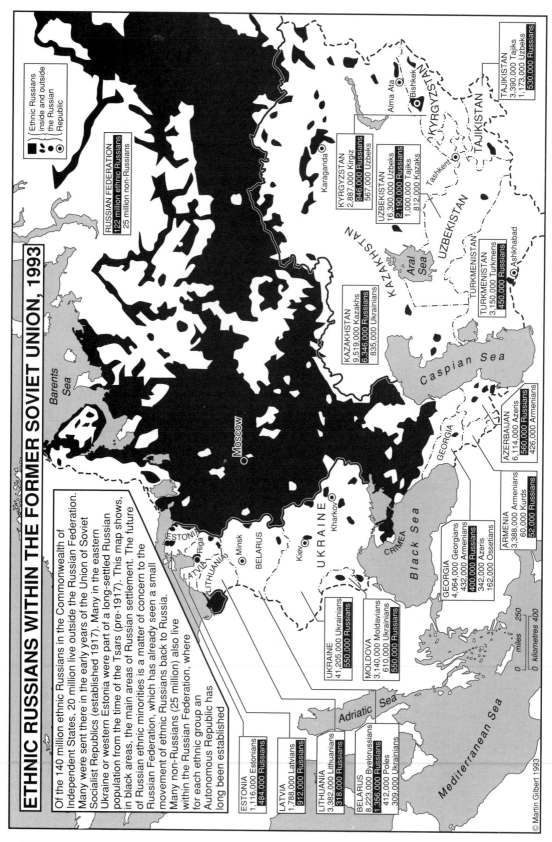

ETHNIC RUSSIANS WITHIN THE FORMER SOVIET UNION, 1993

Of the 140 million ethnic Russians in the Commonwealth of Independent States, 20 million live outside the Russian Federation. Many were sent there in the early years of the Union of Soviet Socialist Republics (established 1917). Many in the eastern Ukraine or western Estonia were part of a long-settled Russian population from the time of the Tsars (pre-1917). This map shows, in black areas, the main areas of Russian settlement. The future of Russian ethnic minorities is a matter of concern to the Russian Federation, which has already seen a small movement of ethnic Russians back to Russia. Many non-Russians (25 million) also live within the Russian Federation, where for each ethnic group an Autonomous Republic has long been established

Ethnic Russians inside and outside the Russian Republic

RUSSIAN FEDERATION
122 million ethnic Russians
25 million non-Russians

ESTONIA
1,116,000 Estonians
484,000 Russians

LATVIA
1,788,000 Latvians
912,000 Russians

LITHUANIA
3,382,000 Lithuanians
318,000 Russians

BELARUS
8,223,000 Byelorussians
1,356,000 Russians
412,000 Poles
309,000 Ukrainians

UKRAINE
41,205,000 Ukrainians
550,000 Russians

MOLDOVA
3,140,000 Moldavians
610,000 Ukrainians
550,000 Russians

GEORGIA
4,064,000 Georgians
432,000 Armenians
400,000 Russians
342,000 Azeris
162,000 Ossetians

ARMENIA
3,388,000 Armenians
60,000 Kurds
52,000 Russians

AZERBAIJAN
6,114,000 Azeris
560,000 Russians
426,000 Armenians

KAZAKHSTAN
9,519,000 Kazakhs
6,346,000 Russians
835,000 Ukrainians

TURKMENISTAN
3,150,000 Turkmens
450,000 Russians

UZBEKISTAN
16,300,000 Uzbeks
2,190,000 Russians
1,000,000 Tajiks
812,000 Kazaks

KYRGYZSTAN
2,887,000 Kirgiz
946,000 Russians
567,000 Uzbeks

TAJIKISTAN
3,390,000 Tajiks
1,173,000 Uzbeks
530,000 Russians

Barents Sea

Moscow

Riga

Minsk

ESTONIA

LATVIA

LITHUANIA

BELARUS

Kiev

Kharkov

UKRAINE

CRIMEA

Black Sea

GEORGIA

Adriatic Sea

Mediterranean Sea

Caspian Sea

Aral Sea

KAZAKHSTAN

Karaganda

Alma Ata

Bishkek

KYRGYZSTAN

Tashkent

UZBEKISTAN

TAJIKISTAN

TURKMENISTAN

Ashkhabad

AZERBAIJAN

ARMENIA

0   miles   250
0 kilometres 400

© Martin Gilbert 1993

Bibliography of Works Consulted

(i) ATLASES

Baratov, R. B. (and others), *Atlas Tadzhikskoi Sovetskoi Sotsialisticheskoi Respubliki* (Dushanbe and Moscow, 1968)

Bartholomew, John (ed), *The Times Atlas of the World*, 5 vols (London, 1959)

Bazilevich, K. V., Golubtsov, I. A. and Zinoviev, M. A., *Atlas Istorii SSSR*, 3 vols (Moscow, 1949–54)

Beloglazova, O. A. (ed), *Atlas SSSR* (Moscow, 1954)

Czapliński, Wladislaw and Ladogórski, Tadeusz, *Atlas Historyczny Polski* (Warsaw, 1968)

Droysens, G., *Historischer Handatlas* (Bielefeld and Leipzig, 1886)

Durov, A. G. (General editor), *Atlas Leningradskoi Oblasti* (Moscow, 1967)

Engel, Joseph, *Grosser Historischer Weltatlas* (Munich, 1962)

Grosier, L'Abbé, *Atlas Générale de la Chine* (Paris 1785)

Hudson, G. F. and Rajchman, Marthe, *An Atlas of Far Eastern Politics* (London, 1938)

Kalesnik, S. V. (and others), *Peterburg–Leningrad* (Leningrad, 1957)

Kosev, Dimiter (and others), *Atlas Po Bulgarska Istoriya* (Sofia, 1963)

Kubijovyć, Volodymyr, *Atlas of Ukraine and Adjoining Countries* (Lvov, 1937)

Kudriashov, K. V., *Russkii Istoricheskii Atlas* (Leningrad, 1928)

Kovalevsky, Pierre, *Atlas Historique et Culturel de la Russie et du Monde Slave* (Paris, 1961)

McEvedy, Colin, *The Penguin Atlas of Medieval History* (London, 1961)

Penkala, Maria, *A Correlated History of the Far East* (The Hague and Paris, 1966)

Oxford Regional Economic Atlas: The USSR and Eastern Europe (Oxford, 1956)

Sochava, V. B. (Principal ed), *Atlas Zabaikalia* (Moscow and Irkutsk, 1967)

Taaffe, Robert N. and Kingsbury, Robert C., *An Atlas of Soviet Affairs* (London, 1965)

Terekhov, N. M. (senior editor), *Atlas Volgogradskoi Oblasti* (Moscow, 1967)

Toynbee, Arnold J. and Myers, Edward D., *Historical Atlas and Gazetteer* (London, 1959)

Voznesenski (and others), *Atlas Razvitiya Khoziastva i Kultury SSSR* (Moscow, 1967)

Westermann, Georg, *Atlas zur Weltgeschichte* (Braunschweig, 1956)

Zamyslovski, Igor E., *Uchebnii Atlas po Russkoi Istorii* (St Petersburg, 1887)

(ii) MAPS

Atanasiu, A. D., *La Bessarabie* (Paris, 1919)

Bazewicz, J. M., *Polska w Trzech Zaborach* (Warsaw, n.d.)

Bazileva, Z. P., *Rossiiskaya Imperia 1801–1861* (Moscow, 1960)

British G.H.Q., Constantinople, *Ethnographical Map of Caucasus* (Constantinople, 1920)

Fedorovskaya, G. P. (publisher), *Promyshlennost Rossii 1913; Promyshlennost Soyuza SSR 1940* (Moscow, 1962)

Filonenko, W. J., *Volkstumkarte der Krim* (Vienna, 1932)

Kuchborskaya, E. P., *Rossiiskaya Imperia 1725–1801* (Moscow, 1959)

Stanford, Edward, *Sketch of the Acquisitions of Russia* (London, 1876)

Wyld, James, *Wyld's Military Staff Map of Central Asia, Turkistan and Afghanistan* (London, 1878)

(iii) ENCYCLOPAEDIAS, REFERENCE BOOKS AND GENERAL WORKS

Baedeker, Karl, *Russland* (Leipzig, 1912)

Cole, J. P., *Geography of the USSR* (London, 1967)

Florinsky, Michael T. (ed), *Encyclopaedia of Russia and the Soviet Union* (New York, 1961)

Katzenelson, Y. L. and Gintsburg, D. G. (eds), *Evreiskaya Entsiklopediya,* 16 vols (St Petersburg, 1906–13)

Kubijovyć, Volodymyr (ed), *Ukraine: A Concise Encyclopaedia* (Toronto, 1963)

Pares, Bernard, *A History of Russia* (London, 1926)

Parker, W. H., *An Historical Georgraphy of Russia* (London, 1968)

Sumner, B. H., *Survey of Russian History* (London, 1944)

Utechin, S. V., *Everyman's Concise Encyclopaedia of Russia* (London, 1961)

Zhukov, E. M. (ed), *Sovetskaya Istoricheskaya Entsiklopediya*, vols 1–12 (Moscow, 1961–69)

(iv) BOOKS ON SPECIAL TOPICS

Allen, W. E. D., *The Ukraine: A History* (Cambridge, 1940)

Allen, W. E. D. and Muratov, P., *Caucasian Battlefields: A History of the Wars on the Turco-Caucasian Border 1828–1921* (London, 1953)

Allilueva, A. S., *Iz Vospominanii* (Moscow, 1946)

Armstrong, John A. (ed), *Soviet Partisans in World War II* (Madison, 1964)

Armstrong, Terence E., *The Northern Sea Route* (Cambridge, 1952)

Avalishvili, Zourab, *The Independence of Georgia in International Politics 1918–1921* (London, 1940)

Baddeley, John F., *The Russian Conquest of the Caucasus* (London, 1908)

Baddeley, John F., *Russia, Mongolia, China*, 2 vols (London, 1919)

Caroe, Olaf, *Soviet Empire: The Turks of Central Asia and Stalinism* (London, 1953)

Chamberlin, William Henry, *The Russian Revolution 1917–1921*, 2 vols (New York, 1935)

Clark, Alan, *Barbarossa: The Russo-German Conflict 1941–1945* (London, 1965)

Conquest, Robert, *The Soviet Deportation of Nationalities* (London, 1960)

Cresson, W. P., *The Cossacks, their History and Country* (New York, 1919)

Dallin, Alexander, *German Rule in Russia 1941–1945* (London, 1957)

Dallin, David J., *The Rise of Russia in Asia* (London, 1950)

Dallin, David J. and Nicolaevsky, Boris I., *Forced Labour in Soviet Russia* (London, 1948)

Dixon, C. Aubrey and Heilbrunn, Otto, *Communist Guerilla Warfare* (London, 1954)

Dubnow, S. M., *History of the Jews in Russia and Poland* (Philadelphia, 1916–20)

Eudin, X. J. and Fisher, H. H., *Soviet Russia and the West 1920–1927: A Documentary Survey* (Stanford, 1957)

Fennell, J. L. I., *Ivan the Great of Moscow* (London, 1963)

Fennell, J. L. I., *The Emergence of Moscow 1304–1359* (London, 1968)

Fischer, Louis, *The Soviets in World Affairs,* 2 vols (London, 1930)

Fischer, Louis, *The Life of Lenin* (London, 1964)

Freund, Gerald, *Unholy Alliance: Russian-German relations from the Treaty of Brest-Litovsk to the Treaty of Berlin* (London, 1957)

Futrell, Michael, *Northern Underground: Episodes of Russian Revolutionary Transport and Communications through Scandinavia and Finland 1863–1917* (London, 1963)

Greenberg, Louis, *The Jews in Russia: The Struggle For Emancipation,* 2 vols (New Haven, 1944, 1951)

Höhne, Heinz, *The Order of the Death's Head: The Story of Hitler's S.S.* (London, 1969)

Indian Officer, An (anon), *Russia's March Towards India*, 2 vols (London, 1894)

Jackson, W. A. Douglas, *Russo-Chinese Borderlands* (Princeton, 1962)

Joll, James, *The Anarchists* (London, 1964)

Kamenetsky, Ihor, *Hitler's Occupation of Ukraine 1941–1944: A study of Totalitarian imperialism* (Milwaukee, 1956)

Kazemzadeh, F., *The Struggle for Transcaucasia* (New York, 1951)

Katkov, George, *Russia 1917: The February Revolution* (London, 1967)

Kennan, George, *Siberia and the Exile System* (New York, 1891)

Kerner, Robert J., *The Urge to the Sea: The Course of Russian History* (Berkeley and Los Angeles, 1946)

Kirchner, Walther, *Commercial Relations Between Russia and Europe 1400 to 1800* (Bloomington, Indiana, 1966)

Klyuchevskii, Vasilii Osipovich, *Peter the Great* (London, 1958)

Kochan, Lionel, *Russia in Revolution 1890–1918* (London, 1966)

Kolarz, Walter, *Russia and her Colonies* (London, 1952)

Krypton, Constantine, *The Northern Sea Route* (New York, 1953)

Lang, D. M., *A Modern History of Georgia* (London, 1962)

Leslie, R. F., *Reform and Insurrection in Russian Poland* (London, 1963)

Lias, Godfrey, *Kazak Exodus* (London, 1956)

Liubavskii, M. K., *Ocherk Istorii Litovsko-Russkovo Gosudarstva* (Moscow, 1910; Russian Reprint Series, The Hague, 1966)

Lorimer, F., *The Population of the Soviet Union: History and Prospects* (Geneva, 1946)

Lyashchenko, Peter I., *History of the National Economy of Russia to the 1917 Revolution* (New York, 1949)

Maksimov, S., *Sibir i Katorga,* 3 vols (St Petersburg, 1871)

Malozemoff, A., *Russian Far-Eastern Policy 1881–1904* (Los Angeles, 1958)

Manning, Clarence A., *Twentieth-Century Ukraine* (New York, 1951)

Mazour, Anatole G., *The First Russian Revolution, 1825: the Decembrist movement* (Stanford, 1961)

Mikhailov, V., *Pamiatnaya Knizhka Sotsialista-Revoliutsionera*, 2 vols (Paris, 1911, 1914)

Miller, Margaret, *The Economic Development of Russia 1905–1914* (London, 1926)

Mora, Sylvestre and Zwierniak, Pierre, *La Justice Sovietique* (Rome, 1945)

Nasonov, A. N., *Russkaya Zemlia* (Moscow, 1951)

Nikitin, M. N. and Vagin, P. I., *The Crimes of the German Fascists in the Leningrad Region: Materials and Documents* (London, 1947)

Nosenko, A. K. (ed), *V. I. Lenin 1870–1924* (Kiev, n.d.). A collection of photographs, with 2 maps

Obolenski, Prince Eugene, *Souvenirs D'Un Exilé en Sibérie* (Leipzig, 1862)

Owen, Launcelot A., *The Russian Peasant Movement 1906–17* (London, 1937)

Park, Alexander G., *Bolshevism in Turkestan 1917–1927* (New York, 1957)

Philippi, Alfred and Heim, Ferdinand, *Der Feldzug gegen Sowjetrussland 1941–1945* (Stuttgart, 1962)

Pierce, Richard A., *Russian Central Asia 1867–1917* (Berkeley and Los Angeles, 1960)

Pipes, Richard, *The Formation of the Soviet Union: Communism and Nationalism 1917–1923* (Cambridge, Massachusetts, 1954)

Platonov, S. F., *Ocherki Po Istorii Smuti v Moskovskom Gosudarstve* (Moscow, 1937)

Pospelov, P. N., *Istoriya Kommunisticheskoi Partii Sovetskovo Soyuza,* 6 vols (Moscow, 1964–68)

Pounds, Norman J. G., *Poland Between East and West* (Princeton, 1964)

Radkey, Oliver H., *The Agrarian Foes of Bolshevism* (New York, 1958)

Rapport du Parti Socialiste Revolutionnaire de Russie au Congres Socialiste International de Stuttgart (Ghent, 1907)

Reddaway, W. R., Penson, J. H., Halecki, O. and Dyboski, R. (eds), *Cambridge History of Poland*, 2 vols (Cambridge, 1941, 1950)

Reitlinger, Gerald, *The House Built on Sand: The Conflicts of German Policy in Russia 1939–1945* (London, 1960)

Riasanovsky, Nicholas V., *A History of Russia* (New York, 1963)

Rosen, Baron A., *Russian Conspirators in Siberia* (London, 1872)

Rostovtzeff, M., *The Iranians and Greeks in South Russia* (Oxford, 1922)

Salisbury, Harrison E., *The Siege of Leningrad* (London, 1969)

Schuyler, Eugene, *Peter the Great: Emperor of Russia,* 2 vols (London, 1844)

Schwarz, Solomon M., *The Russian Revolution of 1905* (Chicago, 1967)

Serge, Victor, *Memoirs of a Revolutionary 1901–1941* (London, 1963)

Seton-Watson, Hugh, *The Russian Empire 1801–1917* (London, 1967)

Shukman, Harold, *Lenin and the Russian Revolution* (London, 1966)

Simpson, Sir John Hope, *The Refugee Problem* (London, 1939)

Skazkin, S. D. (and others), *Istoriya Vizantii*, 3 vols (Moscow, 1967)

Slusser, Robert M. and Triska Jan F., *A Calendar of Soviet Treaties 1917–1957* (Stanford, 1959)

Squire, P. S., *The Third Department: The establishment and practices of the political police in the Russia of Nicholas I* (Cambridge, 1968)

Stephan, John J., *Sakhalin* (Oxford, 1971)

Sullivant, Robert S., *Soviet Politics and the Ukraine 1917–1957* (New York, 1962)

Sumner, B. H., *Peter the Great and the Ottoman Empire* (Oxford, 1949)

Sumner, B. H., *Peter the Great and the Emergence of Russia* (London, 1950)

Suprunenko, M. I. (and others), *Istoria Ukrainskoi RSR* (Kiev, 1958)

Tikhonov, Nikolai (and others), *The Defence of Leningrad: Eye-witness Accounts of the Siege* (London, 1944)

Treadgold, Donald W., *The Great Siberian Migration* (Princeton, 1957)

Trotsky, Leon, *My Life* (London, 1930)

Vernadsky, George, *The Mongols and Russia* (London, 1953)

Wheeler, G., *The Modern History of Soviet Central Asia* (London, 1964)

Woodward, David, *The Russians at Sea* (London, 1965)

Yarmolinski, Avram, *The Road to Revolution: A Century of Russian Radicalism* (London, 1957)

Yaroslavsky, E., *History of Anarchism in Russia* (London, 1937)

Zimin, A. A., *Reformy Ivana Groznovo* (Moscow, 1960)

(v) ARTICLES

Anon, 'How the Bear Learned to Swim', *The Economist* (London, 24–30 October 1970)

Bealby, John Thomas, Kropotkin, Prince Peter Alexeivitch, Philips, Walter Alison and Wallace, Sir Donald Mackenzie, 'Russia', *The Encyclopaedia Britannica* (Eleventh edition, London and New York, 1910)

Carsten, F. L., 'The Reichswehr and the Red Army 1920–1933', *Survey* (London, 1962)

Dziewanowski, M. K., 'Pilsudski's Federal Policy 1919–21', *Journal of Central European Affairs* (London, 1950)

Footman, David, 'Nestor Makno', *St Antony's Papers No. 6: Soviet Affairs No. 2* (Oxford, 1959)

Lobanov-Rostovsky, A., 'Anglo-Russian Relations through the Centuries', *Russian Review*, vol 7 (New York, 1948)

Parkes, Harry, 'Report on the Russian Caravan Trade with China', *Journal of the Royal Geographic Society*, vol 25 (London, 1854)

Stanhope, Henry, 'Soviet Strength at Sea', *The Times* (London, 25 January 1971)

Sullivan, Joseph L., 'Decembrists in Exile', *Harvard Slavic Studies,* vol 4 (The Hague, 1954)

Wildes, Harry Emerson, 'Russia's Attempts to Open Japan', *Russian Review,* vol 5 (New York, 1945)

Yakunskiy, V. K. 'La Révolution Industrielle en Russie', *Cahiers du Monde Russe et Soviętique* (The Hague, 1961)

Index

Mitterand, President: signs Franco-Russian Treaty (1992), 160

Mlava: a centre of Polish revolt against Russia (1860), 53; and German war aims (1914), 80; Germans occupy (1914), 81

Mogilev: Polish invasion of Russia launched from (1610), 30; Alexander I establishes military colonies in Province of (1810–25), 50; peasant discontent and serfdom in Province of (by 1860), 57, 58; anti-Jewish violence in, 69; Jewish political activity in, 70; the Tsar's military headquarters at (1915–17), 84, 86; German SS headquarters at (1942), 123

Mogochin: shipbuilding at (after 1937), 112

Moldavia: declares independence as Moldova (1991), 157, 158; signs agreement with Hungary (1992), 160; ethnic Russian and Ukrainian minority in (1993), 161

Molotov: *for earlier index entries see Perm*: Soviet labour camps established near, 110; factories moved to (1940–42), 113; city of over half a million inhabitants (1959), 138

Monasteries: their foundation and spread within Russia, 16; and the eastern colonization of Novgorod, 19

Mongolia: under Soviet occupation (1945–46), 142; and the Soviet-Chinese border (1970), 143; and Stalin's crimes, 159

Mongols: attack the Novgorodian town of Torzhok (1238), 18; their Empire (by 1300), 21; their conquest of Russia, 22, 146; driven from Russia by the Muscovites, 25; under Chinese control (by 1720), 40; 250,000 in the Bolshevik-controlled Far Eastern Republic (1920–22), 106

Montenegro: and European diplomacy (1890–1907), 64; and Russian policy in the Balkans (1876–1914), 78, 79

Montpellier: Russian students at the University of, 70

Montreal (Canada): Ukrainians at, 99

Moravians: a western Slav tribe, 12

Mordva: a non-Slav tribe, revolting against Russian rule, 29

Moshchny Island (Gulf of Finland): Germans fail to capture (1941–43), 126

Moscow: Orthodox monastery established at, 16; its conquests and expansion (by 1533), 25; and the rivers of European Russia, 27; Ivan IV seizes land in, 28; uprising in (1648–50), 32; peasants flee from serfdom in, to become Cossacks, 35; administrative centre of a Province established by Peter the Great, 38; Napoleon advances towards (1812), 49, 146; railway to St Petersburg from patrolled by a special Gendarme squadron (from 1846), 51; Anarchist group meets in (1840–80), 55; the industrial growth of (by 1860), 56; peasant discontent in the Province of (1827–60), 57; serfdom in the Province of (by 1860), 58; and Russian trade with China (1850–70), 59; and the opening of the Trans-Siberian and Asian railway systems, 62; strikes in (1885–1903), 68; Jews expelled from (1891), 69; Jewish political activity in, 70; and Russian industry (by 1900), 71; political assassinations in, 72; Bolsheviks active in (1903–14), 73; revolution in (1905), 76, 77; anti-war agitation at (1917), 84; secret police headquarters at, burnt (1917), 86; Bolsheviks seize power in (1917), 91; alleged subversive communist activity in, 108; Soviet labour camps to the north of, 110; factories evacuated from (1940–42), 113; Treaty of, with Finland (1940), 115; a German plan for (1941), 122; a German military plan to attack from the east (1942), 124; five million inhabitants (by 1959), 138; twice occupied by the invaders of Russia (1612, 1812), 146; Olympic Games in (1980), 147; an exile returns to (1986), 149; agreements signed in, ending the Cold War (1991–3), 150; and the collapse of Communist power (1989–91), 151, 152, 155, 156; barricades in, against the anti-Gorbachev coup (1991), 157; becomes capital of newly independent Russian Federation (1991), 158

Mozambique: Soviet arms supplies to (1984–8), 148

Mozdok: claimed as part of the Ukraine, 97; part of the Terek peoples' SSR (1918–20), 104

Mozyr: Jews murdered in (1648–52), 31; annexed by Russia (1793), 43

Msta, River: and river systems of European Russia, 27

Mukden (China): and the Soviet-Chinese border (1970), 143

Munich: Lenin in, 73

Munschengratz: Treaty of (1833), 51

Muraviev, Nikolai Nikolaevich: advocates Russian expansion in the Far East, 60

Murmansk: Lenin plans to return to Russia through (1917), 87; occupied by British troops (1918–19), 91, 92, 94; Kara Sea Expedition stops at (1921), 105; labour camp near, 109; and the Northern Sea Route, 112; allied aid enters the Soviet Union through (1941–45), 121; a German plan for (1941), 122

Murom: within Kievan Russia, 13; anti-Jewish violence in, 69, 75

Muromski monastery: 19

Murom-Riazan: a Russian Principality, 17; conquered by the Mongols, 22

Mus: occupied by Russia (1829), 46; occupied by Russia (1916), 83; Armenian claims to (1918), 104

Mylga: Soviet labour camp at, 111

Nachichevan: annexed by Russia (1828), 48

Nagorno-Karabakh: an autonomous region, 144; ethnic violence in (1988), 151; Russian troops evacuated from (1992), 160

Naissus: Roman city in the Balkans, 4, 7; raided by the Goths, 5; *for subsequent references see index entry for* Nish

Nanking (China): Soviet air units defend against Japanese attack (1941), 142

Naples: bombarded by the Russian fleet (1798–1800), 45; Russia opposes national revolution in (1815–25), 50

Napoleon I: and Russia, 49, 146

Narva: ruled by the Teutonic Knights, 20; taken by Russia from Sweden (1721), 36, 37, 47; industrial growth of (after 1860), 56; revolution at (1905), 76; Bolshevik influence in (1917), 89; anti-Bolshevik forces advance on Petrograd from (1919), 93; Soviet partisans attack the Germans near (1941–42), 127

Narym: founded (1596), 33; a town of exile in Tsarist times, 54, 72; a Bolshevik leader in, at the time of the revolution (1917), 88; Soviet labour camp at, 111

Nebolchi: a town in the Republic of Novgorod, 18

Nerchinsk: founded (1659), 33, 40; in the Bolshevik-controlled Far Eastern Republic (1920–22), 106

Nerchinskii Zavod: and the Siberian exiles, 54

Neuri: possible Slav tribe named by Herodotus, 3

Nevel: Jews murdered in (1648–52), 31; Germans driven by the Soviet army from (1943–44), 129

New Archangel (Sitka): Russian settlement in Alaska (founded 1804), 44

New York (USA): Russian Bolshevik leaders in (1917), 88; Ukrainians at, 99; Soviet veto in (1980), 147

Nezhin: anarchists active in (1905–6), 55; anti-Jewish violence in, 69

Nicaea: raided by the Goths, 5

Nicholas I: Russia during his reign (1825–1855), 51; restricts Polish liberties, 52

Nicholas II: and the 1905 revolution, 76; lives in increasing

(1941), 118, 126; Soviet partisans active near (1941–42), 127

Tiksi: a port on the Northern Sea Route, 112

Tilsit: Peace of (1807), 49

Timisoara (Rumania): anti-Communist protesters killed in (1989), 152

Tirana (Albania): anti-communist riots in (1990), 153

Tirgoviste (Rumania): President Ceaucescu executed in (1989), 152

Tisza-Eszla (Hungary): ritual murder charge against Jews in, 69

Tiumen: founded (1586), 26, 33; shipbuilding at (from 1937), 112

Tmutorokan: a Slav town on the Black Sea, 12; part of Kievan Russia, 13

Tobol, River: and the river systems of the Urals and European Russia, 27; early Russian settlements on, 33

Tobolsk: founded (1587), 26, 33, 40; a town of exile in Siberia, 54; and Russian trade with China (1850–70), 59; Soviet labour camps near, 111; industry at (1941–45), 121

Tomi: Greek colony on the Black Sea, 3

Tomsk: founded (1604), 33, 40; a town of exile, 54, 72; Ukrainians at (by 1937), 98; Soviet labour camps near, 111; and the Northern Sea Route administration, 112; a German plan for (1941), 122

Tornea: annexed by Russia (1809), 47

Toronto (Canada): Ukrainians at, 99

Torzhok: attacked by the Mongols (1238) and by the Lithuanians (1245), 18; does not fall under Mongol control, 22

Tosno: anti-Bolshevik forces fail to capture (1919), 93; Germans occupy (1941), 126; Soviet partisans active near (1941–42), 127

Totma: Ivan IV seizes laid in region of, 28; uprising in (1648–50), 32

Trade routes: of Kievan Russia, 14

Transcaucasian Federative Republic: its brief existence (1917), 104

Trans-Siberian railway: and the Siberian exiles, 54; and the development of Siberia (by 1917), 62; Ukrainian settlements along, 98; and the spread of Soviet rule to Central Asia (1917–36), 103; goes through the Bolshevik-controlled Far Eastern Republic (1920–22), 106; Soviet labour camps on, 111; administrative centres of the Northern Sea Route on (from 1920–25), 112; Jewish Autonomous Region of Birobidjan on, 135

Transylvania: a Roman Catholic region by 1000 AD, 24

Trapezus: Greek colony on the Black sea, 3; controlled by Rome, 4; raided by the Goths, 5; *see henceforth* Trebizond

Trebizond: a Byzantine port on the Black Sea, 10; a trading centre for Kievan goods going to India, 14; occupied by Russia (1829), 46; Armenian claims to (1918), 104

Trelleborg: Lenin returns to Russia through (1917), 87

Treviso: Russian campaign in Italy begins at (1798), 49

Troitski-Gledinskii monastery: 19

Troitski-Sergievski monastery: 16

Troki: annexed by Russia (1795), 43; a centre of Polish revolt against Russia (1860), 53

Troppau: conference of, 50

Trotsk: Germans manufacture poison gas secretly at (1922–33), 101

Trotsky, Lev Davidovich: describes life in Siberia (before 1917), 54; in New York at the time of the revolution (1917), 88; returns to Petrograd, and is arrested (1917), 89; and the Bolshevik seizure of power in Petrograd (1917), 90; and the defence of Petrograd (1919), 93; exiled, 113

Tsaritsyn: founded (1589), 26; in area of peasants' revolt (1670–71), 32; a shipbuilding centre, 34; large Cossack settlement in, 35; anti-Jewish violence in, 69, 75; industry in (by 1900), 71; Bolsheviks active in (1903–17), 73; strikes in (1905), 76; famine in (1921), 102; name changed to Stalingrad, 139; *for subsequent index entries see* Stalingrad (now Volgograd)

Tsarskoye Selo: special Gendarme detachment at, 51; Protocols of Zion published in, 69; troops disarmed at (1917), 86

Tsingtao: German port on the China coast, 65

Tskhinvali: anti-Bolshevik revolt in (1920–21), 104

Tuapse: Black Sea coastal town, claimed as part of the Ukraine, 97; Bolsheviks advance into the Caucasus from (1920), 104; Germans fail to capture (1941–43), 128

Tula: dispossessed landowners settle in, 28; within area of peasants' revolt (1606–07), 29; an industrial centre (by 1800), 34; in the most heavily populated area of Russia (in 1724), 38; conversions to Judaism in (1796–1825), 50; centre of an anarchist group (1840–80), 55; industrial growth in the region of (by 1860), 56; peasant discontent and serfdom in Province of (by 1860), 57, 58; industry in (by 1900), 71; peasant uprising in Province of (1905), 75; strikes in (1905), 76; Germans make armaments secretly at (1922–33), 101; Soviet labour camps in region of, 110; German SS headquarters at (1942), 123; Germans driven from (1943), 129

Tunguska, River: and the Siberian exile system, 54

Tura: Ukrainians at, 98

Tura, River: and Russian trade with China (1850–70), 59

Turgai: Ukrainians at, 98

Turinsk: a town of exile in Siberia, 54

Turkestan-Siberian railway (Turksib): and the spread of Soviet rule to Central Asia (1930–36), 103

Turkey: signs Treaty of Kars with the Bolsheviks (1921), 104; Russian refugees in (by 1930), 107; alleged revolutionary activity prepared against, inside Russia, 108; Germans fail to reach Caucasus frontier of (1941–43), 128; and Cold War arms supplies (1984–8), 148

Turkmenistan: independent Republic of, 158; joins Muslim trading group (1992), 160; signs Mutual Security Treaty (1992), 160; ethnic Russian minority in (1993), 161

Turks: settle on the eastern shore of the Aral Sea, 8, 9, 10

Turnovo: occupied by Russia (1810), 46

Turov: Russian Principality of, 17; conquered by the Mongols, 22; conquered by the Lithuanians, 23; Russians advance against Poles through (1654–55), 31; annexed by Russia (1793), 43

Turukhansk: founded (1619), 33; Stalin in exile at, 54; political exiles at, 72; a Bolshevik leader in, at the time of the revolution (1917), 88; Kara Sea Expedition visits (1921), 105; Soviet labour camp at, 111

Tver: Orthodox monastery established at, 16; peasant discontent in the Province of (1827–60), 57; serfdom in (by 1860), 58; political assassinations in, 72; Bolsheviks active in (1903–14), 73; strikes at (1905), 76; name changed to Kalinin, 139

Tyras: Greek colony on the Black Sea, 3

Udskii: founded (1679), 33

Ufa: industrial growth in region of, 34, 56; political assassination in (1903), 68, 72; and Russian industry (by 1900), 71; Bolsheviks active in (1903–14), 73; strikes in (1905), 76; controlled by anti-Bolshevik troops (1919), 92, 146; famine in (1921), 102; anti-Bolshevik revolt in region of

1917), ceded to Russia by Finland (1940), 115, 116; annexed by Russia (1945), 133

Vychegda, River: a trade route of Novgorod, 19; and the river systems of European Russia, 27

Vym, River: a trade route of Novgorod, 19

Vymskii-Arkhangelskii monastery: 19

Wakhan: given to Afghanistan by Russia and Britain (1905), 61

Wallenberg, Raoul: one of Stalin's victims, 159

Warsaw: capital city of the Kingdom of Poland, 23; under Russian rule (1815–1915), contained a large German community, 39; annexed by Prussia (1795), 42; becomes Russian (1815), and centre of Polish revolt against Russia (1831), 52; again a centre of Polish revolt (1860), 53; anarchists active in (1905–06), 55; factory development in (by 1860), 56; Jewish political activity in, 70; industry in (by 1900), 71; political assassinations in, 72; revolution in (1905), 76; Germans hope to annex (1914), 79, 80; Germans occupy (1915), 82; Poles defend from attack by the Red Army (June 1920), 96; communism established in (1945), 113; occupied by Germany (1939), 114, 116; Jewish uprising against Germans in (1942), 123; anti-Soviet revolt in (1956), 134; Communist rule ends in (1989), 152; Stock Exchange opens in (1991), 153; revelation of Stalin's crimes near, 159

Warsaw Pact: and the ending of the Cold War, 150, 153, 156

Washington DC: 'evil empire' denounced in (1983), 147; Soviet-American accord signed in (1987), 150; summits in (1990, 1992), 150

Weihaiwei: British port on the China coast, 65

West Germany: and Cold War arms supplies (1984–8), 148; unification with East Germany (1990), 153; Eastern European asylum seekers in (1990), 154

West Ukrainian Republic: established (Nov 1918), 97

White Huns: settle along the Oxus River, 6, 7

White Russia (Belorussia): annexed by Catherine the Great, 41, 43; occupied by the Poles (1919), 100; occupied by the Germans (1942), 119; a Soviet Republic (since 1945), 144 path to independence of (1991), 156

White Sea: Orthodox monastery on an island in, 16; Principality of Moscow extends its control to, 25; river routes across Russia from, 27; Ivan IV seizes lands along the shore of, 28; controlled by Britain (1918–19), 91, 92, 94; Soviet labour camps established on, 109, 110

Wilson, Harold: signs Helsinki Agreement (1975), 147

Windau: taken by Russia from Poland (1795), 36, 43

Winnipeg (Canada): Ukrainians at, 99

Winter Palace (Petrograd): seized by the Bolsheviks (1917), 90

Wismar: a Hansa town on the Baltic, 20; under communist control (since 1945), 36

Wrangel, Pyotr Nikolaevich: defeated by a joint Bolshevik-Anarchist army (1920), 95; based on the Crimea, 100

Wrangel Island: Soviet-Canadian dispute over (1921–45), 112

Wuhan (China): Moscow establishes Communist Party cell in (1920–24), 142

Xanten (Germany): ritual murder charge against Jews in, 69

Yadrin: in area of peasants' revolt (1670–71), 32

Yakutsk: founded (1632), 33, 40; a town of exile, 54, 72; and the Lena coal basin, 112

Yalta: anarchists active in (1905–06), 55; annexed to the Independent Ukraine (1918), 97; annexed by Germany (1941), 123; allied conference at (1945), 113; Communist Party privileges end at (1990), 155

Yalu, River: Russia fears British expansion in the region of (after 1840), 60; Soviet troops advance to, against Japanese (1945), 142

Yalutorovsk: a town of exile in Siberia, 54

Yama: attacked by the Teutonic Knights, 18

Yamburg: occupied by anti-Bolshevik forces (1919), 93

Yangtse, River: within the Mongol dominions, 21

Yarkand: annexed by China (by 1764), 40; and Russian trade with China (1850–70), 59; Britain wants to extend its influence to, 65

Yarslav: ruler of Kievan Russia, in whose reign the first Russian legal code was compiled, 13; the division of Kievan Russia after his death, 17

Yaroslavl: Russian counter-attack against Poles draws troops from, 30; peasant discontent in the Province of (1827–60), 57; serfdom in (by 1860), 58; strikes at (1905), 76; Polish (from 1918), Germans occupy (1939), 114

Yangulbene: Bolshevik influence in (1917), 114

Yellow River: Eurasian nomads move westwards from, 2; seen as possible southern boundary of Russian territorial zone in China (1900), 65

Yeltsin, Boris: his rise to power (1991), 156, 157; and East-West détente, 150; his first full year of power in Russia (1992), 160

Yemen: Soviet fishing agreement with (1970), 141; Soviet arms to (1984–8), 148

Yenisei, River: early Russian settlements on, 33; and the Siberian exile system, 54; Ukrainian settlements on the upper reaches of (by 1937), 98; Kara Sea Expedition visits lower reaches of (1921), 105; Soviet labour camps on, 111; industrial development of (by 1970), 137

Yeniseisk: founded (1619), 40; and Russian trade with China (1850–70), 59; a town of exile, 72

Yorktown (Canada): Ukrainians at, 99

Younghusband, General Francis: leads British military expedition to Lhasa, 65

Yudenich, General Nikolai Nikolaevich: fails to capture Petrograd (Sept 1919), 93, 100

Yugoslavia: Russian refugees in (by 1930), 107; strongly anti-communist (by 1926), 108; German population of flees to Germany (1945–46), 132; communist regime established in (1945), 133; Soviet control of foreign, economic and domestic policy rejected (since 1949), 134; and Soviet-American arms supplies (1984–8), 148

Yurev: a town conquered by Kievan Russia, 13

Yuzovo: name changed to Stalino, 139

Zaison: and the Soviet-Chinese border (1970), 143

Zakataly: occupied by the Turks (1917–18), 104

Zakopane: Lenin in exile in (1913), 73

Zamosc: Jews murdered in (1648–52), 31; a centre of Polish revolt against Russia (1860), 53

Zaporiye: and the siege of Leningrad (1941–43), 126

Zaporozhe: occupied by the Germans (1942), 119; Germans driven from (1943), 129

Zaporozhian Cossacks: join revolt of Don Cossacks (1707), 37

Zbarazh: Jews murdered in (1648–52), 31

Zelichenok, Alec: imprisoned (1985), 149

Zeya, River: gold fields of, 106

Zhigansk: a town in the Lena coal basin, 112

Zhitomir: conquered by the Lithuanians, 23; Russian (since 1793), acquired (by 1914) a large German community, 39; annexed by Russia (1793), 42, 43; anti-Jewish violence in, 69, 75; Jewish communal charity in (before 1914), 70;